THE Educator's ··········· FIELD GUIDE

THE Educator's ·········· FIELD GUIDE

From Organization to Assessment
(And Everything in Between)

EDWARD S. EBERT II
CHRISTINE EBERT
MICHAEL L. BENTLEY

CORWIN
A SAGE Company

CORWIN
A SAGE Company

FOR INFORMATION:

Corwin
A SAGE Company
2455 Teller Road
Thousand Oaks, California 91320
(800) 233-9936
Fax: (800) 417-2466
www.corwin.com

SAGE Ltd.
1 Oliver's Yard
55 City Road
London EC1Y 1SP
United Kingdom

SAGE Pvt. Ltd.
B 1/I 1 Mohan Cooperative Industrial Area
Mathura Road, New Delhi 110 044
India

SAGE Asia-Pacific Pte. Ltd.
33 Pekin Street #02-01
Far East Square
Singapore 048763

Acquisitions Editor: Jessica Allan
Associate Editor: Allison Scott
Editorial Assistant: Lisa Whitney
Production Editor: Veronica Stapleton
Copy Editor: Matthew Sullivan
Typesetter: C&M Digitals (P) Ltd.
Proofreader: Dennis W. Webb
Indexer: Sheila Bodell
Cover Designer: Scott Van Atta
Permissions Editor: Karen Ehrmann
Illustrator: Seth Johnson

Printed in the United States of America

Library of Congress Cataloging-in-Publication Data

Ebert, Edward S., 1953–

The educator's field guide: from organization to assessment (and everything in between)/Edward S. Ebert II, Christine Ebert, Michael L. Bentley

p. cm.
Includes bibliographical references and index.

ISBN 978-1-4129-6949-9 (pbk.)

1. Teaching—Handbooks, manuals, etc. I. Ebert, Christine, 1946– II. Bentley, Michael Lee. III. Title.

LB1025.3.E235 2011 371.102—dc22 2011002971

This book is printed on acid-free paper.

11 12 13 14 15 10 9 8 7 6 5 4 3 2 1

Contents

List of Figures and Tables

Preface

Start Here

Welcome to the *Educator's Field Guide!* The *EFG* has been compiled particularly as a resource for student teachers and beginning teachers, though as a desk reference it may be a valuable volume to keep close at hand in your professional library. The four units that we have assembled here, focusing upon Instructional Organization, Classroom Management, Instruction, and Assessment, encompass the primary duties of any professional educator. In this edition of the *EFG* you will find both the classic research in these areas of your work as a teacher as well as up-to-date discussions and explanations of key topics such as student diversity, special needs, lesson planning, instructional techniques, and assessing your students' academic progress. If you are facing student teaching (or hosting a student teacher), are in your first years as a professional teacher, or simply want a source you can go to as a refresher on one topic or another, the *EFG* is your book.

THE ORGANIZATION OF THE BOOK ■

There are several aspects to the organization used in the *EFG* that we want to point out to you. As mentioned already, the book is structured into four units. They are sequenced in the order in which you might need them most, though we understand that good arguments (even some of our own!) could be made for a different arrangement. We have placed an indexing mark along the edge of each page so that you can quickly go to the unit you need by either looking at the edge of the book or while thumbing through. Once again, the units are as follows:

- Unit I: Instructional Organization
- Unit II: Classroom Management
- Unit III: Instruction
- Unit IV: Assessment

At the beginning of each unit you will find an outline to help you zero in on the topic you need and also a concept map to help you see the bigger picture of what the unit discusses. And while we are mentioning it, the Table of Contents beginning on page v lists the major headings and subheadings found in the text as a quick reference.

Need a refresher on some of the terms used in education these days? Anything we use in the text that has been identified as a key term shows up in the glossary at the back of the book.

■ HOW TO USE THE *EFG*

Each of the units is organized in the same manner: **First, Second, Now, Tomorrow**, and **Finally**. You can go directly to the level of information that you need based on these category headings. The sections with the heading "**First**" are intended to give you the background information, the "whys and wherefores" of the topic. This section is not intended to tell you what to do in class tomorrow but instead is the foundation information that teachers should have to be professional educators.

In the sections titled "**Second**," you will find what we will call *transition* information. That is, these sections start to bridge the gap between the foundation material found in the previous section and the very practical information to be found in the next section. For instance, in *Unit I: Instructional Organization*, the **First** section discusses long-range planning. You may well be required to do this, but it probably isn't what you are most concerned about doing with your students tomorrow. The next section, **Second**, however, talks about short-range planning—and that's all about what is going to happen in your room tomorrow.

"**Now**" is the section that tells you what to do, well, *now*. For instance, in *Unit II: Classroom Management*, **Now** is a detailed exercise in developing your own classroom-management plan. It begins with writing a mission statement and works its way all the way through to assessing your plan and reflecting on the results.

Preparation on a particular topic should be pretty well under control if you have gone through the previous sections (at least the **Now** section), so "**Tomorrow**" explains how to take what you've prepared and implement it. In *Unit IV: Assessment*, **Now** helps you to prepare strong assessments for your students to complete and **Tomorrow** tells you how to analyze the results of those assessments.

And "**Finally**." We hope that you are feeling pretty confident about your work by this point. However, in the world of teaching and working with other people's children, there is always something else to mention, and that's where **Finally** comes in. Sometimes it's a reiteration of things discussed in the unit. Other times—for instance, in *Unit III: Instruction*—it's a reminder to all of us in education of a little item that can often get lost amid the hustle and bustle of getting it all done: take the time to enjoy your profession!

We have enjoyed putting this guide together for you and hope that you will find the *EFG* to be a useful resource and, perhaps, an anxiety-reducer when you are faced with a task that might require just a little bit of back up. And don't forget the words of Nobel Peace Laureate Nelson Mandela, "Education is the most powerful weapon which you can use to change the world." We wish you the very best in your work—go out and change the world!

Edward S. Ebert, II
Christine Ebert
Michael L. Bentley

Acknowledgments

The authors wish to thank the team of editors who have made this book possible. Jessica Allan has been the guiding force and calming influence throughout the preparation of the *EFG*. Along the way we have been pleased to work with Allison Scott, Lisa Whitney, Veronica Stapleton, and Matthew Sullivan. The authors put words to the page, but it is a team such as this one that puts a book in the hands of readers such as yourself. We sincerely thank all of the folks at Corwin for their helpful and professional work.

PUBLISHER'S ACKNOWLEDGMENTS

Corwin wishes to acknowledge the following peer reviewers for their editorial insight and guidance.

Tonia Guidry
Teacher
Golden Meadow Middle School
Golden Meadow, Louisiana

Amanda J. Hartness
Elementary School Principal
Chapel Hill Carrboro City Schools
Chapel Hill, North Carolina

Alexis Ludewig
Adjunct Instructor—GOAL English
Former Third-Grade Teacher, Resource Teacher, and Title I Instructor
Fox Valley Technical College
Appleton, Wisconsin

About the Authors

Dr. Edward S. Ebert, II is Professor Emeritus of Education at Coker College in Hartsville, South Carolina. He has been teaching for more than thirty years. With a doctorate in Psychological Foundations of Education, Dr. Ebert teaches courses in educational psychology, elementary science methods, child development, classroom management, assessment, and creative problem solving. He has written eleven books, with topics including elementary science methods, creative thinking and science teaching, introduction to education, classroom pragmatics, management and assessment, and educational reform. Dr. Ebert has done numerous presentations nationally and internationally, and has taught science education and educational psychology for a semester at Shanghai International Studies University, Shanghai, People's Republic of China. He resides in Wellfleet, Massachusetts, with his wife, Dr. Christine Ebert.

Dr. Christine Ebert is Distinguished Professor Emeritus of Education and former Dean of the Graduate School and Associate Provost and at the University of South Carolina. She has worked in teacher education on the undergraduate and graduate levels for twenty-five years. In particular, her work in science education focuses on conceptual change and development in students' understanding of science principles. In addition, she has taught courses in thinking and reasoning and is extensively involved with collaboration between elementary schools and the university. Dr. Ebert serves regularly as a program evaluator for national federally funded science initiatives and has coauthored three other books related to science education and conceptual development. Dr. Ebert has presented her work at conferences across the country and around the world. She and her husband live in Wellfleet, Massachusetts.

Photo by Matthew E. Bentley.

Dr. Michael Bentley has authored twenty-three books and chapters in books about science and science education, the most recent being a chapter on eco-justice education in *Cultural Studies and Environmentalism* (2010, Springer). A graduate of the University of Virginia, he taught at Virginia Tech and National-Louis University in Chicago and recently retired from the education faculty at the University of Tennessee. He currently writes and teaches part-time. His career has included teaching in Philadelphia and Virginia public schools, administering a science museum, and founding two innovative high schools in Virginia, including Community High School (www.communityhigh.net). Dr. Bentley serves on the expert panel for Education.com and volunteers for several nonprofits in his community. Dr. Bentley and his wife, the Rev. Susan E. Bentley, have three children, dogs, a lop-eared bunny, a Russian tortoise, a boa, a python, and several corn snakes.

UNIT I

Instructional Organization

■ UNIT I CONCEPT MAP

Unit I

1 long-range planning
- why plan
- prerequisites
- safety
- demographics
- content area(s) standards and assessment

2 short-range planning
- unit plans
- goals and objectives
- lesson plans
- projects and group work

3 classroom organization
- teacher's seating
- independent work area
- resources and storage
- information
- moving from place to place
- scheduling
- educational decoration
- student seating

4 instructional presentation
- technology- old and new
- use of primary writing surface

5 communication with outsiders
- school staff
- parents
- museums and agencies

UNIT I PEP TALK ■

It's time to get organized! Whether you are preparing for student teaching or facing your first few years as a classroom teacher, instructional organization—which includes all four of the units in this book—will be the determining factor in your success or failure, your ease or stress, and your fulfillment as a professional educator. Yes, it is a big topic. No, it is nothing mystical or magical—it is just a matter of doing the things that effective teachers do.

First, let's talk *conceptualization*: This unit is about organizing and planning instruction in the classroom. We will focus here on the nuts and bolts of teaching, the processes that occur inside and outside the classroom that most directly enable students' learning. As a teacher, your primary goal is to create a rich learning environment in your classroom, one that provides many opportunities for your students to engage with content and peers, to study, and to grow.

> Instructional organization will be the determining factor in your success or failure, your ease or stress, and your fulfillment as a professional educator.

Such an environment would contain a variety of materials and supplies, and especially inviting *spaces* that can be used flexibly for different purposes. Nicholson's (1973) classic *The Theory of Loose Parts* states that in any environment, both the degree of inventiveness and the possibility of discovery are directly proportional to the number and kind of variables in that environment. Some classroom environments do not work simply because they do not have enough "loose parts" to generate learning. It is having the loose parts that makes your classroom an inviting and stimulating place. Note, however, that we don't mean your classroom should resemble a junkyard! The loose parts work best when they are well organized. Your aim should be a classroom environment that is aesthetically pleasing to those who study and work there.

Second, *content*: Keep in mind that there is no single right way to go about your curriculum planning as a teacher. Your several million colleagues across the country do their planning in many, many different ways, some more effective, some less so. Also remember that the content of the curriculum can, and should, reflect the uniqueness of your school's locale and the multiple cultures of its patrons. That is to say that the *context* in which education occurs will vary from one place to the next. Fourth graders in an Illinois science class might be studying the prairie environment, while those in Florida would be studying wetlands. Both the *what* of the content and the *how* of the teaching should reflect a consideration of the needs and cultures of your local community.

And think about this classic point: According to Vygotsky (1978), learning occurs when your students interact in meaningful ways. Student-to-student interaction happens naturally in cooperative group work. As you develop your repertoire of teaching strategies, you will naturally want to learn how to use a variety of cooperative learning strategies in your teaching. This is something this book should help you do.

Tomorrow is all about *implementation*: Other teachers will tell you that their classes are different each year. Most teachers recognize that the effectiveness of instruction depends upon the particular students in their classes. Much also depends upon the circumstances of the moment. Thus, even though you have planned your lessons well, a lot of interactive planning often occurs right on the spot in response to students' interests or needs. Successful teachers are flexible enough to respond to each situation and take advantage of the "teachable moment."

And finally, *reflection*: All in all, classroom life is affected by myriad variables. The educational profession has to be among the most complex enterprises in all of society! No one formula for planning and managing a classroom possibly could be applicable in all, or even most, situations. There is no way you can predict every kind of student or every teaching situation with which you might have to cope. Yet, despite the constraints and challenges, teachers and students in different kinds of schools manage year after year to create communities where learning flourishes. Through thoughtful planning, you can anticipate and address many of the tasks and problems involved in enacting your classroom curriculum. Here is one piece of advice based upon our (your authors') own classroom experiences: *Be patient with the complexity and keep yourself open to learning on the job.*

■ FIRST: LONG-RANGE PLANNING

Long-range planning represents the big picture of your work in the classroom. With a solid perspective of this picture, planning the day-to-day activities comes much more easily. However, many teachers try to plan from one moment to the next, believing that they just don't have time to lay out the larger plan. Yet how many buildings are built without blueprints first being drawn? No, far from being an unnecessary exercise, putting together the long-range plan is one of those things that separates the professional from the wannabe.

Why Plan?

Just imagine facing a classroom of children—at any age level of your choosing—*without* a plan for what you are going to do! At the very least, having a plan is a way to reduce stress as you begin your day! And we would add that planning is good for the deportment of the teacher *and* good for the quality of the instruction.

Any teacher will tell you that planning takes place well before class time, perhaps as you drift off to sleep or in the haze of waking up or when showering. Ideas emerge when you are traveling to and from school—and that's why some of us keep a writing pad or a tape recorder handy wherever we are.

What goes into planning for instruction? Always in the back of your mind is who your students are and what their lives are like (demographics). Also very important: what you expect that they already should know. You also have to consider whether or not you have students with special needs. Then there is the matter of what your state or school system requires you to teach in terms of content, skills, and habits of mind (your local or state standards).

Plus, you need to think about the materials you have on hand and whatever else you will need. Then there is the time issue: how much time you will have to spend on the lesson or unit. A further consideration is whether or not you can relate this content to other areas of the curriculum, so that you might integrate lessons. Sounds like it might be getting just a bit overwhelming, but don't worry, planning goes a step at a time specifically to ward off "overwhelming."

After you have settled these matters, you can write unit goals and the objectives for your lessons. Figure I.2 (see page 40) lists some guiding questions that will help you in planning. Lessons should be written to address the objectives, or learning outcomes, that you have set for your students. You will find more details about unit and lesson plans later in this unit.

Three Prerequisites

There are three prerequisites to planning your classroom curriculum. First, it is best that you know your students—their cultural and economic backgrounds and their general family situation—as well as your students' ability levels, interests, maturity, prior knowledge and experience, and special needs or necessary accommodations. You may need to begin your long-range planning, however, *before* you know all this in the detail that you'd like. Regardless, your job is to design and enact a classroom program that will not only meet the needs of your students but also motivate them to want to keep learning.

Second, to plan the classroom curriculum, you will need to know the subject matter that you will teach, that is, the content. *Content* is the body of facts, concepts, skills, habits of mind, and so forth that represent what you will teach. For elementary teachers, it is likely that you will be ahead of your students to start with, but it is still necessary for you to study and update yourself on the content that you will be teaching. You should also review your state standards and local district or school curriculum guides.

> Know your students! To whatever degree possible, include whatever knowledge you have of your students in your planning.

Third, you will need to be aware of what materials you have and what equipment is available. It makes a difference, for example, if you'll have an Internet-connected Smart Board in your classroom or still have to rely upon the chalkboard. Available technology, software, audiovisuals, science equipment, measuring tools, math manipulatives, library resources—all make a difference. And don't forget to consider your local community's resources, such as museums, zoos, nature centers, parks, guest speakers, and volunteers. And it makes a difference whether or not you have help from a teacher mentor or a teacher aide. You will find more about this in the section of this unit titled, *Tomorrow: Instructional Presentation.*

Finally, keep in mind that long-range planning is considered within a larger frame than the school day. One larger frame is the week, while another is the grading period—which could be six weeks, a quarter (nine weeks), or a semester. An example of framing instruction into a weekly schedule is the teacher who, on Monday, introduces the content that is to be addressed by Friday and the assignments students will complete by then. Assignments might include readings, searching for information online or in the library, and responding someway in writing to the concepts and skills being studied.

Safety

Before we continue discussing each of the prerequisites, let's take a moment to consider a key element that must underlie all planning: *safety*. Safety has to be foremost in your mind, both inside and outside the classroom. Plan to engage your students in discussing safety early in the school year. They should be able to contribute suggestions in determining appropriate safety rules, and involving them fosters their investment in maintaining a safe environment. Post the resulting standards for safe behavior prominently in the classroom.

Safety has been described as simply using common sense in planning ahead. Of course, nothing you can do can guarantee that an accident will never happen in your classroom. The best practice is to think ahead and be prepared. For example, locate the fire extinguishers in your school and know how to use them (a practice "shot" is a good idea). Keep your classroom door free from obstructions and never store flammable material near the door. Know your school's procedures for handling student injuries. Unless circumstances offer no alternative, never treat injuries yourself. Excluding lifesaving measures, teachers may only stop bleeding and apply water (as to burns or acid spills).

Your liability as a teacher falls under **tort law**, where negligence or breach of contract or trust results in injury to another person or damage to property. A student generally acquires the status of an *invitee*, which means that no contractual basis exists for assumed risk on his or her part. The law assumes students do not know the potential dangers or appreciate the risks involved. Your responsibility as the teacher is related to the legal concept of *negligence*, which is about neglecting instruction, supervision, or proper maintenance of equipment and supplies. If there is no precedent or statute involved, then your actions or inactions as the teacher are to be measured against what a hypothetical *reasonably prudent individual* would have done under the same circumstances. *The reasonable person is one who anticipates what might happen.*

> When it comes to safety, the reasonable person is one who anticipates what might happen.

For older students, a good strategy is to work with the class to develop safety contracts that everyone in class will sign. These should be kept on file. A simple sample safety contract can be found in Figure I.3 (see page 41). Flinn Scientific offers middle school and high school sample contracts for science on this website: www.flinnsci.com/Documents/miscPDFs/safety_contract_MS.pdf.

Keep in mind, however, that *such a document does not absolve you of responsibility*. While you will never be able to establish an absolutely injury-proof environment, *always* be conscientious about safety.

Demographics

The primary prerequisite to planning your classroom curriculum is knowing your students. Part of this involves knowing about their backgrounds. *Demographics* have to do with socioeconomic status indicators. The demographic variables among your students, such as family income, parental education, mobility, and home language, are a few of the components that define a demographic context and are what make each classroom unique. The demographics of your students are the givens, what you have to start with in your classroom, and there is not much you can do to change them. Remember, what students bring to school accounts for much of the variance in their academic performance. Your understanding of the demographics can enrich your perspective and help you better allocate your instructional time and resources.

Understanding a classroom's demographic context can help remove excuses and increase the positive stress when students are not performing in line with their favorable demographics. Often there is little pressure on some students to improve their achievement, as they already perform better than students in other schools in their area. With a little push, however, these students, with their advantaged demographic profile, can improve relatively quickly. If this is the situation in your classroom, what you have to do is up their positive stress.

Conversely, understanding a classroom's demographic context can also help decrease the negative stress when students are doing well despite a *disadvantaged* demographic profile. When students are doing better than their backgrounds would indicate, this tells you that they are making the right efforts, and this calls for celebrating! Thus, the demographic lens is another tool that can help you plan more appropriately for instruction. We will look at this again when we discuss sociograms.

Special Needs

Special needs represents a category of students that includes everything from the learning disabled to the gifted. Inevitably you will have the opportunity sometime in your career to teach many kinds of students with special needs. Some students have specific disabilities, such as being visually or hearing impaired. Some may be normal in every other way except that English is not their first language. These children are variously called ESL (English as a Second Language), ELL (English Language Learners), or simply EL (English Learners). Other students with special needs may be cognitively or physically challenged.

Special needs represents a category of students that includes everything from the learning disabled to the gifted.

Inclusive learning environments represent a change in how students are to be taught in our schools today. Back in the "old days," students with special needs were segregated for specialized instruction. The preference today, however, is for teachers to provide appropriate instruction for *all* students through differentiating instruction in a heterogeneous classroom. Doing this will require time and patience: you may have to make *accommodations* for some students and *modifications* for others. Providing for the special needs of students will certainly be one of your biggest challenges as a teacher.

Inclusive learning environments represent a preference for teachers to provide appropriate instruction for *all* students through differentiating instruction in a heterogeneous classroom.

Such students may require that you use particular teaching strategies in a structured environment that supports their learning. You may want to learn more about teaching children with special needs by taking special education classes or workshops. The Internet has many websites devoted to teaching children with particular needs. For example, see the National Association for Gifted Children online at www.nagc.org.

Classroom-Management Plan

We will discuss classroom management in detail in Unit II. However, you need to understand right up front that effective classroom management begins with bringing a plan into class. This is not something to start thinking about once all the students have arrived. A key to effective classroom management is to first develop a plan for managing a classroom effectively.

> *A key to effective classroom management is to first develop a plan for managing a classroom effectively.*

There is no one right way to manage a classroom, because every group of students is unique, but your aim should be to create a positive classroom climate, not one based upon fear of retribution. As you grow into your teaching, you will develop your own style of classroom management. Your style may also evolve and will likely remain a work in progress as you gain more experience with the new classes you teach. Thinking about your management plan requires that you seriously consider your values and beliefs about discipline and your social goals for your students.

Conceptualizing a management plan will enable you to better understand how you will teach and increase your confidence in your approach to classroom management. You will want to be proactive rather than reactive to student behavior. The plan can always be amended, and you will want to be flexible. Your management plan should include the following:

- A diagram of how you will arrange your classroom and perhaps the seating arrangements you will use during different kinds of activities, and why you chose the arrangement(s) you did
- What you believe regarding classroom management—this will be based upon your philosophy of education and would include what you know about your teaching style
- Classroom rules and how you will communicate them to your students and parents
- How you propose to manage students that misbehave and how you will encourage positive behavior in your classroom
- Classroom procedures—this includes generally how you will conduct your lessons and assessments

Your management plan also should include a consideration of the unexpected. Interruptions and unexpected events occur periodically, and you should be ready when they do. They range from fire drills, to students getting sick, to your own personal family emergencies. You should have contingency plans ready for such unexpected events.

Routines can help. Among the first tasks of a teacher each school year is to determine how the students will spend their time each day, that is, the daily routines and weekly classroom schedule. Middle school and secondary teachers, who typically deal with a bell schedule and whose students move from room to room, will already have most of the scheduling decisions made for them, but all teachers have to create routines for their classroom time.

We recommend that you make your daily agenda visible to your students each day, such as by using the chalkboard, whiteboard, or electronic Smart Board to display the tasks of the day. Students will be able to see what to expect as they come in. Further, by making a habit of doing this, you will tend to be more organized yourself.

You will also occasionally find that your lesson may move faster than you expected. This is generally not a problem in a self-contained classroom, but it is not so good for students in a seventh-grade class to have a bunch of extra minutes with nothing to do. Even experienced teachers sometimes end up short on their timing. When this happens, don't fill the time by letting students talk. Instead, plug in more instruction, such as a written reflection, a review, or even an educational game. Having available several minilessons for backup can also be helpful when your regular period is shortened, such as for an early dismissal due to weather or for a school assembly.

Remember that classroom management extends to instructional and noninstructional time. That is, whenever students are present—whether or not a planned lesson is underway—classroom management is still your responsibility. *Unit II: Classroom Management* will provide you with a thorough discussion of this critical topic.

Working With Parents

Forging a positive parent–school relationship is very important to a child's development, and you should always remember that parents are the most important teachers in their children's lives. Often it is difficult, however, to get them engaged with their child's school. On the other hand, some parents may become overengaged, even meddling in matters that should only be your province as the teacher. Some parents will claim that teachers give lip service to their involvement but that they disregard their ideas. So you can see that working with parents can be complicated and challenging. It requires respect, humility, openness, and certainly a lot of tact.

> *Working with parents requires respect, humility, openness, and tact.*

A way to get off on a good footing with parents is to visit with them in their homes or on neutral ground rather than at school. This can also be an opportunity for you to invite them into your classroom to observe. Also, it is an opportunity to find out what the parents know and can do that might support your classroom educational program. Perhaps you'll discover one who loves gardening and would help you with creating a school wildflower garden or nature trail. Maybe one of your parents can help with your class website, and so on. Parents can be a great help on field trips as drivers and chaperones, and you can hold brief training sessions with them so that they can help with group activities. Consider that your parents represent a huge resource pool for your classroom-instructional program.

One thing to remember when communicating to parents is to avoid education jargon. Terms like "constructivism," "metacognition," "cooperative learning," and "multiple intelligences" are not in the vocabularies of most parents. Don't try to snow them with your intelligence, just use plain talk and remember to maintain good eye contact and body language, such as favoring an open- rather than a closed-body position. As you get to know your students' parents, you will better understand the community in which they live and its subcultures.

TRY THIS: UNDERSTANDING YOUR SCHOOL (SOCIOGRAM)

Creating a *sociogram* may provide you some insight into the relationships among students in your class or school. This is a tool that can be constructed in a number of ways. A sociogram is a mapping of the interrelationships within a group, conducted to reveal group structure (the pattern of friendships and subgroup affiliations). With an accurate sociogram, you can see how a child in your class relates to others. Referring to a sociogram can help you understand your class's behavior and make better classroom-management decisions.

How to Do It

One way to create a chart of classroom relationships is to use what are called "negative questions" to find out about interpersonal resistance. For example, you could ask students to write down responses to the question, "Which three classmates do you like the least?" This would be called a "fixed negative nomination" technique. If the students were also asked to rank their classmates from most to least disliked, it would be called a "fixed rank, negative nomination" technique. Researchers have found that collecting data for this kind of sociogram sometimes elicits unfavorable emotional reactions from students. It is important to be sensitive in asking these questions and assure your students that you are gathering data to help you understand the class better. So, negative nomination information is useful for getting the big picture of your students as a group.

Of course, there is also a "positive nomination" technique. To go with this approach you ask your students questions about who they "like" or would "like to do" something with. An example would be, "Which three students would you most like to sit with?" What you do is to restrict their choices to only so many nominations, three in this example. You could ask a student to name the three other students in class who are their best friends, or the three students they would want to play a game with. This technique is called a "fixed positive nomination."

It is interesting to compare sociograms constructed using each of these techniques. Your students who get a lot of positive nominations and few if any negative ones are typically considered popular, while those who receive a lot of negative nominations and few if any positive ones are typically considered unpopular or "rejected" (Sherman, 2000). Analyzing further, you can identify your class "stars" (both negative and positive ones), isolates, and "ghosts"—those who are not even acknowledged as being in the classroom. These are the students who haven't received any positive nominations or any negative ones.

You can also identify group phenomena, such as mutual choices (pairs who chose each other), chains (when one nominates another who nominates another—usually leading to a "star"), triangles and circles (when a chain comes back on itself), and islands (when pairs or small groups are separated from the larger patterns and members are not nominated by anyone in other patterns). Mutual negative choices are a red flag, of course, and should never be placed in the same small group. So, you can see how a sociogram would be useful for grouping students into cooperative groups. Other red flags are patterns that potentially reveal threats to a positive classroom climate, such as overactive competition among students or the development of in-groups or cliques and out-groups.

As you might expect, there are commercial software programs available that take a lot of the work out of creating useful classroom sociograms. One inexpensive program is Walsh's Classroom Sociometrics Program, available from www.classroom sociometrics.com.

Content Area(s) Standards and Assessment

Returning again to what you need to know to plan your classroom curriculum, you may recall that one of them is the subject matter. As you begin your planning, be sure to examine your state and national standards for the subject(s) at the grade level you teach, as well as your textbooks and supplemental materials. Standards for the fifty states can be downloaded at www.academicbenchmarks.com/. Studying your state's standards will help you determine what content you must address.

Some teachers find it helpful to extract the main ideas from their standards or curriculum framework and outline them or create a *concept map* (a *semantic web*). Figure I.4 (see page 42) is an example of a teacher-made concept map for Grade 5 science in the Virginia Standards of Learning curriculum framework (Board of Education, 2010). These concept maps can be drawn out by hand, of course, but the one in Figure I.4 was created by Inspiration® software (you can try it free for one month, www.inspiration.com). This program is intuitive to use and creates maps that can be exported into many file formats. It is available for both Windows and Mac operating systems.

If you have a spare calendar or can generate one on your computer, you will find it is a helpful tool in planning. With a calendar you can visualize the time in the month or in the academic term and then map out what you want your students to be studying in a subject over the course of the semester or school year. Think of it as a process of merging your curriculum concept map to your time frame for delivery. Through this process of organizing your lessons, you'll be able to roughly pace yourself as you teach. However, don't let your plan and timeline become a rigid dictate for enacting your classroom curriculum. The plan should only be a rough guide. You must be sensitive to "conditions on the ground" and be ready to modify your plans and timeline as you judge from your ongoing assessments. Remember, you are meeting children's needs and, to a reasonable extent, must "go with the flow."

An assessment simply describes what data you will use to decide whether your lesson objectives have been achieved. This topic will be addressed in detail in Unit IV, but as with classroom management, it is something to consider as part of your planning. Far from just happening when a lesson ends, a good assessment precedes instruction, continues throughout the lesson, and then shows up again when evaluating student progress.

Assessment must be based on your unit goals and lesson objectives. It is about gathering all the information that you will use to *evaluate* your students. Evaluation is the actual judgment you make as to the degree a student has achieved the objectives. Assessment is both *formative* and *summative.* Formative assessment should be embedded throughout your lessons. It helps you determine such things as the pace of the lessons and whether particular topics have already been learned or will need reteaching. Assessment can involve using scoring guides or *rubrics* for projects, written and oral reports, group work, and student journals. As to the summative assessment, it occurs at the end of the unit (or grading period) and can take many forms, typically involving a written test for older students, though it can be a portfolio of the work that a student accomplished during the time the unit was taught. *Unit IV: Assessment* will provide you with a complete explanation of how to go about assessing and evaluating your students.

■ SECOND: SHORT-RANGE PLANNING

Long-rang planning provides the broader perspective of what you want to accomplish with your students and it *informs,* but does not organize, your day-to-day activities in the classroom. For that we take what you have set down in the long-range plan and use it as the guide for developing **short-range plans**, which might include unit plans and daily planning or lesson plans.

Unit Plans

Unit planning begins with identifying the particular content to be taught and your goals for learning outcomes. *Goals* are about your purpose or aim. They relate to your *rationale* for teaching the particular content that your students will study.

Goals help set the stage for study and typically are written as broad statements. Often they are tied to state or national curriculum standards. It is important to always remember that your goals should go beyond the basic cognitive (knowledge) domain. Don't neglect to consider the affective and psychomotor domains (for more on this, you may wish to research the White House Conferences on Education). Note that other scholars have also created models for educational domains. So, using Yager and McCormack's (1989) domains, you will need to go beyond the knowledge (knowing and understanding) domain and also address the creative (imagining and creating), attitudinal (feeling and valuing), process (exploring and discovering), and application (using and applying or connecting) domains.

Your introductory lesson to the unit should be given extra attention. You will want this lesson to grab your students' attention and stimulate them to want to know more. There are many exciting ways to begin a new unit, but reading a chapter out of a textbook is not one of them. Likewise, you should give attention to your culminating lesson. You will want to wrap up your unit by helping students reflect upon and synthesize the content that they studied. If there is to be a final test or exam, you might also plan a review activity that is also fun. Framing a review in a game such as "Jeopardy!" is an example. Another way to wrap up a unit is for students to present individual or group projects. Depending on the project and the quality you expect, you might even consider culminating with presentations to other students, or to family and community members.

Single-Topic Units

Probably the most typical way teachers plan their classroom curriculum is in terms of instruction in units organized around a single topic. This kind of organization generally reflects a daily schedule in which reading, math, science, social studies, and so forth are taught separately and divided from each other by assigned time periods. Many of us have been taught most often this way. Remember the unit on the Civil War? It is likely it was organized this way. Another example would be the math unit on fractions and the science unit on weather.

Thematic Units

Thematic units use a single topic to address several subject areas.

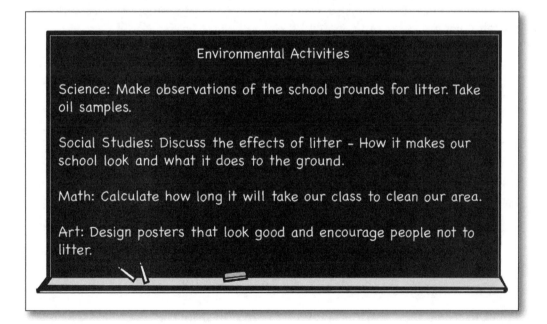

Environmental Activities

Science: Make observations of the school grounds for litter. Take oil samples.

Social Studies: Discuss the effects of litter – How it makes our school look and what it does to the ground.

Math: Calculate how long it will take our class to clean our area.

Art: Design posters that look good and encourage people not to litter.

Instruction through **thematic units** assumes students learn best when the curriculum is a coherent whole and when they can connect their studies to the real world. The challenge for the teacher is to integrate content from many subjects, all the while being specific enough to be practical yet broad enough to encourage creativity.

Instruction in a unit organized around a theme integrates, for example, reading, math, and science through the study of a broad area, like, for example, "energy" or "exploration." The rationale for the thematic approach is that it demonstrates the interdisciplinary nature of learning itself. First among the reasons for using a thematic approach is that student interest and engagement are likely to increase. Thematic planning lets you use collaborative and cooperative learning, as well as classroom computers. Further, you end up with a more compact curriculum—with less content overlap and simpler organization of the content. This approach also expands both your assignment and your assessment options.

Often, thematic units are team taught, and several teachers work together to plan and teach the unit. Either way, you begin by selecting an appropriate theme reflecting the curriculum, student interests, experiences, issues, or problems. Identify the goals you wish students to accomplish by the end of the unit. These can be related to state and local standards and competencies. Select and organize content-rich and challenging activities to use. Activities will be broad based, integrating many subject areas.

When your unit is completed, it should be stored for later access. Probably it will first reside on your computer hard drive. We suggest you back up your hard drive regularly and also store a hard copy of it in a file folder in a filing cabinet, where it will be easy to find the next go round. Alternatively, a loose-leaf binder will do if that works for you. Either way, a hard copy will probably be helpful as a place to make notes for changes as you go, and it can later be used for making revisions on the electronic version. The hard copy in the file cabinet can be altered as your class and the content change and as different teaching resources become available.

Single Topic Units

Most typical. This kind of organization generally reflects a daily schedule in which reading, math, science, social studies, and so forth are taught separately and divided from each other by assigned time periods.

Thematic Units

Assumes students learn best when the curriculum is a coherent whole and when they can connect their studies to the real world. The rationale is that it demonstrates the interdisciplinary nature of learning itself.

Goals and Objectives

Objectives for a daily lesson plan are drawn from the broader goals of the unit plan but are more specific and often stated as learning outcomes that are achieved over a defined time period. In writing lesson objectives, consider first what you want your students to be able to do as a result of the lesson. Also consider the conditions students will work under to accomplish the desired outcomes and the criteria you will use to judge a satisfactory attainment of the objectives—in other words, how your students will demonstrate that they have met the objectives of your lesson. Also consider if your students are ready for the new material or if first they will need some prerequisite knowledge or skills to succeed. This step allows you to factor in any needed preparatory work so that the necessary prerequisites are attained and students are able to meet the objectives. Finally, based on the unit goals, decide how many lessons will cover the unit and write a specific objective for each lesson.

While every education professor will have preferences for how you do lesson plans for his or her class, there really is no single right way to organize your units or lessons. Check to see if your school or school district requires a particular format. Many states will have sample lessons available that illustrate how to teach to their standards, so look for those to see if they are useful for your own classroom. You can always modify such lessons or the lessons you find that are suggested in textbooks. The format of the sample lessons might be useful as well as a guide for your own planning. We will consider a couple of different formats in this unit.

Usually lessons are planned in the context of a *unit of instruction*—a series of lessons organized around a theme or related concepts. In science, for example, a unit might be created on weather or mammals; in social studies, perhaps on Colonial America; in math, on fractions. So, we recommend you first conceptualize your unit. Begin by roughly sketching out what you want your students to learn in general: the unit goals.

In writing your goals, ask yourself why you are teaching this unit. What do you want your students to learn from it (knowledge, skills, attitudes, and appreciations)? How will you answer when a students ask, "Why do we have to learn this?" Consider giving an answer that tells them how learning whatever it is will benefit them now in their daily lives, rather than, for example, when they are in high school or college or working a job.

> *When writing your goals, ask yourself how will you answer when a student asks, "Why do I have to learn this?"*

An example will illustrate how goals differ from objectives. A unit on biomes in science may have the following goal: "Students will understand and appreciate the diversity of plants and animals that make up each of the biomes." The lesson objectives, however, will be more specific and contain indicators that will inform you if the student has achieved the objective, such as, "The student will define diversity in the words of others or in his or her own words," or "The student will explain how maintaining the species diversity in a particular biome can be achieved."

In general, units will have goals, which are more general statements of what is to be accomplished, while *lessons* within the unit will have more specific objectives.

In general, **units** will have *goals*, which are more general statements of what is to be accomplished, while **lessons** within the unit will have more specific *objectives*.

Elements common to most lesson plans include

- Objectives (sometimes combined with the state standards being addressed)
- Activities (read-alouds, investigations, role-plays, WebQuests, homework, etc.)
- Time estimates
- Materials needed
- Alternatives (for students who may be absent during a lesson, or for differentiating instruction for different ability levels or interests)
- Assessment

Sometimes teachers also include *prerequisites* that indicate what the students need to know or be able to do to achieve the objective(s). It is always important to consider prior knowledge and skills when you are planning instruction, since researchers have found that most learning, more than two-thirds, is dependent on how prepared the students are for the instruction.

Activities are the "meat" of your lessons and should be carefully planned. Don't include activities just to keep students busy. Each activity should contribute to the students meeting the lesson's objectives.

Using your calendar as a rough guide, you can write out or word process your units and lessons. Teachers vary a great deal as to the level of detail they create in their lesson plans, and this typically changes with years of experience as well. Some will use an outline with times indicated to help keep track, while others will write out detailed notes on the content. We recommend that you have a daily agenda prepared that can be shared with your students, and this will help you to make smooth transitions as you move through topics and activities.

Here are some variations on the writing of instructional objectives:

Gronlund Objectives

Gronlund (1999) suggests beginning with a general statement and then giving specific examples of topics to be taught or behaviors to be observed. An example of an objective from a Gronlund perspective is,

The student can perform simple multiplication

    a. can define what multiplication means, in his or her own words
    b. can define relevant terms such as "multiplier" and "product"
    c. can solve problems of the type $5 \times 4 =$ _____.

Mager Objectives

Mager (1997) suggests writing very specific statements about observable outcomes. This type is called a *behavioral objective*. An example of this kind of objective is, "The student will name at least seven of ten state capitals." While there are advantages and disadvantages to each approach, we will illustrate most of our examples in this chapter using Mager's approach, since it is the most widely used and perhaps the most inclusive.

Eisner (or Expressive) Objectives

Elliot Eisner (1997) proposes that not all instructional objectives should focus on a specific outcome and that some should focus on the learning process itself. This type of objective is called an expressive objective. Two examples are as follows:

- Students will walk on a trail in the woods.
- Students will use multiplication in everyday activities.

"TSW" Objectives

TSW is an abbreviation commonly used by teachers in lesson plans. It stands for "The student will . . ." The next word that follows will be a verb that both identifies the desired learning outcome and the level of thought required (see Figure I.7, page 45). This is where Bloom's Taxonomy or another scheme of instructional domains, such as the one suggested by Yager and McCormack (1989), is useful. For example, the verbs *recall, describe, apply, analyze, predict, construct,* and *judge* are representative of Bloom, in order from the lowest level to the highest level.

The following are examples of properly written objectives:

- TSW list three characteristics of mammals.
- TSW draw the food pyramid.
- TSW explain the actions of the main character in the book.
- TSW name three conditions that led to the Great Depression.
- TSW solve ten multiplication problems (with two digit multipliers).
- TSW distinguish between elements and compounds.
- TSW compare the health care systems of the U.S. and Cuba.
- TSW label the bones of the torso.
- TSW define three of four vocabulary words.
- TSW order the layers of a soil profile from the ground downward.

Using Bloom's Taxonomy, try to identify the level of each of the preceding objectives (see Figure III.5, page 130).

Here are examples of poorly written objectives:

- TSW mix the ingredients in a bowl to make plaster of paris in class. [What makes this a poor objective? Because this is an activity, not an *outcome of instruction.*]
- TSW work in groups using magnets and other materials. [This is an activity.]
- The teacher will provide work sheets for students to review the story. [This is something that the teacher will do.]

STYLES FOR WRITING OBJECTIVES

Gronlund: Begin with a general statement then give specific examples.

Mager: Write specific statements about observable outcomes.

Eisner: Items focus on the learning process.

TSW: "The student will . . ." followed by a verb that both identifies the desired learning outcome and the level of thought required.

Remember when you are writing your lesson objectives that your students are to be assessed at the end of the lesson or unit based upon them. For this task, a grading rubric is very useful. Rubrics are simply scoring guides that provide criteria that can help you to evaluate the quality of completed work. You create a rating scale consisting of preestablished performance criteria (Parkay & Stanford, 2003). Typically, the rubric is given to students at the time the assignment is given. For them, the listed criteria identify what their work must include for them to be successful. Figure I.5 (see page 43) provides an example of a grading rubric.

Lesson Plans

As is the case with objectives and unit planning, **lesson plans** come in different varieties. Some schools adopt a style that all teachers are to follow. It may also be the case that in your student-teaching experience, there was (will be) a particular format that you were (are) supposed to follow. Of course, in these situations you will need to be sure to meet the expectations placed upon you. However, when it really comes right down to conceptualizing how you will teach something, the format must be something that works for you. We are not suggesting that you try to bamboozle anybody and slide your preferred lesson plan style by them. However, plan in a way that facilitates your work and then, if need be, you can write it out in a format that satisfies your other requirements. It will not be difficult to do because your plan will already have the necessary elements.

Traditional Lesson Plans

A traditional lesson plan is the generic format that is used in most introductory methods courses. It looks like this:

GRADE LEVEL(S): 5
SUBJECT(S): SOCIAL STUDIES/U.S. HISTORY

Description

This unit begins with students identifying their ancestors, identifying their ethnic backgrounds, connecting historic events with the lives of their ancestors, and growing into their own unique personal identities, and leads to students developing a better understanding of the U.S. as a melting pot. We will focus upon the concept of immigration and relate the past to the current issues of immigration in the U.S.

Goal

The primary purpose is to foster an understanding that America is politically, ethnically, culturally, and economically a nation of immigrants. Study will focus on the motivations for immigration, the dangers of the journey to America, the challenges in adapting to a new world, and the development of a melting pot culture in this country.

Objectives (Days 1–5): The students will

1. record and transcribe an interview of their families,

2. provide documentation of immigrant ancestors,

3. write an overview of the country after researching their country or countries of origin.

Materials

The main resources will be family interviews, documents, records, and pictures. For interviews, students may use tape recorders, digital cameras, notebooks, and pens/pencils.

Procedure

Family Tree Activity

Students will trace the family tree, if possible as far back as their ancestors who were immigrants.

Diagram the family tree

Place of birth

Pictures (if available)

What brought them to the U.S.

Summary of their lives in the country of origin and in the U.S.

Research the history of U.S. immigration

Examples of customs, dress, music, religious traditions, etc.

Written overview of the country of origin (2–3 pages)

Family traditions that relate to ancestry

Report will be written and shared orally

This assignment can be a resource throughout the school year in teaching the history of the U.S.

Assessment

The oral presentations and reports will be graded using two teacher-created rubrics.

Note that the objectives are written using behavioral verbs that indicate what the students will do (e.g., interview, seek, research, and write). Conceptualizing objectives in this way emphasizes student engagement in the lesson. Figure I.6 (see page 44) provides you with a traditional lesson plan template. Figure I.7 (see page 45) provides you with a list of behavioral verbs as suggestions.

Some traditional forms also include other sections, such as "anticipatory set," "extensions," and "modifications." Another traditional lesson plan format is taken from Madeline Hunter's planning model. The basic format for that model is illustrated below. Figure I.8 (see page 46) provides a template for using this lesson plan format.

MADELINE HUNTER LESSON PLAN FORMAT

1. **Anticipatory set**: a brief activity or prompt that focuses student attention at the beginning of a lesson; can be a discrepant event, a handout, or focusing question

2. **Purpose**: the objective(s), what is to be learned and/or what students will be able to do

3. **Input**: procedure, what the teacher will do. Includes vocabulary and skills, etc.

4. **Modeling**: what you will show or demonstrate so that the students understand what is expected of them, what a finished product will look like

5. **Guided practice**: how you will lead the students step by step using the trimodal approach—hear/see/do

6. **Checking for understanding** (CFU): using questioning strategies to find out if the students have achieved the objectives and to help you pace the lesson

7. **Independent practice**: what students will do to practice on their own

8. **Closure**: how you will end the lesson; can be a review or summary or the "L" part of a K-W-L

Learning Cycle Lesson Plans

The **Learning Cycle** planning format is based upon a *constructivist* perspective on learning that can be traced back to John Dewey. In this view, ideas are not transmitted by teachers telling them to their students but are actively constructed by the students themselves. Among the founders of this view of learning were Piaget and Vygotsky, and from their theories, an instructional model emerged in the 1960s that would later be called the Learning Cycle. This format is most popular among science teachers but has relevance for other subjects as well. The original format for the Learning Cycle had only three steps (Exploration, Invention, Discovery), but the format evolved into five steps and most recently seven (Eisencraft, 2003). The purpose of changing the model to the 7E format is to remind teachers of the importance of eliciting students' prior knowledge and the extending of concepts to the real world and to other areas where they may be relevant. Here are the steps with a brief description of each phase:

1. **Elicit**: You assess the students' prior knowledge of the content, which can be a pretest or a K-W-L chart, or simply by conducting a talk with your class about what they know.

2. **Engage**: You do a demonstration or pose a problem that helps focus student attention to the topic, helps them make connections, and gives them a heads-up as to what they will be studying.

3. **Explore**: Now your students are at the center of the action as they seek information or collect data to solve a problem.

4. **Explain**: Here students report what they did and what answer(s) to the problem emerged while you introduce new vocabulary and use questions to assess their understandings of the concepts.

5. **Elaborate (or Expand)**: You offer new information that adds to the study and you pose problems or issues that students solve or discuss by applying what they have learned.

6. **Evaluate**: Students self-assess, and you evaluate by whatever means you choose to find out what they have learned.

7. **Extend**: Here you help students connect newly acquired skills and knowledge to new situations within the subject area or to other subject areas.

Much research has been conducted on the effectiveness of the Learning Cycle approach and supports the conclusion that this planning model, compared against traditional approaches, results in better student achievement and retention of concepts, as well as improved attitudes, more sophisticated reasoning ability, and better performance of process skills (Gerber, Cavallo, & Merrick, 2001). Using a Learning Cycle format can help you develop a conceptual storyline that accommodates both selection and sequencing of teaching activities so that you avoid fragmented activities (Ramsey, 1993). But always remember, there is no one best lesson-planning model. Elements of the models presented here can be used to create a framework that best fits your own teaching philosophy. Figure I.9 (see page 47) provides a template for using the learning cycle format.

Projects and Group Work

Social studies and science are subjects amenable for long-term, challenging projects, something that your students might take on over the course of several weeks. Such projects provide opportunities for students to work together to conduct investigations, and some projects can contribute to integrating your classroom curriculum.

An example of such a project is a project that involves students in building a catenary arch. The social studies connection is history, while the science is forces. A catenary arch is an arch that distributes the forces evenly throughout the curve of the arch. Once the keystone, or top piece of the arch, is put in place between the two ascending sides, the arch will support itself. Students would first research the meaning of the term, perhaps by doing an Internet search. The actual construction would begin with a drawing of the arch on paper.

Patterns made from the drawing would then be used to cut pieces from corrugated cardboard boxes. The pieces would be glued together with white school glue (or by using a hot-glue gun) and the arch assembled by stacking the pieces on top of each other, without glue or fasteners. You can view an example of a constructed arch at www.coker.edu/educationdept/arches_of_ the_world.htm.

Another example of an integrative project would be to have students build a working greenhouse. The basic ingredients would include PVC pipe, PVC fittings, and plastic sheeting. After the construction is completed, students can plan investigations related to plant growth and life cycles by planting seeds and recording plant growth measurements. Visit this website to see a student-built greenhouse: www.coker.edu/educationdept/tomatopage.htm.

There are a number of strategies that you can use to manage student group work. You can assign your groups and have each group commit to a contract that outlines what each member is responsible for and the consequence for not contributing to the group (i.e., they would have to leave the group or lose points). As a reminder, you can post the contract so the groups can refer to it when a group member is off task. Further, you can have the groups select a leader who will be held responsible for keeping the rest of the group on track. You could create added incentives by awarding bonus points to leaders whose group meets all the deadlines. Plan to meet with your group leaders periodically for them to report what progress they have made. The group leader can alternate daily or weekly depending upon the extent of the project, so that everyone will have a chance to be the leader.

Another management strategy is to give each group a pacing guide and have them fill in the due dates. Have the groups record what they are going to do during their class time and what each group member is responsible for. You can give points to the groups that accomplish their goals each day or week. Group projects also provide an opportunity to use student notebooks or journals. Have students write a reflection in their journals at the end of each day or week that describes what they have done and learned. You can use this as one way to assess the group's progress and understanding. This process also encourages the group members to communicate and reflect.

Sometimes disagreements will crop up if students are in groups with classmates that they do not like. While students should learn to work with others, you can avoid this predicament by using the sociogram you created at the beginning of the year in assigning groups. If you don't have a sociogram, you can have your students write down a list of, say, ten or fifteen students they would like to work with and one student that they do not want to work with. From the lists you can then assign groups that are more likely to work well together.

Each group should have a place in the classroom to store all of their project work. You can also do periodic checks of their cubbies or folders to monitor the groups' progress. Figure I.10 (see page 48) presents additional tips for managing groups.

NOW: CLASSROOM ORGANIZATION ■

If you are a teacher who has a home-base classroom, as is typical of elementary teachers, among your first tasks each year is deciding how to organize the classroom space. Depending on the type of school furniture, you may have some options in how to arrange the desks and how to store and make materials and equipment accessible. Take a moment to consider the following questions:

- Given how you prefer everyone to interact, how should the classroom furniture be arranged—your own desk, the students' desks, tables and chairs, and so forth?
- What will work best for materials storage and independent or group work areas?

Even when they are empty, classrooms can be all kinds of spaces, and this is especially true for classrooms in elementary schools. Some of those are the traditional rooms not much different from what existed in the one-room schoolhouse, while others are organized in multiclass open spaces. These days many classrooms at all levels are located in transportable modules—"double-wides." Some classrooms have sinks and water. Some have nooks and crannies and even separate breakout rooms for preparation and storage. In some classrooms, students keep their books and belongings in their desks, while in others they use lockers or cubbies that may be located in the classroom or out in the hallway.

Student Seating

A big advantage of self-contained classrooms is that teachers usually have some latitude in deciding details of how the room is to be organized. You may or may not have a choice as to what kind of seating your students will have. But small things like the type of furniture and how it is arranged can make a big difference in facilitating student learning. Slant-topped desks and desks or tables bolted to the floor would be an obstacle for many kinds of activities. Movable furniture and flat-topped desks offer more flexibility and more options for student interaction, and from a learning theory perspective, interaction is what it is all about.

Let's assume your students will have movable, flat-topped desks. Some teachers prefer student desks to be separate from each other and typically arrange them in rows facing a chalkboard or whiteboard. This traditional setup reflects a teaching style that emphasizes individual work. Alternatively, you could group four desks together or use tables instead of desks as workspaces. Desks in clusters would better facilitate students' conversations, cooperative learning, and your own movement around the classroom. On the other hand, having desks in the traditional rows and columns arrangement provides independent work spaces and a more structured atmosphere. Even if your intention is to eventually group student work desks, you may find it advantageous to begin with the row and column layout as a start.

Student seating can be flexible, organizing desks and tables to suit your instructional needs.

Teacher's Seating

Consider, too, the location of your own desk in the classroom. What's the message to students when your desk is in the back versus the front of the classroom? Have you ever seen one in the center?

Even in the most activity-rich classroom, there will be times when your students will be working at their desks or in groups while you are at your desk. Certainly you won't want your desk placed in such a position that your back will be to your students! Find the spot and place your desk where you have the best view of your classroom.

Placement of the teacher's desk in the front of the room, and used as the place from which class is conducted, is rarely used. The placement of a desk between the student and teacher establishes a barrier between student and teacher. More typically, with the desk used primarily for administrative activities (rather than as a teaching station), it is positioned in a less conspicuous location.

Independent Work Areas

Centers are special classroom workplaces. They are more common in elementary classrooms but are useful throughout preK–12 and are especially helpful for teachers who differentiate instruction. Your classroom might have one or more subject-related centers, or a single center might be used for different subjects at different times. A math center will have measuring devices and various manipulatives. A science center can be supplied with materials that allow for independent or small-group investigations and study. There can be centers for reading and social studies too. You can guide your students to share responsibility with you for recording work done for center assignments.

Here is an example of a fourth-grade teacher who has a science and math center. It consists of a table and several shelves for storage. On one shelf is a terrarium housing a pair of anoles. Another shelf contains math manipulatives—Cuisenaire rods, pattern blocks, attribute blocks, Unifix cubes, number bars, chip trading materials, geoboards, and color cubes. Another shelf has materials used in both math and science, such as blank paper and graph paper, calculators, rulers, measuring cups, plastic beakers, a trundle wheel, meter sticks, spring scales, and an equal-arm platform balance. Science supplies in the center include microscopes, containers, eyedroppers, magnifiers, magnets, a collection of seashells and various other specimens, and reference books and data sheets for recording observations.

A center also can be created to complement a particular instructional unit. For example, if you are teaching a fifth-grade unit on insects, you could create a center featuring Peterson's *A Field Guide to Insects* (Borror & White, 1998), containers with various examples of insects, an ant farm (or butterfly hatchery), and magnifiers for students to examine different specimens. The center might also be decorated with colorful posters and include periodicals with features on insects (like *National Geographic Kids*), a computer connected to the Internet, and interactive games like Predator–Prey. If you are aiming for a differentiated classroom, be sure to provide reading materials at different levels.

Students can use a center if they are working on individual or group projects or working with computers, but that is not the only way to use centers. In some instances, you may want all students to gain particular experiences in small groups. This can be accomplished by creating several centers and then having assigned groups of students rotate through them during the same class time or on successive days. Figure I.11 (see page 49) illustrates one hassle-free procedure for moving groups of students from center to center (Novelli, 1995).

Resource Storage/Availability

You have probably noticed that teaching requires *stuff* (remember *The Theory of Loose Parts*?). Some stuff will need to be stored much of the time. You may be fortunate to have an adequate storage area, but in many classrooms, space for storing materials and equipment is at a premium. Teachers often use cardboard file boxes or plastic containers and bins of different sizes to store materials. *Organizing* your materials for easy retrieval is a key to making teaching manageable.

There are many ways to organize. For example, you might color-code your storage bins and label them clearly. You might want to use shelves so that each bin is accessible without requiring removal of the ones above. Whatever system you choose, don't be afraid to modify it so that it works for your particular situation and style.

In addition to storage space, there is a need for space in the classroom for students to temporarily house projects and work that is in progress. Access to the Internet is typically needed, requiring space for one or more computers and their peripherals—printer, scanner, external hard drive, and so forth.

Two points are significant: One is that the success of your classroom program can be facilitated by classroom design, and the second is that teaching requires *stuff* and *space,* for its doing and for its preparation, as well as space for storage. Hence you as teacher will contribute much *behind the scenes* to maintain a quality classroom program by handling logistics and organizing materials for use and for storage. One plus to all this is that being prepared will give you more confidence as you move through enacting your classroom curriculum.

Communication

From rules to sign-up sheets, part of your overall organizational plan will include how to get information out to the students.

In any classroom, there is no shortage of information to be disseminated that is not part of the explicit curriculum. From rules to sign-up sheets, part of your overall organizational plan will include how to get information out to the students.

Class Rules

Ideally, class rules should be negotiated early on between you and your students (see Unit II). This process can begin with the question, "What rules can we all agree upon that will make our classroom life together more pleasant and supportive of everyone's learning?"

Typically, things go better in classroom life if students

- arrive to school (or class) on time;
- come to class prepared, with required books, paper/notebook(s), and pens or pencils to class;
- attend to personal needs before class time starts;
- turn off all cellular phones;
- do not eat or chew gum in class;
- stay seated unless given permission to stand and move;
- raise a hand if they want to speak;
- respect the person who "has the floor";
- use respectful language when speaking;
- respect the personal space of others;
- respect other's and school property;

- do not interfere with the learning of others;
- submit only work that represents academic honesty (meaning that the borrowed work of others is cited and referenced).

One K–8 school has only one schoolwide rule, which students call *the Big One*, which everyone memorizes. It states, "Treat yourself, others, and the environment with care." Though we will discuss rules in detail in *Unit II: Classroom Management*, we want to mention here that rules of which the students are not aware are not rules at all. Whatever rules you ultimately use in class, it will be necessary that they are posted somewhere easily seen and that students know the rules of your classroom.

Assignments

In the past, homework was often dry and boring stuff . . . "Read the chapter, answer questions 1–6 at the end of the chapter" or "Look up the vocabulary words in the glossary and write the definitions." This kind of homework rarely challenges students and rarely results in meaningful learning. On the other hand, linking classroom instruction with the home can be motivating. There are many simple activities that students and their parents or guardians can conduct at home. Instructions can be provided on a take-home handout, or you can let the investigative teams come up with their own procedures. It is these kinds of activities that strengthen the connections between student, school, and home, and give a student's caregivers opportunities to help and show interest in their child's work.

One elementary teacher sends the students in her third-grade class home on Friday with a science activity packed in a ziplock baggie. Included in the baggie are the science materials, instructions for carrying out one or more investigations, a data sheet or worksheet, and a "Science Wizard Form" for the parent to verify that the student completed the activity at home. On Monday, the teacher recreates the activity that the student and parent have done at home. This teacher says that she receives immediate responses from most students because they have done the activity. Students are encouraged to discuss questions that came up at home. Examples of some take-home activities include exploring magnets or the properties of Alka-Seltzer (effervescence); building an aluminum-foil barge and then estimating the number of pennies that can be placed in it before it sinks; seed sorting and graphing; completing estimation activities; graphing and sorting gummy bears; and finding the center of gravity of a ball of clay.

If you are a secondary teacher, this theme can be adapted to your situation as well. It is not likely that you can prepare enough ziplock baggies for all of the students you will see in a day, but preprinted assignment/activity/investigation/research sheets (call it what you like) can always be on hand and in a convenient location. You may distribute these to students or establish a routine that students retrieve them on their own.

Sign-Up Sheets

A sign-up sheet can be a useful way to recruit parent volunteers for your classroom. During your initial conference with your parents, have in plain sight a sign-up sheet with column headings such as

Name—Phone—E-mail–What I can do to help—When I can be available

Sign-up sheets can be used for many purposes, such as a sign-up list for bringing in classroom supplies, signing up for a field trip, scheduling parent–teacher conferences, creating snack sign-up, organizing a fundraiser, recruiting volunteers for work days, orchestrating a car pool schedule, and planning a class party.

Strategies for Moving From Place to Place

Many middle and high schools operate on "bells," and classrooms in these schools are departmentalized in areas of the school as to their subjects: math, science, English, social studies, and so on. Unlike elementary teachers, who are typically generalists, teachers in these schools specialize in one or more subjects, and students move at the bell from classroom to classroom. In these schools, the instructional day usually begins after a homeroom period in which announcements are made and attendance taken. Changing classes every fifty or so minutes occurs throughout the rest of the school day.

There are many variations on daily schedules. For example, the period around lunchtime might be longer and subdivided into thirty-minute or less periods for eating lunch. There are also many variations in middle school staffing and scheduling. For example, in one school, a core team of teachers is responsible for the main subjects, which are block scheduled. Within that large block of time, the teaching team and the students can allot the time as they choose. One advantage of this approach is that it enables each subject to get taught in an integrated fashion with other subjects.

However, within the classroom, there are also many instructional activities that require students to be up and out of their seats, and that is a good thing as it stretches the body and can focus and energize the mind if done right. If not done right, chaos may result and little or no learning may result.

Figure I.11 showed you an example for a middle school history class where the teacher has created five stations for different activities in the room. After announcements at the opening of the period, the three or four member student teams are assigned group names and then given the go to move to a station. After fifteen minutes, students are told to rotate in the fashion depicted in Figure I.11. For example, in one center, the Gammas might be at the classroom computer entering data they collected interviewing their neighborhood old-timers about their experiences during the Depression. The Thetas are at a second station and are using headphones and taking notes as they listen to taped recordings from an NPR special. The Omegas are working together to create and practice a skit based on a book that they have been reading together, while the Betas are examining a photograph and comparing the objects in the photo to depictions on a map of the city. Meanwhile, the Alphas are measuring out a table on graph paper.

Scheduling the Day in a Self-Contained Classroom

A big advantage of self-contained classrooms is that teachers usually have some latitude in deciding details of the daily and weekly schedule. In terms of scheduling, the professional wisdom is that "students become more engaged in their own learning when the daily routine is predictable and consistent" (Fisher, 1992, p. 57). Opening and closing routines and transitions throughout the day are especially important. One teacher, for example, begins his third-grade students' day with sharing time and typically ends in the afternoon with a journaling activity. The routine that opens the day can serve as the "set" or advanced organizer for the day's learning tasks.

According to Fisher (1992), "Students become more engaged in their own learning when the daily routine is predictable and consistent." (p. 57)

Here is an example of a daily schedule a teacher created for her first-grade class:

8:40 am	Settling-in time
9:00	Group meeting—community circle
9:30	Science and/or workshop
11:00	Snack and recess
11:20	Math
12:10	Specialist (art, music, physical education, etc.)
12:45	Lunch
1:30	Social studies and/or workshop
2:10	Shared reading
2:30	Independent and collaborative reading or second specialist
2:55	Group meeting, community circle
3:10	Dismissal

You can infer from this schedule what this teacher considers important in her classroom curriculum. Prime time for instruction is in the morning and early afternoon. You can also see what the teacher values pedagogically. Emphasized in this schedule are both individual and group activities. This primary teacher seems to do some subject integration in the classroom curriculum and uses methods such as projects and group work.

Another consideration is that student learning of some subjects can be improved when longer periods are provided for more intensive studies. This is the rationale for **block scheduling**, which has become a popular way to create longer periods of student engagement, such as for project work or science labs. An example of this would be to designate Mondays, Wednesdays, and Thursdays with hour-and-a-half periods while Tuesdays and Fridays would have the regular fifty-minute periods. In our experience, most students are flexible enough to handle some daily variation. The professional wisdom is to aim for a predictable schedule for students but not necessarily with the same exact routine every day.

Even teachers in self-contained classrooms don't have complete control over their days, however, because they often have to work around the schedules of others, including the specialist teachers (music, art, physical education, ELL program, gifted program, etc.). Further, teachers may be compelled by school or district policies to divide the teaching time in a particular way. Such constraints aside, however, the teacher's personal pedagogical priorities are revealed in his or her scheduling. Typically, elementary teachers schedule reading and math in the morning and science and social studies in the afternoon. It is in the afternoon that our bodies experience the *postprandial dip*—a low energy and low attention period that is part of everyone's diurnal metabolic cycle. In recognition of this natural down time, some countries even shut down commerce for afternoon siestas. The early afternoon is not a time your class is likely to be the most creative or excited about schoolwork. Another thing about instruction in the afternoon slot is that this is most often the time when schools schedule assemblies and parent–teacher conferences, and this is the slot that is cut off for half-days.

Educational Decoration: Avoiding Overstimulation

Classrooms should not be overly decorated, especially with commercial products. Instead, have your students help you display their work around the room: their lab reports, sketches, concept maps, and so forth. This shows that you value their work and encourages them to take ownership and contribute to a positive classroom environment. Avoid, however, the tendency toward overstimulation. You likely have seen rooms that exemplify this—not a square inch of wall space is left exposed due to all of the posters, signs, charts, and other decorations. In such a setting the items displayed become nothing more than wallpaper from the students' perspective.

Whatever level you teach, the room to which students come to learn should be inviting and *comfortable.* Display those items to which you want your students to pay attention. Your classroom represents you, and that should represent a professional educator providing an environment conducive to learning.

A simple way to enhance the classroom environment is to add plants. The same plants can be a source of investigations. Dependable choices include geranium, begonia, coleus, impatiens, spider plants, tradescantia, ivy, snake plants, nephthytis, pothos, Chinese evergreen, and philodendron. Hardy plants that can tolerate water are best for the primary classrooms because young students like to care for them often. If the room has good sun, you might try miniature roses, sensitive plants (*Mimosa pudica*), and dwarf and scented geraniums. African violets also make good classroom plants, and forcing daffodil or tulip bulbs is a great activity.

> *Your classroom represents you, and that should represent a professional educator providing an environment conducive to learning.*

An aquarium can house aquatic plants and fish, or it can be used as a terrarium for many kinds of organisms. If your budget is tight, a terrarium can be made in a large jar, like a supersize pickle jar, or even in a two-liter clear plastic bottle. There are many interesting investigations involving plants. Using hydroponics is an example. A terrarium could be modified to model or simulate different ecosystems, such as a desert or wetland.

We need to point out that some animal-rights advocates claim that the educational benefits of having animals in the classroom are overstated and that the suffering of the animals involved is underestimated. What do you think about this issue?

TOMORROW: INSTRUCTIONAL PRESENTATION ■

So far in this unit we have considered practical matters, such as scheduling, arranging the classroom, and managing student work. Now we want to stress that learning is a *social* process. Knowledge itself is a social construct that is influenced by the cultures of the classroom, family, and community. And don't think that a student reading a book in a corner is constructing knowledge in isolation. Rather, that student is engaged in a social process; the student is interacting with the authors and illustrators of the book, assimilating and accommodating while pondering the ideas encountered, the familiar and the new. We know from Vygotsky (1978) that learning happens in the *interactions*, student-to-student, student-to-adult, student-to-author, and so forth, and thus it is the *quality of these interactions* that you will want to consider as you develop your teaching. You will want to plan activities that optimize the interactions. Students will demonstrate their knowledge, skills, attitudes, and appreciations from what they write or say, as, for example, they consider the merits of different ways of solving a problem.

> *Learning is a social process. A student reading a book in a corner is not constructing knowledge in isolation. That student is engaged in a social process; interacting with the authors and illustrators of the book, assimilating and accommodating while pondering the ideas being encountered, the familiar and the new.*

Vygotsky (1978) claimed that cognitive functions in general are internalizations of social actions. If you provide students access to appropriately nourishing experiences, such as opportunities to carry out investigations or to read a good science book, learning will come about naturally. The experience of the activity itself (reading the book) does *not* produce the knowledge. Vygotsky and others argue that knowledge does not derive directly from experience per se, from the sensory data alone, but rather that the student *makes sense* of the experience, actively constructing knowledge through the interaction, through inquiring in the context of a particular cultural setting (reading the book). Thus we come back to Dewey's claim that we *learn by thinking*.

Since learning is a natural consequence of positive social interactions focused upon challenging problems and issues, you can do much to enhance students' opportunities for learning by attending to the cultural setting of your classroom. Your task is thus to facilitate students' engagement with each other and with the subject matter. As Chaillé and Britain (1991) point out,

> Good environments for young students permit, encourage, and even necessitate interaction with others, from simple communicative interaction to the complex negotiation of conflicts. But social interaction is important not only because it is a part of life, but also because it actively contributes to students' theory building. (p. 9)

That is, their explanations and understandings. Unfortunately, the social interaction between students is often neglected in the classroom while attention is focused on the teacher–class interaction.

Use of the Primary Writing Surface

At the time of this writing the primary writing surface for teachers in the U.S. is still one of two things, either an old-fashioned blackboard/chalkboard or its modern counterpart, the dry-erase board. Slowly overtaking these primary writing surfaces in use in classrooms is the **interactive whiteboard** (IWB).

The oldest form of instructional technology is the slate, or blackboard, and it is one of the most basic forms of instructional media. The chalkboard/whiteboard helps you to emphasize key points. You can use the board to list assignment due dates and focus of the day's lesson. You can use the board to present a problem to the class that you will later address. You can use the board to present graphics, math problems, a vocabulary list, timelines, and so forth.

If you have a whiteboard, we recommend you use different colored markers to highlight important points or to create graphic organizers. You should try to write legibly and horizontally, making certain your writing is large enough for students to read from the most distant point in the room. You should be aware of any obstructions that may block your students' view of the board. If your students are taking notes, give them enough time to copy what's on the board, and don't erase anything while students are still copying. Though while you write on the board your back may be to the students, be careful to speak toward them, not toward the board. With practice, you'll be able to write while being attentive to the class.

The IWB is an electronic whiteboard writing surface that can capture writing electronically. The IWB is designed to allow interaction with a computer display. IWBs are becoming increasingly common in schools, and new skills and understanding are required to use them effectively in teaching. IWB is a versatile teaching tool and well worth the effort to learn to use.

> *Though while you write on the board your back may be to the students, be careful to speak toward them, not toward the board.*

Many classrooms have an **overhead projector** (OHP)—or its electronic version, a **document camera**—a technology that has the advantage of letting you face your class as you do your presentation. The overhead projector is one of the few teaching tools that was actually invented for educational use rather than adapted from an entertainment device.

The OHP will show a series of images (overhead transparencies—OHTs) in sequence. Such a series of OHTs can relieve you from looking at your notes so you can pay more attention to your students. The OHP really allows you to be more spontaneous in your teaching without constantly turning your back to a chalk or whiteboard. When using an OHP in a presentation, you can use a piece of file folder or cardboard to mask part of the image you don't want your audience to see until you are ready to reveal it.

Further, the OHP can be used in novel ways, other than showing commercial or teacher-made slides, or for outlining lesson notes as the class progresses. One possibility is to use a photocopier to make an OHT from a book or magazine, such as a map. Another strategy would be to distribute a blank OHT to each student group and have them create a graph, drawing, or concept map related to the content. Data collected in an experiment could be graphed, or the plot of a story outlined or webbed. The finished transparencies could be displayed while a group spokesperson explains.

You can have a copy of the class rules on an OHT and have it ready to display when necessary. You can have instructions for a lab activity or for a center assignment on an OHT for frequent reuse.

Another advantage of the OHP is the flexibility it provides in an interactive presentation, where you may have to jump around. You can easily take OHTs out of sequence to review or to jump ahead in response to a question. Plus, you can write on and amend OHTs, easily keeping them up-to-date.

Some negatives of OHPs are that they are bulky and the bulbs can burn out. Plus OHTs can smear, and both commercial and teacher-made ones often fade or wear with use.

Some tips for using the OHP effectively:

- First position it for optimum image size and be sure it is focused before the class starts.
- Be sure all your students can see the screen. This done, you do not have to look at the screen again and can concentrate on the class.

- If you need to point, use a pen or pointer and point to the OHT, not to the screen itself. Remember that you can also lay the pointer on the OHP so it stays pointing at the part you are focusing upon.
- Don't stand in front of the screen because some of the image will be projected onto you and that will be a distraction, plus there will be a large shadow on the screen.
- Remember to remove an OHT after you have finished with it and when you have moved on to talk about something else. It can be effective to switch off the OHP between sequences or to expound upon a point (though turning an OHP on and off seems to set you up for a burned-out bulb right in the middle of a presentation).

One thing that all three primary writing surfaces that we have discussed are capable of doing is expressing graphic organizers. Graphic organizers are one way for visual thinkers to work with content, and there are many expressions possible for visual ideas. Graphic organizers are variously called concept maps, mind mapping, semantic webs, brainstorms, idea showers, and visual organizers. An example in this unit is Figure I.4 (see page 42) illustrating the Grade 5 science content in Virginia schools. There are books, articles, and websites that can provide more examples. Other visual organizers include simple drawings, Venn diagrams, skill triangles, chain of events, K-W-L charts, and bar and pie graphs.

Technology (the Old and the New)

We have just considered some of the most useful educational technologies, the black-/whiteboard, the overhead projector, and the interactive whiteboard. Of course, there are many more tools available for the contemporary teacher.

Document cameras are devices that allow you to display magazine pages, books, graphics such as charts and maps, and even three-dimensional objects. Generally, the same suggestions that we made for the use of the OHP also apply to document cameras, especially the suggestion to use a piece of file folder or cardboard to cover part of a document so that only the aspect being discussed can be seen by the students. Three-dimensional objects show up more clearly when placed on a darker background rather than on white paper or directly on the platform. Glossy pages in books and magazines may produce a glare, but you can work with the settings to improve the image.

LCD projectors are used with a computer to project an image onto a screen or wall. Many classrooms have now been provided with this technology, which provides you more flexibility in the media that you can use in your classroom. One advantage of LCD projectors coupled with a computer is that you can access a large amount of text and a great variety of images from your computer to project for instruction. Further, you can project presentations made with software like Microsoft's PowerPoint or Apple's Keynote.

Our tips for PowerPoint/Keynote or web-based class presentations are the following:

- Begin your presentation with a title or main topic focus of the lesson.
- Continue with slides displaying key vocabulary and questions for student engagement, and highlighting main ideas.

- Telling a story is always engaging, so if you can arrange your slides to tell a story, you'll probably keep their attention.
- Engage your students in talking about the visuals, and talk to your students, not at them.
- Use the last slide as a discussion starter. Encourage your students to summarize and synthesize the content.
- Spice your presentations up by embedding animations, videos, and sound clips.
- Don't make the show too long and don't spend beyond a few minutes talking about each slide.
- Cite your sources and provide your references at the end, even though you might be tempted to neglect this when pressed by time—you never know when you might want to use the presentation again in the future, perhaps sharing with colleagues, so you want to know where you got your information and visuals.
- *Do not compile a presentation and then just read it off the screen to your class or audience.* Use your slides to highlight key points that you discuss further.

LCD projectors also allow you to project videos and films. Such media can help you present abstract ideas in an engaging and realistic way. Of course, if you have access to still and video cameras you can take photos and make movies of your students in action doing their projects or classwork, which can be shared with their parents and can be motivational or used to extend instruction. Consider why you plan to use a DVD and show only the part that applies to your lesson, not the entire program, unless it is necessary. Also, it is wise to pause the program at particular preselected scenes to engage students in analyzing what they are watching. One strategy is to prepare a number of questions that students could discuss or answer after watching. Before beginning the video, use an anticipatory set so your students have a notion as to what the video is about and so that they know what to look for as they watch.

There are always emerging technologies, and it will be a challenge just to keep up. It is likely that you will find, as have your authors, that once you have mastered one presentation technology, it will become obsolete and something new will take its place. There is much buzz as this is being written about the educational potential of iPods, iPads, Twitter, and other kinds of online applications. Simulations and electronic games are getting ever more interactive and realistic and offer much promise for classroom applications. Some see potential in social networking and in web-based collaborative writing and blogs. And then there is YouTube with its incredible inventory of videos, many specifically created for teaching some content or another.

However, here are two cautions: Whenever depending upon technology of any sort, always have a Plan B. You should know enough about your content to teach the lesson without the "crutches"—valuable as technology can be. Something can always go wrong or break down. However carefully you plan, you cannot anticipate every situation that may occur. Be prepared so that if you are left on your own in front of the class you can still carry through with a productive lesson.

> ALWAYS *preview all instructional media before using them in class or online. Knowing the suitability of such material is the teacher's responsibility!*

And the second caution: Be sure that you preview all instructional media before you use them in class or online. If you do, you will be more familiar with the content and how it is presented. As you might guess, some teachers have found themselves quite embarrassed when mix-ups have occurred or inappropriate material has been presented to the class. And again, always remember that effective teachers talk to their students, not to the visual aids.

■ FINALLY: COMMUNICATION WITH "OUTSIDERS"

"Outsiders" is not meant to sound as scary as it may seem. There are, however, a number of constituencies with whom you must interact other than your students. What you need to understand is that each group needs to be approached in a different way. Horace Mann, who pioneered the cause of schooling for all children in this country, was known to be a master at tailoring his remarks for maximum benefit whether he was speaking with educators, legislators, parents, or community members. This is a lesson that you should take to heart.

School Staff

School staff include secretaries, custodians, cafeteria workers, social workers, people who used to be called truant officers, safety officers and crossing guards (who also may be volunteers or safety patrol students), and others. Some would list the principal and assistant principal in this list, that is, the administrators. These people provide for the physical plant and do all the work in the background that allows a school to operate. These are the people teachers often find themselves depending upon in a crunch.

School staff people, just like your fellow teachers, want to be appreciated and recognized for the work they do to help the school function. So, your attitude toward them should be appreciative and respectful, and you should cultivate positive professional relationships with them. Just remember that many of your colleagues and support people have families and other lives and want to balance work and family needs. Everyone has a life outside of school. By recognizing others' lives and supporting their need to juggle work and home, you are creating a relationship with your co-workers that communicates to them that you know they need that balance.

Parents

We have already discussed working with parents in the context of you being their child's teacher. Parents, however, can contribute to your classroom in other ways, and you might want to keep this in mind as part of organizing for instruction.

Teachers frequently overlook the human resources their community offers. Students in your classroom may have relatives who work in various subject-related fields or who have to use particular technologies or methods in their work. Some connections might even surprise you. For instance, examples of simple machines are to be found in the toolbox of a carpenter or plumber. There are always parents and community members who are willing and interested in helping students learn, and many willing to help with student investigations. Knowledgeable parents are a source of information about community resources and field study sites.

Museums, Agencies

Try to break free of the idea that all instruction must occur on the top of a student's desk. Look outside the classroom window and consider how you can make what's out there a part of your classroom curriculum.

Every community has resources you can tap to enrich your classroom curriculum. Among the most underused resources of all is the great outdoors. School grounds are underutilized for academic learning as are the outdoors around schools—the neighborhoods, local parks and public spaces, footpaths and biking trails, and resources you might never have thought about, such as the farm owned by one of your students' grandparents. Your local community represents an even broader category of resources, with institutions such as a museum, library, theater, art gallery, visitor center, zoo, aquarium, arboretum, botanical garden, nature center, planetarium, children's museum, and parks and recreation department. These can be among your greatest allies in teaching. Museums, cultural centers, and public-service agencies are not just places where exhibits are stored; each represents a treasure trove of possibilities for investigations. Plus they have people with special expertise and hands-on resources for investigations.

Field trips are often among students' most memorable school experiences. They require advance planning and attention to detail, but a good field trip can enrich classroom life for days and weeks, before and after the trip. Field trips should be planned that fit naturally into the curriculum. For example, a visit to an aquarium or a saltwater marsh would be appropriate when teaching a unit about marine life or the oceans.

If you are new to a locale, you can find out about its resources by visiting the public library, or contacting the Chamber of Commerce, the local newspaper, a nearby museum or nature center, or faculty members in the field of study at a local community college.

In planning excursions you will need to be aware of school and district policies and regulations regarding field trips. There might be constraints as to the number of field trips per class per year, or a limit on the amount students' caregivers can be asked to pay for transportation, admissions, or other costs. Typically, a field trip request form must be submitted to your school administration for advance approval. Such forms ask you to indicate the date of the proposed trip, site address, and the name of an on-site contact. You may be required to provide a rationale that specifies your objectives and states how the field trip activities fit into the curriculum. There is considerable administrative input required in arranging a field trip, and those skills of communicating with the school staff will pay off when it comes time to put this all together.

We recommend you involve your students and their parents or guardians in planning trip logistics and in deciding which activities will take place. If your students are invested in the process, more will be learned and there will be fewer management problems. Most students recognize that excursions are special learning opportunities and are eager to cooperate. The countdown days before the trip can be used as a series of deadlines for getting tasks finished and getting everyone prepared for the special event.

You will probably want to solicit parents to participate as chaperones. At the elementary level, "room mothers" (or fathers) often can provide the extra support you need. You will have to send a notice about the trip home with students a week or more in advance, and most schools require a permission form signed by parents or guardians.

Field trip success is enhanced if you create an investigative atmosphere—one of excitement and expectancy of different possibilities and discoveries. It is hard to fail if students go off on the field trip with inquiring frames of mind, confident in their roles as observers, problem solvers, and data recorders. On the other hand, failure is almost assured if students head off on a field trip not knowing what they are responsible for doing.

> *Field trip success is enhanced if you create an investigative atmosphere—one of excitement and expectancy of different possibilities and discoveries.*

The problems or questions that provide the focus for a field trip are established during pretrip activities. Some teachers have students keep logs or journals, and these are often very useful on field trips for sketching and recording observations. Depending on the field trip, other tools and materials also might be useful. Figure I.12 (see page 50) provides a list of things frequently used to support students' observing and learning on school excursions.

Making a field collection is an educational and rewarding activity for students on field trips. Before collecting organisms, however, check with your county extension agent or a park agent regarding regulations that prohibit collecting particular plants or animals. Never collect rare, threatened, or endangered species. Generally, most insects will be OK to collect.

If you are going to be on private property, always get a landowner's written permission to visit or collect. A major rule should be that everyone picks up after him or herself: "Leave nothing but footprints." Encourage students to show respect for wildlife, for example, by replacing logs, rocks, and so forth that they have moved back into their original position and, after having examined them, releasing organisms back into their natural habitats.

As we have mentioned, your school grounds and neighborhood are valuable as resources. One elementary school in Winnetka, Illinois, is located next to a forest preserve. A fifth-grade teacher in the school used the site for students to study native flora. She invited a local forester to help. This led to the beginning of a project for the class. The students learned to identify and remove alien plant species that had invaded the native prairie. The teacher and forester trained parent volunteers to take groups of students out on study and work expeditions periodically throughout the year. Each group was responsible for caring for an area in the preserve. The students' enthusiasm in tackling the project to restore the native flora led to a lot of worthwhile physical exercise and environmental education, as well as helping restore the local natural ecosystem of the prairie.

Few schools may be so fortunate to be located adjacent to an area managed for nature, like the forest preserve. Regardless, there are many other valuable activities and investigations that can be done outdoors. Gardening is one of them. A school garden can offer lots of opportunities for lessons in both science and social studies, connecting with topics such as reproduction; growth; plants; the structure of flowers, seeds, leaves, stems, and roots; photosynthesis; capillarity; nitrogen-fixation; the water cycle and other biogeochemical cycles; food chains; trophic levels; parasitism; as well as local agricultural business, among others. There are many kinds of gardens: butterfly, rock, herb, vegetable, flower, desert, and so on. An example of a project would be an heirloom seed garden (note that seed catalogs often have interesting historical and scientific information), a project that could be tied into both social studies and science. Information and assistance is available in every part of the U.S. from land-grant university extension agents. Local garden clubs also may be willing to contribute.

A variation on the garden idea is a nature trail. In this case, what grows around your school is left undisturbed except for establishing a path through the area. Once a pathway is cleared, the plants that are indigenous to the area can be identified and labeled. In addition to seeing what is there, students can observe and record changes over time—both in writing and by photographs. Over the course of several years, these changes could be dramatic. A marker indicating the height of a sapling when initially measured would be interesting years later to another class.

CONCLUSION ■

Planning for instruction has been our focus here. We've looked at how teachers can work with students to plan and manage an effective classroom curriculum. Your goal is to create an inviting place as your classroom, a place where students' interests and ideas are respected and are the starting point of program planning. We have addressed practical matters, such as safety, organizing the classroom space, scheduling, selecting tools and resources to support learning, and conducting excursions.

How you set up your classroom reflects what you think is important about the learning that is to go on there. Providing the right kind of time for learning is important too—students need time to investigate and to reflect through discussions, drawing and writing, and other process activities.

> *How you set up your classroom reflects what you think is important about the learning that is to go on there.*

We also have mentioned the importance of working with students to establish reliable classroom routines. But remember that unit and lesson plans are meant to *guide*, not *bind*. Excitement about learning grows when routines give way to exploration and adventure, as in taking studies into the field and community. As a teacher you not only present a lesson, you create an environment where learning is invited to occur.

Unit I Appendix

Figure I.2 Example of Guiding Questions to Facilitate Planning Units and Lessons

Guiding Questions for Planning

Think about the following:

1. Where do you take your students? That is, what is the topic (theme, content, issue, or problem)? What is (are) its source(s)?

2. Why is this topic (theme, issue, problem) important? Why should students learn this? What, if any, influence will it have on their lives?

3. What do the students already know? How do their explanations or beliefs differ from those of the scholarly community?

4. What knowledge will students construct? What "big understanding(s)"? What major concept(s)? What important facts?

5. What processes and skills will students develop? What knowledge acquisition skills, thinking processes, manipulative or social skills?

6. What "habits of mind" will students develop? What attitudes and dispositions, what values?

7. What other parts of the curriculum can be naturally integrated with this content?

8. What resources are available?

9. How will students be engaged and stimulated to investigate the topic(s)?

10. What can be done so that students share their knowledge with peers?

11. How can students be motivated to apply and extend what they know?

12. How will I assess what they learned?

13. How will I evaluate my teaching? (Powell, Needham, & Bentley, 1994)

Figure I.3 A Sample Student Safety Contract

Safety Rules

1. Know the class emergency plan.

2. Follow the teacher's instructions. Ask if you do not understand what to do.

3. Do not taste, eat, drink, chew gum, or inhale anything used in science activities unless the teacher gives you permission to do so.

4. Avoid touching your face, eyes, and mouth during science activities, and wash your hands after science activities.

5. Always wear eye protection when using chemicals, glass, or flames and when there is a risk of eye injury.

6. Tell the teacher if you see potential dangers or someone being unsafe.

7. Notify the teacher immediately if you have an accident or an injury.

Safety Contract

I have reviewed these safety rules with my teacher and my parent/guardian. I agree to follow these rules and any additional instructions, written or verbal, given by the school and/or teacher.

Student's Signature	Date
Parent's Signature	Date
Teacher's Signature	Date

Figure I.4 Example of a Teacher-Made Concept Map for Grade 5 Science in the Virginia Standards of Learning

Virginia Standards of Learning for Grade 5 Science

©Michael I. Bentley, 2006 Board of Education. (2003). *Standards of learning for Virginia public schools.* Richmond, VA: Commonwealth of Virginia.

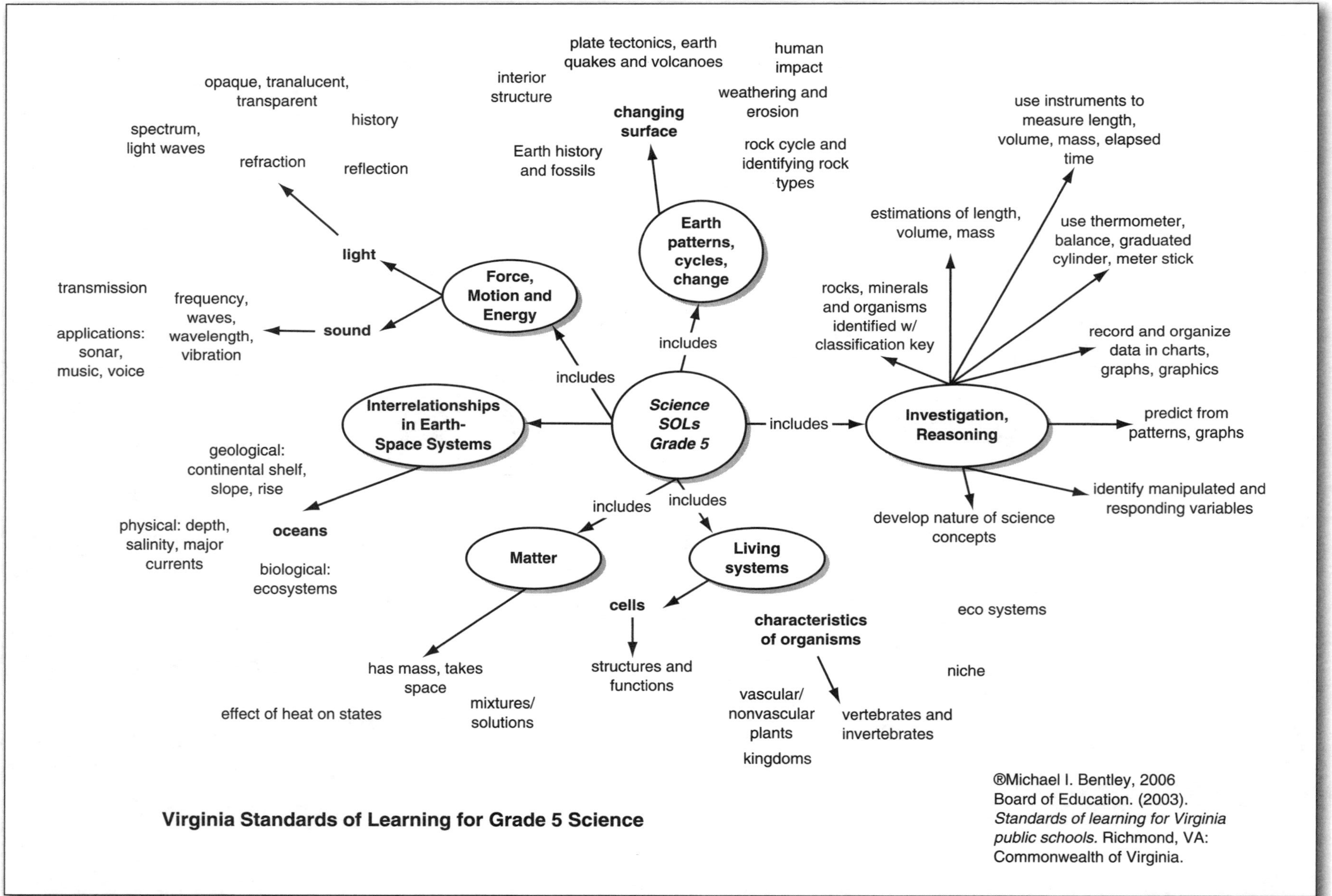

Figure I.5 A Generalized Rubric for Grading a Student Assignment

Category	Needs work (1)	Satisfactory (2)	Proficient (3)
Understands concept	Contains inaccurate information	Mostly accurate Information, most is appropriate	Accurate and appropriate information
Originality and clarity	Not a clear and original presentation	Mostly clear and in student's own words	Information clearly presented and in student's own words
Mechanics of sentences	Few clear and complete sentences	Most sentences complete	Clear and complete sentences
Spelling	Many misspelled words	Mostly correct spelling	Correct spelling

Figure 1.6 Traditional Lesson Plan Template

Teacher: _____ Subject(s): _____

Grade(s) or Level(s): _____ Date: _____

Description: Content, subject matter, concept(s), skill(s), or state/district standards

_____

_____

_____

Goal: What students should know or be able to do as a result of the lesson.

_____

_____

_____

Objectives: What is to be learned. Use behavioral verbs. Your objectives need to be related
to your assessment. _____

_____

_____

_____

Materials: _____

_____

_____

_____

Procedures: What students will do in the lesson. _____

_____

_____

_____

Assessment: _____

_____

_____

_____

Figure I.7 Behavioral Verbs for Writing Objectives

A verb is an action word. In a lesson objective, the verb specifies an observable outcome of instruction. Sometimes you will see objectives written such as, "The student will understand such-and-such," but understanding cannot be observed. Hence, we recommend that you use verbs that specify what behavior or product will be observable as a result of the lesson.

Activate	Compare	Differentiate	Integrate	Question	Schedule
Adjust	Compute	Distinguish	Interpret	Rank	Score
Analyze	Complete	Draw	Introduce	Rate	Select
Appraise	Compose	Dramatize	Investigate	Recall	Sequence
Arrange	Conduct	Establish	Judge	Recognize	Simplify
Articulate	Construct	Estimate	List	Recommend	Sketch
Assemble	Contrast	Evaluate	Locate	Reconstruct	Solve
Assess	Convert	Examine	Manage	Record	Specify
Build	Coordinate	Explain	Modify	Relate	Summarize
Calculate	Count	Express	Name	Reorganize	Tabulate
Catalog	Criticize	Extrapolate	Order	Report	Theorize
Categorize	Critique	Formulate	Organize	Reproduce	Track
Change	Define	Generalize	Point out/to	Research	Translate
Cite	Demonstrate	Identify	Predict	Restate	Use
Classify	Describe	Infer	Prescribe	Restructure	Verify
Collect	Design	Illustrate	Produce	Revise	Visualize
Combine	Develop	Implement	Propose	Rewrite	Write

Figure 1.8   Madeline Hunter Lesson Plan Template

Date: _____

Grade level and subject(s): _____

Objectives: _____

Materials: _____

Anticipatory set: _____

Teacher procedure: _____

_____

_____

_____

Checking for understanding: _____

Guided practice: _____

_____

_____

_____

Independent practice: _____

_____

_____

_____

Closure: _____

Evaluation: _____

Accommodations for individual children's needs: _____

_____

_____

_____

Figure I.9 Learning Cycle Lesson Plan Template

Date: _____ Grade(s) or Level(s): _____

Elicit: _____

_____

Engage: _____

_____

Explore: _____

_____

Explain: _____

_____

Elaborate (or Expand): _____

_____

Evaluate: _____

_____

Extend: _____

_____

Figure 1.10   Strategies for Using Cooperative Learning Groups

Tips for Managing Group Work

- Arrange student desks to allow discussion between students—think circular instead of straight lines.

- Early in the school year provide some explicit instruction in communication, conflict management, and leadership prior to assigning group work. Have students practice listening, taking turns, disagreeing politely, managing time, asking for help, being supportive, sharing feelings, keeping everyone involved, paraphrasing, expressing appreciation, making everyone feel important, and making eye contact.

- Design tasks to encourage all students in the group to contribute, with everyone having a stake in the learning of others in the group. This might be achieved by assigning a group grade or by assigning roles and dividing labor.

- Avoid providing opportunities for some students to hitchhike on the work of others in the group. This may be achieved by individual accountability, such as by questioning students at random or by having students share in the reporting back to the whole class.

- Use pairs whenever possible, avoid trios and groups larger than four; group members can self-select or you can use structured procedures for forming groups, for example, by counting off, by drawing a playing card, or by pairing up within categories ("Walk around and pair up with red as the category—those wearing red pair and those not wearing red pair").

- Use a paired reading strategy for getting students to read texts—have partners take turns reading aloud to each other and, when they have completed the reading, have each pair talk about the reading, write in their journals, or prepare to report to another group. Pairs can rotate for another task ("Okay, identify a person in your pair as 'A' and the other as 'B'— the As remain seated and the Bs move to a new 'A' to be your partner. Bs will share . . .").

- Option display: A group works on a problem or issue, aiming to display (a) several options for solving the problem or addressing the issue, (b) the likely consequences of each option, and (c) the group's overall recommendation.

- Best choice debate: Pairs prepare either a pro or con position on an issue; a "pro pair" and a "con pair" then meet to explain their position to each other and seek an agreement on an overall recommendation (similar to Johnson and Johnson's [2009] constructive controversy method).

- Project work usually aims to produce a product; teams can be organized around an action project whose focus is taking action rather than studying; projects may be based on student interests; guidelines should include clear timelines and progress reports (tasks might involve interviewing, comparing opinions, making models, designing an ideal something, finding contrasting views, producing a graphic, creating a dramatic skit for another class, etc.).

- Allow students both to celebrate a group success and to consider how their work could have been improved. Students should ask questions like, "What contribution did each of us make?" and "How could our work together have been better?" (Jensen, Moore, & Hatch, 2002)

Figure 1.11   A Simple Procedure for Moving Groups Through Classroom Activity Centers

Scheme for Moving Groups Through Five Stations

1. Divide the class into groups (here, e.g., Alphas, Betas, Gammas, Thetas, and Omegas).

2. Create a framework such as the following with center names or numbers going across and days (or times) going down. Write group names on small cards (or use color-coded cards if you're using colors to differentiate groups). To start, assign one group to each station (going across) on Day 1 (or Time 1) by putting cards into place on a schedule board.

3. Explain the rotation schedule and have students take a practice run. Soon, with a quick glance, they will know exactly where they are supposed to be and what center is next.

	Center 1	Center 2	Center 3	Center 4	Center 5
Time (Day) 1	Alphas	Betas	Gammas	Thetas	Omegas
Time 2	Omegas	Alphas	Betas	Gammas	Thetas
Time 3	Thetas	Omegas	Alphas	Betas	Gammas
Time 4	Gammas	Thetas	Omegas	Alphas	Betas
Time 5	Betas	Gammas	Thetas	Omegas	Alphas

Figure 1.12 Items Typically Useful on Field Trips

Considering What to Take on Field Trips

- A first aid kit

- Depending on season, insect repellent

- Maps (road maps, topographic maps, geological maps, etc.)

- Paper, pencils, colored pencils, or markers

- Tape recorders and blank tapes

- Field logs or journals

- Film or digital cameras—still or video

- GPS devices

- Cell/mobile phones (or not)

- Field guides (to historical sites, cities, or organisms such as insects, wildflowers, trees, birds, rocks and minerals, etc.)

- Plastic bags and/or containers—bug boxes, small cages, or collection jars

- Magnifiers, such as hand lenses or jeweler's loupes

- Microscopes

- Tweezers, scissors, probes (or dissecting kits)

- Nets (aquatic or insect)

- Compasses

- Flashlights

- Portable radio

- Binoculars

UNIT II
Classroom Management

UNIT II OUTLINE

■ UNIT II CONCEPT MAP

Unit II

1 Keys to successful classroom management
- perspectives on approaches to management
- basic terms
- management as the basis for success

2 Establishing a management-based learning envionment
- the management structure
- teacher behaviors
- noninstructional tasks
- communicating expectations
- planning

3 Compiling a plan: A template
- deciding consequences
- the discipline program
- procedures
- ancillary personnel
- assessing your management system
- reflection
- writing rules
- writing a mission statement

4 Implementing the plan- responding to student behavior
- a signal
- inform
- practice
- reinforce

5 Assessing your classroom management plan

UNIT II PEP TALK ■

Are you preparing for student teaching? Perhaps it is time to begin your first year as a classroom teacher. Or it could simply be the case that you are at your wits end over what to do to feel better about the management of your class. In preparing to become a teacher, perhaps you discovered that the curriculums had changed, instructional techniques had changed, and, of course, technology had changed. You may also have been dismayed to find that children have changed as well. You may agree with the statement, "Children today are tyrants. They contradict their parents, gobble their food, and tyrannize their teachers." And you may be wondering how that ever happened. Whatever became of the good old days when children came to school and respected their teachers and did as they were told? Well, if that's what you are thinking, we may have some bad news: The comment that we just quoted about children being tyrants is attributed to Socrates around 2,400 years ago! Yes, indeed, children are still children.

But wait, all the news isn't bad! In fact, the good news is that children can be *expected* to act like children. What is more, they are typically willing to be led, to be guided, to be directed toward accomplishing things. All we need is a teacher with a plan. And the really good news is that before long, that teacher is going to be *you*.

It is usually the case that beginning teachers spend a lot of time going over the fresh new curriculum materials that the school principal has placed in their hands. In those weeks before school they cut out letters, prepare bulletin boards, and perhaps even practice a "good morning" or two. These are good things to do. But before the fruits of any of those instructionally oriented labors can be realized, it is necessary to have a solid system of classroom management in mind and in place. But who has time for that?

It actually seems just a bit ironic, doesn't it? You probably spent a lot of time in your teacher-education program learning *about* children (of whatever age), learning what to *do* for children, learning what to *teach* to children, and even learning about technology to be *used* with children. Yet in its most fundamental form, organized education is primarily about working *with* children. It almost seems as though the single most important aspect of any teacher-education program should be the thorough study and practice of *interacting* with children and *managing behavior* so that learning can take place. Well, that's what this unit is about.

Our intent is not to show you how to be the tyrant in the classroom rather than letting the students tyrannize you. Instead, our intent is to prepare you to take charge of your classroom by first building a strong management plan. With that in place, all of those visions of a classroom alive with wonder and filled with enthusiasm for learning (however subtle some children and especially adolescents might be about showing it) can become the rewarding reality of your professional life. So, no, behavior issues in school today are not new. But neither is the remedy—it is simply the case that the professional educator (you) needs to know how to manage a classroom.

CLASSROOM MANAGEMENT

■ FIRST: KEYS TO SUCCESSFUL CLASSROOM MANAGEMENT

"Effective classroom management," according to Darling-Hammond and Bransford (2005), "starts with the creation of curriculum that is meaningful to students and with teaching that is engaging and motivating" (p. 37). The majority of your teacher-education program will, or did, focus on preparing you to do just that. However, that's the start. Despite your best efforts to design the perfect lesson, it will not be perfect enough for the child who comes to school the day after their parents announced that they are getting a divorce, or who forgot to bring in a signed permission slip and so cannot take part in some special function, or who just got back a failing grade on a history paper just before coming to your class. The behavior of your students involves many factors that you cannot anticipate. And that's where a classroom-management plan becomes important.

> The behavior of your students involves many factors that you cannot anticipate. And that's where a classroom-management plan becomes important.

Long and Morse (1996) remind us that no other topic in education receives greater attention or causes more concern for teachers and parents than that of classroom discipline. These authors continue on to say that it is the lack of effective classroom discipline or behavior-management skills that is the major stumbling block to having a successful career in teaching. Cangelosi (2004) notes this about the range of teacher effectiveness in classroom management:

> Some teachers orchestrate smoothly operating classrooms where students cooperatively and efficiently go about the business of learning with minimal disruptions. Other teachers exhaust themselves struggling with student misbehaviors as they attempt to gain some semblance of classroom order. Those from the latter group who remain in the teaching profession eventually give up the struggle, deciding that today's students are so unmotivated and out of control that it is futile to attempt anything more than surviving the school day. (p. 4)

A survey of K–5 and 6–12 teachers (Shuler, 1998) revealed the following about student behavior:

1. 40 percent of K–5 students and 71 percent of students in Grades 6–12 cheated "often" or "almost always."

2. 35 percent of K–5 and 34 percent of Grades 6–12 students often or almost always made verbal wisecracks about the teacher.

3. 36 percent of K–5 and 73 percent of Grades 6–12 students were tardy often or almost always.

4. 30 percent of K–5 and 31 percent of Grades 6–12 students engaged in disruptive personal grooming activities.

5. 38 percent of K–5 and 42 percent of Grades 6–12 students often or almost always tried to humiliate the teacher in class.

6. 28 percent of K–5 and 49 percent of Grades 6–12 students often or always talked back to the teacher.

7. 40 percent of K–5 and 52 percent of Grades 6–12 students often or almost always lied or made ridiculous excuses.

This is not meant to discourage you if you are about to start teaching or to confirm your suspicions if you are already in the classroom. But it is meant to address the topic of student behavior in a realistic light. As much as we all hope to have a classroom full of little angels, it is important that you understand that teaching is just one aspect of your job. While teaching and management are at the heart of the educator's profession, they are by no means the same thing.

Management as the Basis for Effective Teaching

Management as the basis of effective teaching? That sounds a bit incongruous, doesn't it? Well, yes, if you consider that the vast majority of time in a teacher-education program focuses on the theory and practice of teaching and learning. However, the simple fact is that no matter how wonderful a teacher you may be, in the absence of good classroom management, little learning will occur.

As an example, let's compare this to driving a car. Wherever you received your driver training (high school, driving school, patient friend, stalwart parent), it is likely that you learned those things you need to know to safely operate a car. Your local Division of Motor Vehicles probably required that you not only demonstrate those skills but also pass a written test about the rules of the road. However, did your instruction or testing make any reference to changing the oil in the car or recognizing the signs of worn brake pads? Were you required to change a flat tire or to mix up a batch of antifreeze and water and fill the engine's cooling system? Probably not. Yet these are among the many maintenance activities that have to be accomplished before you can get around to turning on the engine and cruising off to the mall. In the absence of good maintenance, the best driver in the world will not be able to operate the vehicle. Having an operable car comes *before* driving it.

Well, that's what we mean about classroom management: You can only get around to doing effective teaching if the classroom is managed in a way that allows learning to take place. The bottom line? Your life will be easier, your work more rewarding, and your teaching more successful if you spend some serious time becoming an outstanding classroom manager. And the other teachers in the school will flock to you for advice.

> *You can only get around to doing effective teaching if the classroom is managed in a way that allows learning to take place.*

Management Facilitates Instruction

It is important that you realize that we are not just talking about the "troublesome" student in your class. When misbehavior occurs, we will address discipline. Management, however, attempts to head off discipline problems, provide a code of appropriate conduct, and inform students about how to get

> *In the final analysis, with an effective classroom-management plan in place, it is actually the students' behavior that facilitates the teacher's work.*

things done. When such a program is in place, it will be the students' own behavior that facilitates instruction in your classroom. Now that's a neat idea, isn't it? Rather than trying to figure out what you are going to do to keep these students "in line," it will be *their* behavior that allows you to get the work done! That actually sounds pretty exciting!

Preserving the Dignity of the Individual

As you work to become a master of classroom management, there is a particular notion that we recommend you always keep in mind: *As an advocate of children (students, if you prefer) it is your responsibility—however challenging—to help preserve the dignity of the individual.* From time to time students will dig themselves into a hole, and before they know it they have no way out that isn't damaging to their self-esteem or self-concept in their eyes as well as those of their peers. In such a situation they will often find it preferable to appear as the "tough guy" and wind up in more trouble rather than to be humiliated in front of their friends. This is by no means a suggestion that you ignore inappropriate behavior! Quite the contrary, you will see that we advocate the consistent use of appropriate consequences following the choices that students make. However, "Job 1" when misbehavior occurs is helping the student to get out of that hole with his or her dignity intact. Here, as an example, is a true-life story from an assistant principal on her first day as an administrator:

> Being an administrator always allows for new and exciting experiences. I was a third-grade teacher closing out the year on a Saturday workday. I became an assistant principal on the following Monday and I did not learn that much at church on Sunday. But I do think being a teacher/administrator allows you to always be thinking about what someone else may be thinking. Especially these "little body people" who have such great minds when it comes to controlling adults.
>
> It was a typical Monday at school, everyone was rocking and rolling with the teaching and learning except maybe one young man. I was called to our EMD classroom because the teachers needed some assistance. When I walked in the classroom, the teachers calmly walked over and stated that they could not get "Troy" out from under the table. Usually we would have ignored this but Troy was making his presence quite well known.
>
> Now in these days my dress attire was usually a suit with the hose and pumps to match. I could feel myself getting a little warm in my suit wondering how I was going to get Troy out from under the table. I slowly moved toward the table trying to act like Troy did not have my attention or of the rest of the class. I could feel my own anxiety as Troy began to direct definitively inappropriate phrases toward me.
>
> I decided at that time that the best course of action would be the direct approach. I simply leaned down and gave Troy a firm, administrative directive to get out from under the table. At about that time, Troy grabbed me by the leg, getting a fistful of pantyhose in his little hand, and pulled me under the table! I went totally under, suit and all. As I was trying to unpeel Troy's death grip one finger at a time, Dr. Inabinet (the real administrator, the principal) walked in. He, like any man might, took one look and stated, "I will handle this."

> *It's surprising to find out when teachers suddenly pay close attention to administrators, and this was apparently it as they did their best to withhold their laughter as I crawled out from under the table. Dr. Inabinet then leaned down to give his direct command. As he did, Troy grabbed him by the tie and down he went! If nothing else, I felt vindicated.*
>
> *We had decided at that point to take the audience away from Troy and so moved the rest of the class next door while we "waited out" the situation. After Troy learned what was going on next door, like most children, he came out and wanted to participate in the teaching and learning.*
>
> *We have laughed often about this and always make reference to the pantyhose story. By the way, I learned something too. To avoid a similar situation, I usually go bare legged to school, and Dr. Inabinet does not always wear a tie.*

Notice in this story that despite yanking two administrators under the table, Troy was never treated with disrespect, never chastised, and not made a fool of in front of his peers. Instead, the assistant principal and principal found a way (removing the rest of the class) to preserve the dignity of this child while helping him "out of the hole" that he had dug. Some situations may be more challenging than this, but in all cases *you* will be the adult, the professional, the one who comes to the situation with a reasonable perspective—and so it will be up to *you*, not to the student, to preserve that individual's sense of dignity.

The Basic Terms

As with any concern, it is worthwhile to take some time to define our terms so that, as topics are discussed, we can all speak the same language. This does not necessarily mean that you must agree with our definitions, but the following sections will explain what we mean as the terms are used in this book. We will consider each of these terms in greater detail in the next section of this unit.

Classroom Management

Classroom management is not something to be considered *after* the students have arrived. It is not something that one can simply spend a few minutes thinking about when all of the other instructional concerns have been addressed. It is a big topic in and of itself. As Weber (1990) points out, teaching involves two major activities: instruction and management. The former is concerned with the presentation, demonstration, and assessment of a curriculum. It is that part of being a teacher that people tend to think of when considering what it is to be a teacher. The latter, management, involves those activities in which a teacher engages before, during, and after interacting with children to allow instruction to take place.

> **Classroom management** refers to those activities in which a teacher engages before, during, and after instruction to allow instruction and learning to take place.

Classroom management refers to the things a teacher does to organize students, space, and time to prevent or minimize behavior problems that would interfere with instruction. Among the concerns that fall under this heading are behaviors that the teacher will expect of the students, the materials that will be needed for various lessons along with the convenient storage and retrievability of those materials, the consequences for inappropriate behavior, and the means by which those consequences will be meted out. And here are the important distinctions: *classroom management* differs from *discipline*, which differs from *rules*. Understanding the difference between the terms, which unfortunately are often used interchangeably, will greatly facilitate developing a clearer picture of management in the classroom.

Discipline

Discipline refers to actions a teacher will take *after* misbehavior has occurred. While classroom management focuses on the *prevention* of misbehavior, *discipline* is concerned with addressing misbehavior that has occurred. Clearly, planning for how the class is to run is a different matter from planning for what to do if things run awry. Keeping the distinction between management and discipline in mind will help you plan for each with much greater clarity of purpose.

Discipline refers to those actions a teacher will take *after* misbehavior has occurred.

The efficacy of discipline in a teacher's classroom will be directly related to the rules established for the class, the consequences announced, and the enforcement, or nonenforcement, of the consequences. We will discuss rules in greater detail in the next section. For now, the pertinent notions to keep in mind about a discipline plan are these:

- Merely posting rules does not constitute planning for discipline.
- Rules are enforced by imposing consequences.
- Whether or not rules are made to be broken, for one reason or another, at one time or another, they will be broken—so be sure the announced consequences are something you can comfortably impose.

The discipline portion of your overall classroom-management plan will revolve around rules, consequences, and enforcement.

Rules

Class **rules** represent the code of behavior that a teacher expects the students to follow (Burden, 2003). As such, they are clearly a part of the greater classroom-management plan. Through the course of your teacher-education program, you will (or did) spend time observing, assisting, and eventually practicing in real classrooms with real students. During those observation opportunities, and even perhaps right now if you have your own classroom, the class rules will be posted somewhere in the room. But what *are* class rules? Only those "rules" that are enforced are actually the rules of the class.

Rules represent the code of behavior that a teacher expects the students to follow.

Of particular importance is that the students should be aware of the rules, that the rules are considered fair and reasonable (and that doesn't mean that everybody has to like them), and that it should be evident that abiding by the rules serves the best interests of everyone. Without doubt you have seen lists of rules that say "Don't do this, don't do that," and so forth. In such a situation the only motivation to abide by the rules is to avoid some sort of punishment. So rather than focusing on "don't" rules, the teacher may emphasize "do" rules. For example, "Don't be late" could be written as "Be on time and ready to begin class." In this way, the teacher can continually emphasize the behavior that is *desired* rather than emphasizing the behavior that is considered inappropriate.

Consequences

Consequences are the results that follow from the making of a choice. We have a life lesson for you here: Throughout our lives we make choices, and for *every* choice there is a consequence. OK, perhaps you already knew that. There's a good chance, however, that your students have not yet come to appreciate that fact. It is a lesson that they need to learn and understand, and believe it or not, the classroom teacher is one of the key players in the teaching of that particular lesson. So let's not keep this lesson a secret or hope the students absorb it on their own. Instead, let's make that an explicit lesson that we intend to teach.

Consequences are the results that follow from the making of a choice, and for *every* choice there is a consequence.

When we talk about rules in the classroom, we want you to appreciate the fact that there should be consequences for not following the rules *and* for following the rules. In either instance, consistent enforcement will be imperative, and so the consequences that you identify must be made as clear to the students as the rules themselves.

Procedures

Procedures detail the manner in which particular activities are to be carried out. At first blush it might seem that rules and procedures are the same. They are not! Rules represent a code of appropriate behavior. Procedures represent the method for accomplishing a task. The failure to follow a rule must be met with an aversive consequence. The failure to follow a procedure, however, is not met with punishment because it merely indicates the failure to accomplish something in a particular manner. It is not a disciplinary situation, but rather a learning situation.

Procedures detail the manner in which particular activities are to be carried out.

Of course, during the school day, there are many different procedures that must be followed. At the elementary levels, there may be procedures relating to different spaces within the room (e.g., individual desks, study centers, group work), throughout the school (e.g., walking in the hall, eating in the cafeteria), whole-class and small-group activities, and miscellaneous procedures. At the secondary level, you might group the procedures as those for beginning class, during class, ending the class, and miscellaneous (Jones & Jones, 2001). Just as some examples, there are procedures for taking attendance, for collecting lunch money, for walking in the hallway as an individual or as a class, for fire drills, and for putting a heading on a paper. This is a short list; certainly you could think of many more examples.

Routines

Routines are those procedures that are used to the point of being "automatic" behaviors. For example, a teacher's process of taking attendance may become a routine. For students, the manner in which they are expected to enter the class and begin work (procedure) can become something they can do on their own without the teacher having to instruct them to do so—a routine.

Routines are those procedures that are used to the point of being "automatic" behaviors.

Wong and Wong (2009) assert that rather than discipline being the Number 1 problem in classrooms, it is instead the lack of procedures and routines. The irony is that procedures are a major part of any school day and a major part of any person's life. And yet learning to follow procedures and to develop routines is often left to chance. In your classroom, procedures and routines should be explicit, that is, specifically taught. In fact, the teaching of procedures, which carries with it a clear description of behaviors expected of students, should be part of instruction during the first weeks of school each year (or at the beginning of each semester if your placement is in a school on a semester system). The learning of procedures not only makes classroom tasks easier to accomplish but also minimizes the opportunities for misbehavior.

Figure II.2 The Basic Terms

1. **Classroom management** refers to those activities in which a teacher engages before, during, and after instruction to allow instruction and learning to take place.
2. **Discipline** refers to those actions a teacher will take after misbehavior has occurred.
3. **Rules** represent the code of behavior that a teacher expects the students to follow.
4. **Consequences** are the results that follow from the making of a choice, and for *every* choice there is a consequence.
5. **Procedures** detail the manner in which particular activities are to be carried out.
6. **Routines** are those procedures that are used to the point of being "automatic" behaviors.

Some Perspectives on Classroom Management

There are many different perspectives and theoretical approaches that can be taken in a discussion of classroom management. For example, the *Assertive Discipline* program developed by Lee and Marlene Canter (1976) puts the teacher squarely in control of the classroom environment. This would be a teacher-centered approach. The assertive teacher that they speak of is

> one who clearly and firmly communicates her wants and needs to her students, and is prepared to reinforce her words with appropriate actions. She responds in a manner which maximizes her potential to get her needs met, but in no way violates the best interests of the students. (p. 9)

In a sense this approach might be thought of as teachers taking back control of the classroom.

At the other end of the spectrum are those who argue that the traditional notion of teacher as controller is not necessarily a good thing. Author Alfie Kohn (2003) writes, "Educators . . . may find themselves caught in an undertow, pulled back to traditional assumptions and practices that result in their doing things *to* students rather than working *with* them" (pp. 26–29). In his view the student is at the center of the educational enterprise, and we might well expect that the student should also be at the center of an effective approach to classroom management. Such a perspective sees the student in a collaborative relationship with the teacher.

William Glasser (1997), as another example, suggests that teachers "must give up bossing and turn to leading" (p. 600). The loss of instructional time due to misbehaviors has led to an increasing sense of the teacher as the boss and the students as the followers. However, in an enterprise such as education—one in which the students are not willingly trading their time for an agreed-upon compensation (as in an employer–employee relationship)—there exists a very special relationship motivating the behaviors that occur. Glasser recommends that "quality" learning environments be established in classrooms in accordance with *choice theory*. The idea is that people make choices that help them satisfy four needs: 1) the need to belong, 2) the need for power, 3) the need for freedom, and 4) the need for fun. The misbehaviors that you see occurring in classrooms are indicative of students finding that the classroom environment is preventing them from creating their own quality worlds.

What approaches to management you see when you observe the classrooms around you depends on many factors. In some school districts, a particular classroom-management/discipline program will be adopted for all of the schools, or there may be a districtwide policy, with the expectation that all teachers will follow it. In many situations, however, it is likely that the teachers you observe will demonstrate some combination of approaches. It is not at all uncommon to find as many variations on the classroom-management theme as there are teachers on a given faculty. We first introduced you to Beth with the story of the student under the table. When Beth was a teacher she recognized the need to develop her own management style, and she tells you about it in the following passage. (Note: This passage is written from Beth's perspective working with a fifth-grade class. Everything she says, however, can be adapted to younger or older students.)

My father used to ask me if I wanted a straight answer. I always said no because I knew that it simply meant the answer was "no." Do you want a straight answer to successful classroom management? The answer is not so simple, but yet it really is . . .

I went into teaching to be the deliverer of content and to truly make a difference. I just knew the children would come to me ready to learn and engage in all of my planned activities. Well, I was in for a surprise!

Let's just say my lovely class of 30 fifth graders chose to chew me up and spit me out. After many tears (in private) and talking with my school mom and friends, I knew I would have to make a change if I couldn't figure this out. Then the answer was so close: a Saturday classroom-management workshop. Finally, an answer to my prayers!

With my new legal pad, a fresh pen, and eager ears, I was ready for this lady to tell me how to do it. Being a most conscientious student, I sat on the front row ready to take down each and every direction. I left disappointed. I realized that there is really no straight answer for questions of classroom management.

Classroom management is a mindset. It is a personality, a climate, or a perception. When I realized this I became a teacher watcher. I watched my colleagues and then began experimenting though putting my own personal twist on things. I began to analyze what worked and what motivated my students. I began to get to know my students and used interpersonal relationships to build classroom community. I saw a tremendous change when my attitude changed. At that point I viewed classroom management with excitement and became very motivated to learn what made students tick. It was amazing how the pieces started meshing together, and teaching and learning was now falling into place.

Though the pieces never fit together perfectly, I have found that these components helped me learn to love the classroom-management part of teaching:

1. ***Recognize the Differences in Children**: Many children come from unstable environments. The teacher should be a constant factor in the child's everyday experiences. A warm, inviting teacher is reassuring to the child, and this climate sets the tone for the day's activities. Children can sense if people like what they are doing, and a friendly, happy teacher gives the child an opportunity to experience a good feeling. All children need many opportunities to feel successful.*

2. ***Teach Discipline**: Teach discipline techniques throughout the day. Use a lot of positive reinforcement. For example:*

   I like the way Antwon is walking down the hallway.

   Suzy is listening so well.

   Who will be a good citizen and lend Billy a pencil?

   Thank you, class, for sitting so nicely.

   When you set up your class rules, discuss together why we walk in a straight line. Explain to kids how if other classes are coming down the hallway, you will have enough space. We walk quietly down the hallway so we will not disturb other children's learning.

3. ***High Expectations for Behavior**: Most kids today are asking for structure. Let kids know exactly what you expect, and it will be done in that manner. If they aren't sure about how to do it, model the behavior. Show kids how to sit on the rug properly. Then let them practice and praise them for their practice. Expect your class to be the best!*

4. **Role-Modeling Behavior:** *You are going to hear arguments on both sides of the issue as to whether teachers are (or should be) role models for students. All I can tell you is that my experience as a teacher tells me that students—of any age— learn from watching their teachers in all sorts of situations. The older kids might not be as obvious about wanting to emulate their teacher but they are internalizing what they see. So if I want my students to walk quietly in the hallway, I can't walk along with them and chat with another teacher all along the way. If I want my students to learn preparedness and responsibility, I have to be prepared for class and I have to demonstrate that I take responsibility for my actions. And above all, if I want my students to have a positive and caring attitude, then that's what they have to see from me in all situations—at school and away from school as well.*

5. **Model Happiness and Show Humor:** *I believe that you need to teach your kids how to laugh and enjoy. Sure, children know how to laugh, but it is in school that they learn the difference between appropriate and inappropriate situations in a social setting. Humor is wonderful and modeling happiness gives kids a real respect for your commands. Let loose a little bit—do the Hokey Pokey, the Teaberry Shuffle (if you remember that!), and a few basketball shots. My kids would focus an hour on math skills just to see me do the Teaberry Shuffle for thirty seconds.*

   Another important skill to teach is how to cut it off and get back on task. This again has to be taught, not just expected. Let them know what your signals are for getting back on task.

6. **Be a Motivator:** *Get excited about what you are going to teach! Try to take the positive route because positive energy increases the odds for success. The bases are loaded with two outs, and your team is behind by one run. You are up to bat. You view this as a challenge, a chance to succeed! The burnouts view it as an opportunity to fail, and then the odds are greater that you will fail.*

   Plan your lessons so they will enable you to share your excitement and enthusiasm for learning. This climate will draw the excitement for good behavior. "Speaking of exciting lessons, we are going to do one right now," I would say. "I need good listeners so you will know exactly what to do." This style of teaching will motivate the children to be good learners. They want to know what you are going to say and do next. Excitement prevails and children are tuned in.

7. **Hands-On Materials for "Doing" Learning:** *Hands-on materials provide many creative ways to teach a skill. The use of these manipulatives helps children to understand concepts and gives them concrete practice. Hands-on materials help to make the learning real. Many educators agree and research supports that doing is the best road to learning.*

8. **Nonverbal Communication:** *I discovered nonverbal communication accidentally. With trepidation I walked into a fifth-grade classroom one day with no speaking voice. Relying on my nonverbal communication skills proved to be one of my most successful measures of control. Thanks to this powerful tool, I had a great day.*

   One of the most effective ways to change a behavior is eye contact. Along with eye contact, closeness with calmness will aid in changing behavior. This often avoids power struggles and allows you to emerge from the situation without breaking stride. For more blatant behavior, eye contact with wait time will sometimes solve the problem. Know your kids and know what will work best with each individual. With some children a comforting hand on a shoulder will remind them to stay on task. While moving around the room monitoring activities, I walk toward children who need to feel my presence.

Beth Elliott is Principal at Pontiac Elementary School, a Presidential Blue Ribbon School.

You may want to spend some time considering different perspectives on management in more detail. Table II.1 lists a variety of approaches to classroom management. It could be the case that one "speaks" to you, that is, as you read about it you find that it has a comfortable fit with your style. Or, as was the case with Beth, you may need to develop a plan that is all your own, an eclectic blending of several perspectives. Our intention in this unit is to provide a pragmatic—practical—look at classroom management. We don't argue for one best approach because classroom situations and teacher personalities comprise multivariate, complex, and chaotic systems. And there can be a blending of many perspectives. But as you will see, we recommend that, whatever plan you put together, you do include a "reflections" component. This is to emphasize that a management plan (a) must match with the person *you* are and (b) has to develop over time. Making changes to your plan is not a sign of failure, it is a sign of continuing development.

Table II.I Perspectives on Classroom Management

Theorist	Strategy	Perspective
B. F. Skinner	Behavior Modification	Use of positive/negative reinforcements and punishment to shape behavior
William Glasser	Choice Theory	Helping to satisfy students' psychological needs and add to their quality of life
Thomas Gordon	Teacher Effectiveness Training	Teach self-discipline, demonstrate active listening, use "I messages" rather than "You messages"
Lee and Marlene Canter	Assertive Discipline	Teachers and students have rights. Insist upon responsible behavior and use consequences
Jacob Kounin	Instructional Management	Use effective instructional behaviors to influence student behaviors
Linda Albert	Cooperative Discipline	Influence rather than control students. Develop a conduct code for a positive classroom climate
Carolyn Evertson and Alene Harris	Managing Learner-Centered Classrooms	Provide learner-centered classroom, behavior management, and begin with clear rules and expectations
Alfie Kohn	Beyond Discipline	Consider students from positive perspectives (not punitive) and believe students will make correct decisions

Abridged from Manning and Bucher (2007, pp. 22–23).

SECOND: ESTABLISHING A MANAGEMENT-BASED ■ LEARNING ENVIRONMENT

Establishing a learning environment will involve planning, communicating expectations, implementation of the plan, and practice.

> No matter what the physical arrangement, management involves the whole class at all times.

Planning

Establishing a learning environment begins with *planning* for classroom management. Much as we all would like to have this element of education take care of itself, the bottom line is that it will not. The teacher must be well ahead of the students long before any one of them sets foot in the classroom. Planning. Let us say that another way just so that you will understand how important it is: planning. OK, that was the same way, but that's because there is no getting around it. As Wong and Wong (2009) say, "Readiness is the primary determinant of teacher effectiveness" (p. 92). They're not talking about the teacher's knowledge of subject material in this instance. No, they're talking about readiness for managing the class.

Through work done by the Research and Development Center for Teacher Education at the University of Texas, it was found that effective classroom managers are nearly always good *planners* (Evertson, Emmer, Clements, & Worsham, 2000). This is to be expected, when you think about it, for despite the fact that curriculum does not change much from year to year, the combination of students that enter your classroom most certainly does. In fact, if you are teaching above the elementary level, those combinations change several times a day with each new class period. Though planning for classroom management is definitely an exercise in preparing for an unknown quantity, so to speak, there are some consistencies that can guide that planning and preparation. Understanding that planning itself is imperative is the first step. Understanding what must be planned comes next.

Shown in Figure II.3 is a list of items that a teacher needs to address when conceptualizing a classroom-management plan. The list is certainly not exhaustive, but the intent is that you understand the broad range of concerns that fall under the heading of managing a classroom. Diverse as they may seem, however, the underlying theme throughout is organizing for maximum instructional effectiveness and limiting opportunities for behaviors that interfere with learning.

Figure II.3   Classroom-Management Concerns

- Student seating:

  Assigned?
  Group?
  Rows?

- Traffic flow in the classroom
- Learning centers (if any)
- Emergency management
- Responding to student behavior
- Storage:

  Teacher materials
  Student materials

- Preparation of materials
- Assignments:

  Academic
  Student responsibilities

- Handling student birthdays and holidays
- Class rules
- Routine procedures:

  Collecting lunch money
  Beginning the day
  Attendance
  Leaving (bus, parent pickup, walking, driving)
  Bathroom breaks

- Practicing procedures
- Grading
- Parent contact
- Disciplinary consequences
- Decorating the room:

  What's enough?
  What's overstimulating?

Do you get the idea? If all a teacher had to be concerned with was keeping students in their seats, classroom management might not require quite the finesse that it does entail. In fact, a mark of a truly effective teacher is so much finesse that one doesn't even notice that a classroom-management program is in place and running. Anybody can spot a poorly managed class, but leave a room that has a well-thought-out and well-implemented program and you are likely to think that you didn't see any evidence of classroom-management techniques. They were there, and that's *finesse*! And, what is more, the planning and organization involve activities before school starts as well as on opening day (Flaxman, 2000).

Implementing a program of classroom management means *practicing* using the rules, following the procedures, and developing the routines that the teacher expects of her students. Think about this for just a moment. How often do people learn a new skill or behavior without practicing it for some period of time? Everything from handwriting to painting masterpieces requires practice. Yet how often is it the case that teachers present students with a list of rules and an explanation of procedures they want the students to follow but fail to allow time to practice? We all know that repetition facilitates developing a new skill, but it is also true that practice provides the opportunity for students to *experience the specific behavior* the teacher is requiring. Through practice they come to know what expectations the teacher has for them.

Implementing a program of classroom management means *practicing* using the rules, following the procedures, and developing the routines that the teacher expects of the students.

Particularly with elementary children, but not to exclude secondary students (or college students, for that matter), time spent at the very beginning of the school year (or in beginning a new course of instruction) practicing procedures, developing routines, and demonstrating appropriate behavior will be time that more than pays for itself through the *prevention* of lost instructional time later in the year. This can be an enjoyable experience that brings the class together around a common goal.

Practice provides the opportunity for students to *experience the specific behavior* the teacher is requiring.

As we mentioned with regard to classroom rules, it is also important to keep in mind that practice is not something done in a few weeks and never done again. Consider the medical and legal professions. Those folks refer to their entire careers as *a practice*! Similarly, be prepared to practice again when skills seem to be slipping. And by all means, be sure to acknowledge both the demonstration of appropriate behavior and procedures or routines carried out well *and* the positive results of having done so.

Communicating Expectations to the Students

The following three guidelines will help ensure that your students understand and accept your classroom-management plan as something that is in their own best interests:

1. Communicate expectations to the students.

2. Involve the students (and others) in the development of the rules and behavior management procedures.

3. See that the rules and procedures are positive behaviors that facilitate instruction and the development of positive self-esteem.

As long as the rules are reasonable and clearly communicated to the students, many of the arguments about "not knowing I couldn't do that" are eliminated. But, of course, there's more to it than that.

It is not reasonable to argue the position that teachers should set up the classroom in a manner that allows children to simply do whatever they please. Actually, the understanding of limitations within a society is part of the educational experience. In the section on classroom-management terminology, we discussed rules as being the behavioral guidelines for your classroom. Here we want to elaborate by suggesting that students can be involved in the formation of class rules under the teacher's guidance and thereby feel that they have a stake in how the class will operate.

> *Understanding the limitations within a society is part of the educational experience.*

Note that the recommendation being made is to help students follow the rules by allowing them to help make the rules. This is a far cry from the typical attempt at "buying" rule conformity by offering gifts, candy, and even the trade-off of instructional time for free time. If the rules are worth following, the following of them should be rewarding in itself. The Principles of Effective Discipline (Wong & Wong, 1991) listed in Figure II.4 tie together this idea of rules as instructional tools for enhancing the learning environment and positive self-esteem.

Figure II.4   Principles of Effective Discipline

1. Treat students with dignity and respect.

2. Effective teaching reduces discipline problems.

3. Students need a limited say in what happens in the classroom.

4. It takes time to develop an effective classroom-management plan and style.

5. Most discipline problems are created by how teachers teach and treat people.

6. Bored students become discipline problems.

7. Lack of self-esteem is a major reason why students act up.

8. No one wants to fail. A student would rather be bad than appear to be stupid.

9. Anything you can do to make people feel good about themselves will help to minimize discipline problems.

10. People who feel powerless will find ways of expressing their lack of power.

11. We deny most the students who need to learn responsibility, by denying them the experience to have responsibility.

Source: Wong & Wong (1991, p. 149).

Notice the degree to which the list of Principles of Effective Discipline swirls around *interpersonal relationships* much more so than adopting the notion of "my way or the highway," so to speak. Perhaps you can see the three underlying themes (communicating expectations, involving students in the development of rules and procedures, and seeing that the rules and procedures are positive parameters) as being very much evident in this list. How difficult do you think it would be to garner the support of parents and your school administrators for a program based on principles such as these?

The Management Structure

The management structure for your plan will consist of the rules, consequences, procedures, and routines.

Rules

To begin, teachers could go about establishing class rules with the assistance of the class. When doing so, it is important to keep in mind that the task at hand is not to take on the legislative load of Congress. We don't need 113 rules governing every contingency that may arise in a classroom. Rather, the teacher and students simply need a brief list of, say, perhaps five rules to govern the class. It is generally suggested that when you make rules for a classroom you stay with about five rules, and no more than seven. There should never be more rules than can be readily remembered. If your students cannot effortlessly recite the rules, then they aren't rules.

Make the rules positive, make them descriptive of the behavior you require, make them observable, and make them enforceable. Something like "Think happy thoughts" sounds nice, but it is not something you can observe nor can it be enforced. A rule such as "Treat others as you wish to be treated" is also a nice rule but subject to individual interpretations as to how one may want to be treated. You may find it helpful to discuss, role-play, and display behaviors which follow or which violate the rules (Jones & Jones, 2001). It can be beneficial to have the rules drafted by the students themselves because this ensures that they are understandable by those who are expected to abide by them (see Figure II.5). In keeping with this, the rules should be simple. If extensive discussion is required to clarify a rule, the rule is too cumbersome. Break it into two rules or decide what is to be expressed and then rephrase the rule more succinctly. Emphasize the appropriate behaviors that are expected rather than focusing on examples of inappropriate behavior. You don't want them to practice bad behavior just so you, the teacher, can say, "And then I would tell you to stop doing that." And finally, academic issues should not be a part of the rules as prescriptions for behavior, and certainly not as consequences for misbehavior. Keep the two separate.

Communicating expectations to the students, involving them in establishing the rules that will guide their behavior, and using rules that foster positive classroom participation are the themes that drive an effective management program. Relinquishing some of one's own sense of control, or "power," is necessary for empowering others. This is as true in the teacher–student relationship as it is in the administrator–teacher relationship. Interesting how that happens, isn't it?

Figure II.5   Involving the Students in Making the Rules

1. Communicate your expectations to the students.

2. Involve them in establishing the rules that will guide their behavior.

3. Use rules that foster positive classroom participation.

4. Keep the list of rules to about five so that they are easily remembered.

Consider some of the following rules. These are examples that we have seen or heard from teachers. Which of them match up with your own expectations? Which lend themselves to multiple interpretations?

- Act in a respectful manner at all times.
- Academic honesty is required.
- Keep feet, arms, legs, and objects to yourself.
- Be on time.
- Enter the classroom quietly and begin working promptly.
- Raise your hand when you have something to say, and wait patiently for permission to say it.
- Follow all directions from the teacher immediately.

A few of these rules may be better classified as something that will be discussed in another section of this unit: procedures. For instance, when driving a car the rule (law) is that you obey the speed limit signs. Failure to do so may result in a ticket that carries a number of penalties. Being a courteous driver, however, is not a rule (there's no fine for being discourteous unless you do damage to someone else's property—and you will be fined for something other than being discourteous), but it is a good procedure to follow. Consider carefully whether the items you classify as rules represent *codes of behavior*. And, being very practical about this, be certain that the rules actually reflect behaviors that if violated can be punished. For example, suppose you have a rule such as "Have two pencils sharpened and on your desk before class begins." You might find that sending a child with only one sharpened pencil to the principal's office might land *you* in more trouble than the student.

Consequences

As was the case with the rules, the consequences must be fair and reasonable even though they will necessarily be unpleasant from the students' perspective. But the teacher's perspective is important here as well. If a teacher announces a consequence and is uncomfortable administering it (or perhaps one that could lead to problems—such as sending too many children to the office), then those consequences need to be reconsidered. We cannot overemphasize that if rules and consequences are part of the classroom-management plan, *they must be consistently enforced.* The teacher who believes the rest of the class will not notice when failing to enforce the class rules makes a serious mistake. Innocent though they may appear, students of all ages always test the limits. Within a week they will know whether or not the teacher means what he or she says.

According to Borich (1996),

Consistency is a key reason why some rules are effective while others are not. Rules that are not enforced or that are not applied evenly and consistently over time result in a loss of prestige and respect for the person who has created the rules and has the responsibility for carrying them out. (p. 364)

Note that Borich doesn't mention in this passage that instructional time is lost or that students fail to learn necessary lessons. Rather, he makes it clear that *the teacher loses prestige and respect* in the eyes of the students. This, in itself, is an important lesson for any prospective teacher to learn very early on. Classroom management is not only a matter of what the student may lose (in terms of educational opportunities), but also very much a matter of what the teacher stands to lose.

Consequences for Appropriate Behavior

For rules to be effective in managing behavior and fostering prosocial behavior, the following of rules must be acknowledged by the teacher. This can be done in a positive way. In the early weeks of the school year, a teacher can bring rule-following behavior to the students' attention daily. As time goes by, acknowledgment of appropriate behavior may come less often, but nonetheless it must be made evident to the students if the teacher wishes to see that behavior continue.

Consequences for Inappropriate Behavior

Inevitably, some student will violate the established rules of your classroom. It will happen for a wide variety of reasons, but the teacher must keep a particular perspective in mind. Part of that perspective is to remember that (a) the focus should be on the behavior, not the person, and (b) discipline and academics are two different entities. With any discipline problem at least one person will be operating from an unreasonable position. Whenever possible, that person should not be the teacher. Keep a clear head and clear focus, and address the behavior.

> *With any discipline problem at least one person will be operating from an unreasonable position. Whenever possible, that person should not be the teacher.*

Responding to Student Misbehavior

Students will be very much attuned to a teacher's enforcement or nonenforcement of the class rules. If the students were involved in establishing those rules, they will be even more aware of whether or not violations occur and whether or not the teacher responds as promised. In your own classes in college there are/were students (certainly not *you*) who would test the limits, and children are no different. A teacher's response to violations of the rules tells the students whether or not the teacher is serious. If the word is out that he or she doesn't follow through, then one can expect that many more transgressions will start occurring. The teacher will ultimately decide that it's a "bad" class, but in actuality it is that teacher's behavior that led to the situation.

Consequences for Misbehavior

We have indicated more than once, and in more than one way, that rules are only effective when there are consequences to enforce them and attractive benefits for following them. Since we are now discussing a teacher's response to misbehavior, our focus is on the aversive consequences of misbehavior. Whether your approach to classroom management tends toward full involvement of the students, full control by the teacher, or somewhere in the middle, it is imperative that the students know and understand that *whatever* the consequences are, the teacher *will* enforce them.

> *Rules are only effective when there are consequences to enforce them and attractive benefits for following them.*

Identifying consequences is something that can be done with the assistance of the students. In this way the students are more likely to embrace the rules and perceive the consequences as fair and agreed upon. Some schools have an established discipline code that must be followed. If such is the case, that discipline code must be explained to the students. In either situation, it is important that the consequences for infractions be perceived as reasonable (in light of the violation) and fair. Consequences that work best are those that will enable a student to choose between acceptable and unacceptable actions. It should be clear that unacceptable behavior is not worth the administration of the consequence. Even better—and this becomes the teacher's task to demonstrate—students should clearly understand that *following* the rules is *beneficial* to them.

It is unlikely that a school's discipline code will impose *academic* penalties for misbehavior (e.g., lowering a grade or failing the student in an academic subject). The same should be true for consequences established within the classroom. Lowering a student's grade in a subject area for arriving late or talking out of turn dilutes the efficacy of assessment. Keep student behavior and academic achievement separate and in proper perspective.

When dealing with misbehavior, make every effort to address the behavior and not criticize the person. No student comes to school wanting to have their dignity, intellect, or decision-making ability insulted. Doing so will only exacerbate an already difficult situation. The effective teacher is one who can maintain a calm demeanor and enforce the rules quietly and without anger or accusations. The particular infraction can be pointed out to the student, along with the agreed-upon consequence without further discussion. If the student persists, the teacher can quietly speak to the student and indicate that the rules and consequences were established by the class as a whole and that the student was the one who chose to violate the rules. Additional discussion about the situation, if necessary, could be held at an appropriate time if the student so desires.

Enforcement of the Rules and Consequences

It is obvious that having rules and consequences is not going to be enough when a child wishes to challenge all that has been presented. At this point the teacher is very much engaged in a decision-making process. With a solid classroom-management and discipline plan in place, these decisions can be much easier to make. The teacher must remember that allowing infractions to go by without attending to them is a mistake. Reference to the rules and consequences, as well as indicating who "owns" this particular problem, only takes a few seconds. When a student protests ("I'm late because my last teacher let us all out late!"), a teacher can offer the chance to discuss the matter outside of class time but indicate that it is a separate issue. The issue that is obvious is that the class rule has been broken. Keep a clear head and clear focus and address the behavior. We've said that once already, and here it is again at no additional charge.

This issue of students protesting the consequence because of extenuating circumstances is a good argument for choosing consequences that are reasonable and justifiable. If such is the case, the consequence can be enforced immediately, as briefly as possible, and even be mildly severe, as Brophy (1983) recommends. Instruction need not be brought to a halt, and in fact should not be stopped. In this case a student is not ruined for life or shamed beyond redemption. But it is imperative that some action be taken so that the message is clear: the rules will be enforced, and the teacher will not acquiesce based on insufficient information. Next time around, the student who was detained by another teacher will ask for a note or some sort of pass to present in the next class. There are multiple lessons to be learned.

Beyond the Rules: Recognizing Extenuating Circumstances

For the vast majority of situations, reference to the class rules and pointing out the clear fact that a rule has been violated will be sufficient to defuse the situation and allow instruction to continue. There is no need for the teacher to enter into a power struggle with the student if a quiet demeanor can be maintained along with a focus on the behavior. The teacher may even tell the student that she has no argument with the student; it's just that this particular behavior does not serve the best interests of the student or class. In fact, the teacher must avoid a power struggle with a student at all costs, for in such a struggle the student has nothing to lose, and the teacher has everything to lose. If you find yourself in this sort of situation, ask yourself who is controlling the event. If you are losing your temper and saying things that will only make matters worse, then the child is controlling you. Think about that: A child is controlling you and your reactions. This seems like a good place to repeat a particular line again: Keep a clear head and clear focus, and address the behavior. Factors may well be at play that will require you to think beyond the rules and consider a broader perspective. Let's consider what some of those factors might be.

> The teacher must avoid a power struggle with a student at all costs, for in such a struggle the student has nothing to lose, and the teacher has everything to lose. If you find yourself in this sort of situation, ask yourself who is controlling the event.

We would be remiss if we did not acknowledge that teachers work with students in an environment that differs from virtually all others. Particularly when dealing with children, inappropriate behavior can be the result of factors that have absolutely no relationship to school. Students can come to the classroom with problems, worries, and concerns that make a set of classroom rules inconsequential. Parents argue and sometimes separate from one another. Family members, or pets for that matter, become sick and sometimes die. Lunch money is lost on the way to school. Some children pick on weaker children. Medications kick in, don't kick in, or wear off. There are more possibilities than we can imagine, and children are not necessarily going to show up at school with a note pinned to their collars explaining every situation. What all of this is leading to is that sometimes a teacher will have to take a situation beyond the rules. It is too much to ask that a teacher solve the domestic problems for all children in the class, but an astute teacher needs to be aware that inappropriate behavior can have origins well beyond what occurs in class.

The Problem-Solving Conference

A **problem-solving conference** is one attempt to go beyond the rules with a student while still focusing on the behavior. As we've said, the teacher can't be expected to solve all of the student's problems, and the primary goal at this point is to defuse the situation, preserve instructional time, and, if necessary, direct the child to resources better equipped to work with the particular problem. With that said, the problem-solving conference helps a student take responsibility for his or her actions and find a way to resolve the situation without losing their sense of dignity. Problem solving, sometimes called conflict resolution, has several general steps:

1. Have the student evaluate and take responsibility for the behavior.

2. The student should make a plan for a more acceptable way of behaving. The teacher can help with this, and agreement is reached on how the student will behave in the future along with identifying the consequences for failure to follow through.

3. Require the student to make a commitment to follow the plan.

4. Avoid the use of punishment or reacting to a misbehaving student in a punitive manner. Instead, remind the student that there are consequences for failing to follow the plan.

5. Stay with it! Reinforce good behavior and ask for the student's perspective on how it's going.

> The problem-solving conference is not an alternative to consequences. Nor does this process release the student from being accountable for their behavior.

These steps are not an alternative to consequences. Nor does this process release students from being accountable for their behavior. It does, however, allow the student and teacher to come to terms with a situation that may have distinct outside influences involved. So while the teacher has gone beyond the rules, the rules have not been forsaken. As a result, the integrity of the learning environment and the classroom-management plan is not lost.

Implementing Procedures and Routines

There is a key word involved with the implementing of procedures and routines. The word is not control. The word is not authority. The word is *practice.* Practice is something to be done *with* the students. As the school year begins, the teacher will be well aware that there are many procedures and routines that will contribute to a smoothly running classroom. We are not suggesting at all that children become automatons or mindless followers. Such could not be further from the truth. Instead, it is now that the teacher teaches and practices those activities (skills) that are performed for the very purpose of enhancing the overall learning experiences that the students will encounter.

The teaching of procedures follows the same process as the teaching of any other skill: Explain, rehearse, and reinforce. If the school in which you teach requires that the class walk on the right side of the hallway, in line, silently, then you must explain this to the students. Do you have to justify every policy and procedure for your class? No, but it is reasonable to assume that you should be able to explain why the procedure is of value. Even if you don't particularly agree with the procedure but are expected to abide by it, find some understandable explanation for it and make that clear to the students. Then, go out and practice. If the students in the class need to walk up and down the hallways for half an hour to learn this, then walk up and down the hallways for half an hour. All the while find examples of appropriate "hall walking" behavior and reinforce it with well-directed praise. Students may need to practice each day for a week or two. If that is the case, then that is what needs to be done. This is a learning experience with goals, objectives, and observable outcomes.

Following procedures and accomplishing beneficial routines is a good thing. For that reason, the teacher needs to bring to the students' attention that their conscientiousness is worthwhile and appreciated. Such activities can actually become a source of pride. The teacher must also keep in mind that many factors affect performance, and so when those procedure and routine skills start to slide, there is nothing wrong with practicing again to bring them back up to an acceptable level. The value of the lesson just presented here is often lost on preservice and beginning teachers. However, many overwhelming days, frustrating sleepless nights, and hours of trying to figure out what's wrong can be avoided by spending real instructional time at the very beginning of the year teaching students how to behave as you want them to behave.

Classroom procedures differ from rules in that procedures tell the student *how* to do something. There are likely going to be many more procedures for your students than there are rules. For that reason, practicing the procedures will be very important. Try this:

1. Select a grade level that you are interested in teaching, or use the classroom that you are working with.

2. List as many procedures as you can think of that would help your class run smoothly. We have mentioned some already (e.g., taking attendance and walking in the hallway). What others can you think of? If you are stuck, think of your own experiences as a student in some class. What procedures can you identify?

3. From your list, consider how you would teach that procedure to your students. Also, how will you let the students know that they are carrying out the procedures appropriately?

4. If you are observing a classroom, ask the teacher about procedures that have been implemented in the classroom. Are there more or less than you had expected?

The list in Figure II.6 offers some ideas for procedures that you might want to consider. As you can see, when it comes to running a classroom there are probably many more procedures involved than you would have thought. Doing a good job of identifying procedures gives you the opportunity to think more critically and creatively about the overall task of managing a classroom environment.

Figure II.6 Examples of Classroom Procedures

Procedures for Students

Entering the classroom	Distributing supplies
Walking in the hallway	Eating in the lunchroom
Asking questions in class	Permission to go to the restroom
Turning in assignments	Headings on papers
When a guest is in the class	During emergency drills
Storing supplies/books	Leaving at the end of class
Passing in papers	Morning/bell work
Responding to questions	Working in groups
Working at study centers	Finishing early (ahead of others)

Procedures for Teachers

Taking attendance	Sending students to nurse, office, guidance, etc.
Collecting money	
Beginning lessons	Reporting to parents/guardians
Collecting assignments	Dismissing class
Monitoring group work	Returning assignments
Addressing discipline problems	Getting assistance from colleagues/administrators
Preparing the classroom	Acknowledging student work
Assessing the management plan	Closing down the classroom

Teacher Behaviors

We become increasingly specific as we work our way through this topic of classroom management. Now let's look at what the teacher might be expected to do from Kounin's classic work on the characteristics of effective teachers (1970) to physical features of the classroom, plus a few other notions along the way.

It would be wise for you to expand your perspective on classroom management to include preventing inappropriate *teacher* behaviors as well as student misbehaviors. What teacher behaviors might one want to avoid? An example would be leaving the students unattended, and another would be sending a student out to retrieve papers or materials needed for a lesson. In both cases instructional time would be lost because of something the teacher has failed to accomplish. Lowering a student's academic grade as punishment for misbehavior is another example of inappropriate teacher behavior because academic achievement and discipline should be kept as separate issues.

In 1970 Jacob Kounin conducted a study of what made a teacher effective, and it turned out that a common theme was that effective teachers were good classroom managers. Three key characteristics of effectiveness he identified were "withitness," an ability to supervise several situations at one time, and the adept handling of transitions from one task to another. Over four decades later, his findings are still illustrative of teacher behaviors that lead to well-managed classes. Though it's easy to say that we should still be doing what Kounin advises, it may even be more important to realize that teachers have been doing some very effective things for a very long time—and so let's emulate those effective teacher behaviors (see Figure II.7 on page 80).

"Withitness"

Effective teachers, Kounin concluded, had a certain "withitness" that allowed them to know what was going on throughout the classroom. Have you ever had a teacher who seemed to have eyes in the back of her head? That's what Kounin means. These teachers stay in touch with what's happening in the class at all times. Perhaps they will make a comment to a student or quietly walk around the room to place a hand on a student's shoulder. It is not a mystery, really, it's paying attention—and effective teachers do this.

Supervising Multiple Situations

Another characteristic of effectiveness is the ability to supervise several situations at one time. A key here is to know what needs to be done in each situation and how to do it. From that point on it is a matter of being able to focus on what needs to be done and not be flustered by distractions. This is by no means a matter of ignoring particular situations or events, but rather having the confidence and expertise to take them in stride and deal with them effectively. Multiple situations might entail attending to a student working at the board while also monitoring several small groups pursuing related activities in other parts of the classroom.

The Effective Handling of Transitions

Effective teachers are also adept at handling **transitions** smoothly. This refers to bringing one activity to an end and moving efficiently to the next. In some cases the transition is from one subject to the next, or it could be completing a lesson and then taking the children to lunch. These are not actions that are accomplished automatically. Though the lesson has ended, the teacher's work has not. Transitions may not be instructional periods, but they are very much management zones. Transitions are not student downtime. Effective teachers are very much attuned to this. Did you know that at the elementary level there are thirty-one major transitions occupying 15 percent of the school day (Burns, 1984)? Well, now you do. Fifteen percent of the day spent in transitions; that represents about one hour out of a six-hour day!

Arranging the Classroom for Effective Management

When arranging the layout of the classroom, avoid congestion in what will be high-traffic areas such as near the doorway or teacher's desk, around the pencil sharpeners, and around storage areas (particularly if they must be accessed during teaching time). Be sure that you can see all students and can monitor their activities. Arrange teaching materials and supplies so that time is not lost during class. Be certain that whatever seating arrangement is used, it allows all students to comfortably see and participate in all the activities of the day.

Proximity to Students

Along with the idea of being able to see all of the students and keeping the arrangement of furniture such that one can easily move about the room, effective teachers will move around the room and attempt to maximize their proximity to the students. Often beginning teachers will plant themselves at the front of the room and will seem to attach themselves to the chalkboard. Granted, this may be done out of nervousness; nonetheless, a teacher's proximity to students is a major force in minimizing student misbehavior. Students need to know that a comic book hidden in their social studies textbook is eventually going to be discovered.

Figure II.7 Effective Teacher Behaviors and Classroom Arrangements

Teacher Behaviors

- "Withitness"—knowing what's going on throughout the classroom and indicating, quietly, that you know
- Being able to supervise several situations at once
- Handling transitions smoothly

Classroom Arrangements

- Avoid congestion in "high traffic" areas.
- Be sure that furniture, work centers, and desks are arranged so that you can see all students at all times.
- Organize your teaching materials so they are readily available.
- Arrange furniture so that you can move easily throughout the room and maintain proximity to students as necessary.

In summary, the teacher's behavior when establishing rules, acknowledging the value of abiding by those rules, and following through with consequences in a calm manner when violations occur will set the tone from the very beginning. As David Berliner (1985) has stated, "In short, from the opening bell to the end of the day, the better classroom managers are thinking ahead. While maintaining a pleasant classroom atmosphere, these teachers keep planning how to organize, manage, and control activities to facilitate instruction" (p. 15). There really are very few "bad" children, and children will typically allow the teacher to take charge of the classroom and lead them. Whether or not the teacher seizes this opportunity will determine the tone of the school year. So the real choice of what type of classroom to have rests with . . . *the teacher.*

Without a doubt, classroom management is a complex and challenging aspect of being a teacher. It is not something that new teachers should be learning on the job. Our discussion of classroom management and discipline has been organized around key aspects of the topic, and so you should be able to watch for those elements during visits that you make as part of observations in schools. You could look for examples of what has been discussed in your college classes as well. What has been discussed here can be seen in class meetings of adult learners as well, for, as is the case with so much of education, the fundamental aspect of teaching is that it is first and foremost an exercise in interpersonal relationships.

Noninstructional Tasks

The heading for this portion of Unit II is "Establishing a Management-Based Learning Environment." With that in mind, it is important to address the reality of noninstructional tasks. Though these concerns typically do not involve the amount of time and consideration that goes into developing instructional strategies and classroom-management plans, they do occupy some of a teacher's time and always come with a measure of responsibility. Some tasks are carried out as part of the classroom routine. Some tasks are within school but in addition to classroom responsibilities. And of course, there's that whole life outside of school! In any event, they must be factored into your overall management plan—perhaps most appropriately as time management—so that the rest of your management tasks can run smoothly.

Outside of the Classroom

The extent of responsibilities that teachers bear outside of the classroom varies from school to school. Teachers must, and should, expect to be involved in the running of the school beyond the walls of their own classrooms. Many schools require teachers to rotate through a bus-duty schedule in the mornings and afternoons. How would such a task affect your procedures and routines for starting and ending the class day? Elementary school teachers often spend their lunch period with their classes, and middle and high school teachers usually serve on a rotating schedule of lunch duty. How will your expectations for student behavior be maintained in these out-of-the-classroom environments?

Teachers are also asked to sponsor clubs and activities that may be conducted during the day or after school. Advising school-sponsored clubs, chaperoning on trips, and supervising school social functions are other typical teacher tasks. Granted, these can be enjoyable experiences (well, maybe not lunch duty), but it has to be remembered that these are still responsibilities. Students enjoy seeing their teachers outside of school, but like it or not, teachers must be aware that they are teachers 24/7/365 in the eyes of their students. This is an exceptional and deeply rewarding responsibility that teachers bear.

Then there are also parent conferences, school open houses, and PTA or PTO meetings. Parents are a very particular audience indeed. Some will see the teacher as a godsend. Others see the teacher as the source of all the child's difficulties. Yet the teacher must work with all of them in a manner that brings credit to the student, the school, and the profession. Veteran teachers can offer excellent advice about working with and even enlisting the aid of parents. As a preservice teacher, you would be wise to use your practicum or internship time to seek out some words of wisdom from a number of teachers.

Committee Work

Schools, like most organizations, function by assigning tasks to committees. It may not seem that way when a principal lays down the law without discussion. But even so, teachers have many opportunities to work collaboratively with one another. Typically these opportunities may involve teachers from other schools and also extend to the district level as well. True instructional leaders will find themselves engaged with committee work on the state or regional level or as members of professional teacher organizations.

Also, some schools are moving toward a site-based management program. Though the school remains accountable to the local district, much of the day-to-day decision making is left to a council composed of building administrators, teachers, parents, and perhaps college or university educators. These site councils depend to a large degree on the principal's willingness to relinquish a measure of traditional control. However, the empowerment that is afforded to teachers can send a wave of professionalism throughout the school.

Planning for a Substitute Teacher

We've discussed planning quite a bit already, but one aspect we have not discussed is that of preparing for someone else to do the teacher's job, temporarily of course. That is, when a teacher takes a "personal day" or is just too sick to come to school (and for teachers this is often a matter of being *really* sick). In such cases, plans must be in place for someone else to take over. Teachers cannot just call all the parents and cancel school for the day. Plans need to be drawn up, in advance, and materials need to be ready to go. Though this sounds instructional, it actually contributes to maintaining the flow of your classroom-management system.

No doubt you have had a substitute or two during your PreK–12 experience. You know how students typically respond to a substitute. One cannot expect that a stranger can walk into a classroom on short notice and simply pick up where the teacher left off the day before. That's why it is very much a teacher's responsibility to have contingency plans in place when a day simply must be missed. Substitutes have gotten a bad reputation and have suffered a lot of grief because of a teacher's failure to take some time to prepare for being away. Even worse is that in a school year already packed to bursting with instructional objectives, the loss of an entire day or more can be difficult to overcome. All it takes to avoid this is some planning. You could even start right now to develop a dossier of educational activities that can be left ready to use when the time comes that you miss a day of school. Collect these activities over the years (good substitutes and veteran teachers you know will be an excellent source of this information). Organize the ideas and update them, and substitutes will love coming to your class—and of course will lament how rarely the opportunity arises!

Though not often mentioned, electronic technologies offer the classroom teacher an unprecedented means for avoiding the downtime that might occur when it is necessary to call in a substitute teacher. A lesson plan folder maintained in a computer's desktop file can hold subfolders for long-range and short-range plans. A substitute may only need the long-range plans if hired to fill in for an extended period of time, but the short-range folder can always have up-to-date lesson plans that keep instruction moving with the least amount of interruption. Setting aside just fifteen to thirty minutes a week would allow a teacher to revise lesson plans based on the progress of the class, and the result is that a substitute could come in at any time and know just where the class is with regard to each subject area. It could also be the case that there is a third subfolder, "Substitute Teacher," that has information and activities that the classroom teacher compiles specifically for those days when being in class is just not possible. If the substitute is not going to have access to the teacher's computer, these electronic files are something that the classroom teacher could easily attach to an e-mail message to the school secretary.

As we have already mentioned, preparing for substitute teachers does not at first blush sound particularly management oriented. However, taking advantage of the opportunities afforded by electronic technology and preparing materials in advance for contingencies is what management is all about. It's not so much that there's a substitute in the classroom that students latch onto, it's that there is an unprepared individual in the classroom.

> It's not so much that there's a substitute in the classroom that students latch onto, it's that there is an unprepared individual in the classroom. Preparing materials in advance for contingencies is what management is all about.

It might seem that noninstructional tasks alone could occupy a full workday. The keys are planning and organizing. If you have not already developed the habit of writing down appointments and assignments, now would be a good time to start. Al Devito of Purdue University has said, "The dullest pencil records what the sharpest mind forgets." That's difficult to argue with. If you want to be high-tech about it, use an electronic organizer. In any event, start practicing your organizational skills. That way, everyone can go ahead and believe that you are indeed superhuman, and we'll just keep the secret to ourselves. We encourage you to see the noninstructional tasks associated with teaching as a way of extending your managerial skills beyond the classroom to other facets of the school experience. Demonstrating the same commitment to well-managed behavior that facilitates the work of others, whether you are working with students, colleagues, administrators, or parents, will serve you well throughout your career.

■ NOW: COMPILING YOUR PLAN: A TEMPLATE FOR CLASSROOM MANAGEMENT

We have discussed all of the background elements, and it is now time to compile a plan of your own. We suggest that you get a three-ring binder that you can use for this purpose. Why? Because if you actually commit your plan to paper it will (a) force you to articulate each element of the plan, (b) provide you with a ready reference for assessing your plan and making changes as needed, (c) make it easy to distribute elements of your plan to appropriate individuals (e.g., students, parents, school administrators), and (d) demonstrate to you that you are serious about becoming an effective classroom manager.

Take the time to prepare this document. You make a mistake that will be difficult to overcome if you believe that you can just make it up as you go along.

Write a Mission Statement

ATTENTION: If you decide to skip this step because you already "have it figured out," you are making a mistake that may well undermine the rest of your plan. Take some time here to complete this very important aspect of putting together a classroom-management plan!

No matter what stage in your teaching career brings you to this task, begin by writing your classroom-management **mission statement**. Our recommendation is that your mission statement be just a single paragraph, a few sentences, and that it represents a brief conceptualization of your management perspective. Follow that paragraph with an elaboration of what you say in the statement. Think of it this way: A parent comes to see you at open house and on a poster you have displayed your mission statement, or perhaps you have it printed on pieces of paper that you hand to each parent. The parent reads it and then engages you in conversation about what you have stated. You want to have a nice statement of the mission *and* be able to explain it.

There are several things to keep in mind as you begin drafting this statement. First is to keep your focus—this particular statement is about classroom management, not about instruction. An instructional mission statement is important, of course, but for this exercise the topic is all about the person you intend to be, the environment you intend to establish, as the *manager* of behavior in your classroom. Second, and in keeping with the first, this is your opportunity to clearly articulate—for yourself as well as for others—those things that are important to you in the establishment and maintenance of a learning environment. If you believe that you function best as the "ruler of the classroom domain" (an *authoritarian* approach), then say so. If you see yourself as one who collaborates with the students even in matters of behavior (an *authoritative* approach), then make that clear. Take the time to examine the person you are and to identify the needs and expectations that you bring to *your* classroom. It is very likely that you will write several drafts of this statement before finally coming to the version that speaks for you. Take that time. Here are several versions that teacher-education students have written in the past. Some students are very parsimonious with their words, and others like to elaborate. No matter, this is *your* statement and simply must satisfy *you.*

In each case we have included only the mission statement paragraph and not the supporting rationale that these teachers included with it. This should, however, give you an idea of the direction to take in putting such a statement of your mission together.

> My mission is to provide a safe and secure learning environment for all of my students. It will be an environment that encourages student, teacher, administrator, and parent cooperation in taking responsibility for the role each is to have in establishing and maintaining this desired environment for the class. I will adopt an authoritative style with my main focus being on the best interests of the students. I plan to implement a management program to facilitate an enjoyable task-oriented atmosphere. I see the advice and support of my fellow teachers and principal as a plus in my management plan becoming a workable element in the classroom. It is my desire that the students understand the rationale and necessity of classroom rules and consequences and that these rules and consequences be presented in a positive manner. Praise in moderation is but one of several rewards that will be earned by the students to encourage them to continue their positive behavior. In time, I hope the students will come to realize that the real reward is in their academic achievement.

Some teachers prefer a briefer statement such as this one from a middle school teacher:

> I will adopt a style to meet the needs of my classroom. I will have student involvement and cooperation in all activities and learning experiences. My perspective is for me to have a cooperative style of classroom management. I will set the stage by being prepared. My plan will be to have relatively little wasted time, confusion, or disruption. My classroom will be work oriented, but pleasant and relaxed. I will expect a very high level of student involvement with work.

And here's one from a high school teacher:

> I want to establish a trusting and comfortable relationship with my students—one in which they feel comfortable asking questions and offering feedback. It is not my intention to humiliate or degrade any student. My intentions are to maintain an orderly classroom in which all participants have the opportunity to learn and thrive. I plan to establish a relationship with my students so that they know me as an encouraging and supportive adult in their lives. I want my students to be active participants even if that means that my class may get a little noisy. I will treat them as adults in this respect, and my expectations will be high and unwavering. A high school classroom should not be likened to a military boot camp or to an elementary school playground. I intend to keep my students in control, while also allowing them to have some control. My approach will be authoritative as opposed to authoritarian.

Whether your statement is brief and tightly focused or takes a little more explanation to verbalize, it simply needs to be a statement of who you are in the classroom as a manager of people. Don't be at all surprised if this is just a bit more difficult to write than you might first expect. But stay with it and keep refining it until you feel that you have a paragraph that you could hand to a colleague or a parent (perhaps to a student if you are teaching at the secondary level) that expresses what it would mean for a student to be in your classroom.

Write Your Rules

It may seem a little strange to include a list of rules if your plan is to involve the students in this task. However, even if your students will take part in this activity, you should already have in mind the rules that *you* need for the class. With your students you will help to clarify their thinking so as to reflect the rules you require. And if they come up with something else that you hadn't considered, so much the better! The final phrasing of the rules should certainly come from them simply because it ensures that they understand the rules. On the other hand, if your situation or preference is that you will supply the rules, now is the time to list them in your classroom-management notebook.

We have already discussed how to go about writing rules (see page 71). In this section of your notebook include *two* lists of your classroom rules. The first version should be just a simple listing of the rules you believe will be necessary to accomplish the mission statement you have provided. This list is what you might eventually copy onto a poster or a transparency, or turn into an electronic presentation.

The second listing of the rules should begin with a brief explanation of how the rules will be presented to the class. Will each student get a copy? Will they be sent home? Will they be displayed in the classroom? Where? In more than one place?

Follow the preceding explanation with an *annotated* listing of the rules. For each rule indicate (a) exactly what the rule means (rules are often general in nature to keep the number down—but remember that if too much explanation is needed, the rule needs revision) and (b) what following each rule will accomplish. That is, if the rule is worth following, what will it do for you and your students? What is the purpose? The particular exercise not only helps you to clarify exactly what you mean by the rule, but also prepares you to articulate that meaning if a student, administrator, or parent should happen to ask about it.

What Consequences Will You Use?

This is the section where you detail the consequences that accompany the rules. There should be two parts to the section: consequences for following the rules and consequences for not following the rules.

Consequences for Following the Rules

Because the rules are supposed to benefit the class in some way, it would be worthwhile to acknowledge rule-following behavior rather than only emphasizing what happens when rules are broken. Note, however, that this is not a matter of buying appropriate behavior by rewarding your students with treats or prizes for doing what you expect them to do. Possible consequences include pointing out to the students what they have accomplished as a result of their behavior. You may praise individuals or the entire group for following the rules. In younger grades, an occasional note home would be a pleasant respite from the typical note alerting parents to inappropriate behavior. Passing on compliments from other teachers or classroom visitors would also be a good way to help your class bond into a smoothly running learning environment.

Now here's the part you don't want to hear. We do not advocate using homework passes (i.e., exempting a student from a homework assignment) or free time (unless that means an opportunity to engage in some other academically purposeful activity) as consequences. Items such as homework passes send the message that homework is only of secondary importance. Similarly, rewarding a student by allowing him or her to trade instructional time for free time makes instruction sound like something to be avoided, or at least to be freed from. To whatever degree possible, encourage the recognition of intrinsic rewards so that students build pride in their behavior and in their ability to control their behavior. It will take your conscientious attention to accomplish this, but that's what makes you the professional educator in the classroom.

Consequences for Not Following the Rules

We are all much more familiar with this sort of list. As we have discussed previously, your rules are only effective if there are real consequences to enforce them. It is not right to humiliate a student in the name of enforcing rules, but it is requisite that the consequences for violating a rule are unpleasant in the eyes of the student. Just between us, writing a student's name on the board is an aversive consequence only for the child who innocently and rarely ever is a behavioral problem. If you need to keep track of student names for later enforcement of a consequence, unobtrusively keep a list on a handy piece of paper—*and then be sure to address that child at the appropriate time.* Conversely, it may be your intent to enforce the consequence for inappropriate actions immediately. It's up to you—but be consistent about it. Otherwise it becomes a game.

Be sure to keep in mind that the consequences you identify must be actions you are comfortable taking. Remember, a rule essentially becomes a dare to a student, and so you must be prepared to follow through with your announced consequences without hesitation. Identify consequences that keep behavioral issues within your classroom. Save sending students to an administrator as the consequence of last resort (unless, of course, the student's behavior is such that it endangers the student or others in the classroom).

Discipline Program

You are probably thinking, "Wait a minute, I thought the rules and the consequences *are* my discipline program." Well, yes and no. By "discipline program" we mean how you intend to handle misbehavior at the moment of its occurrence. We know what the rules are—and that's how you know there's been misbehavior. And you've identified the consequences to follow that misbehavior. The question here is what are you going to do right *now*? Will you address the student (good idea)? Will you write down the student's name and mention that you will have to talk with him or her? Will you move closer to that student in the classroom? Perhaps you will bring instruction to a stop while you administer the consequence. Some teachers write a name on the board. Some have a tag system. Some bring the immediate behavior of the student to a stop and then quietly address the student with regard to consequences at the first available noninstruction moment. Think this over and then be specific about what action you will take at the time to enforce your announced consequences.

List Procedures for Your Classroom

If this is your first attempt at compiling a classroom-management notebook, you likely will not know all of the procedures that eventually will be required to run your class. But for now, put together as comprehensive a list as possible of procedures that you and your students will need to accomplish. We offered a list of some possibilities in Figure II.6 on page 78.

Once you have a good list of procedures (understanding that you will very likely add to the list as time goes on) go back and consider each one. Place an asterisk (*) beside any procedure that you want to become a routine. For example, you will likely have a procedure for how students are to enter your room and prepare to begin (there will be a significant difference between these for elementary school students and secondary students). These particular procedures are the sort that you will want your students to routinely accomplish without your direction each time. Mark any of the "routines-to-be" that are on your list so that you know to specifically indicate to the students that you want them to learn to do this on their own.

Take another look at your list and place an exclamation point (!) beside any procedure (or routine) that needs to be taught in the very first week of school. There are many procedures that can wait until an appropriate time to be taught. It would simply be overwhelming to the student to try to learn them all at once. So mark those that you will need to address immediately so that classes can begin and progress smoothly right away. The routine for students entering the classroom, as mentioned already, would be an example. In the elementary grades, procedures for walking in the hallways and for preparing for lunch would be additional examples. In the secondary grades you may well have procedures for putting a heading on papers and for turning in homework.

Identifying those procedures that will become routines and those that must be taught to the students right away (notice we said "taught" and not "told") will help you to conceptualize the presentation of your classroom-management plan. As you likely understand by now, we don't advocate "winging it" in the classroom. It doesn't take much time for you to accomplish the tasks we are outlining here, and each and every one of them better prepares you to spend time being that outstanding teacher that you want to be.

Ancillary Personnel

Ancillary personnel refers to people other than you and your students who need to be "in the loop" with your classroom-management plan. For instance, this can include administrators, other teachers, and parents. Often students with special needs will have aides that accompany them during the school day. Identify the individuals or groups of ancillary personnel that will have an effect on your classroom-management program. An elementary school teacher might want to ask other teachers to keep them informed of student behavior (good or bad) that they observe. A high school teacher may let coaches and other sponsors of extracurricular activities know about expectations for students. Certainly you will want parents to be informed of your plan and, hopefully, to endorse and support that plan. In this portion of your notebook, explain how those people will be involved in making classroom management in your room work. Then be sure to contact those people and explain your plan.

Assessment of Your Classroom-Management System

An important, and often omitted, portion of your plan should be attention to assessment of the plan itself. Note: We are *not* referring to checking to see whether your students are following the rules and using the procedures. That would be an assessment of your students' behavior. What we mention here is more introspective than that.

At some point you need to take the time to consider how well your plan is working. Are you pleased with the behavior of your students? Are you comfortable with the rules and the consequences? Have *you* been consistent and fair in the enforcement of those rules and consequences? Are there changes that you need to make so that the plan works just a bit better? Or, perhaps, do you need a whole new plan? (Probably not if you've been following our suggestions, but it could happen.)

Also in this section, identify *when* you will do this assessment of the plan. It would be a good idea to set aside some time—and it doesn't have to be an entire weekend, just an hour or so—at the end of the first week of implementation. Perhaps you can schedule another assessment session after a month and another at the end of the semester or the winter break. Look through your notebook during these moments of reflection and go to the three "Reflection" pages (see next section) and jot down some thoughts on each page. And remember, you can always add more pages! You will likely find that you enjoy accomplishing this task and your self-confidence as a teacher will grow as you notice an increasingly professional tone to your observations and ideas for change.

Reflection

In this last section of your notebook include three blank pages. On one page include the heading "Keep." On another page put "Change." And on the third page put "Throw Away." These pages will be used for making changes to your program as your student teaching or full-time teaching proceeds. Having these pages in your notebook will serve as a reminder that this is a plan always in progress and that it's OK for you to be open to change.

■ TOMORROW: IMPLEMENTING THE PLAN AND RESPONDING TO STUDENT BEHAVIOR

Tomorrow is looking like a really exciting day! Whether it is your very first day as the classroom teacher or just the first day in your new career as a teacher-with-a-plan, tomorrow will be a special day. Don't kid yourself; those students are not at home right now in restless anticipation of the new plan you're bringing to class. No, this is the distinction that makes you the teacher and those folks the students: *you know* what your plan is, and you know that your task is to bring them on board with that plan—and this is true whether we are talking about a management plan or a daily lesson plan. Really, it's the same distinction between the author of a book and the reader of a book. The author knows where he or she wants to take the reader and does so a little bit at a time. So, as the author of a new plan, you know that you must implement the plan step-by-step so that they will come to understand it as well as you do.

CLASSROOM MANAGEMENT

A Signal

Begin by establishing the signal you will use whenever you want your students' attention. We would encourage you to avoid techniques that are punitive in nature such as turning lights on and off, or using phrases such as "I will wait until you are ready" or "I'm warning you." In each of these cases the teacher is working from a position of disdain, and that colors what happens next. Rather—and no matter what age level you are working with—establish a signal, a phrase, a word, a chime that all in the class will recognize as meaning they are to stop whatever they are doing and pay attention to the teacher. You've likely heard of the "Give me five" routine, or when teachers begin counting "One, two, three."

We once worked with a student teacher who couldn't seem to get his third graders to pay attention. The more he told them to quiet down and do this or that, the louder they talked. A high school teacher found that as she tried to get her students on task, they just kept talking over her until she was nearly shouting. Does any of this sound familiar?

The third-grade teacher was advised to talk to the class and come up with a word—unique to the class—that would be the signal to pay attention. The word they chose? Cheeseburger. Yes, cheeseburger. You see, the word is just a signal, not a statement. The next time we visited the classroom, and the same behavior occurred, the teacher quietly said "cheeseburger." Whispered throughout the room was "cheeseburger, cheeseburger, cheeseburger," and then everyone was silent. Students will respond, they really will—you just need to give them something to respond to. When cheeseburger no longer seemed to work, they came up with a new word. From the students' point of view it was a matter of the novelty wearing off and needing something new. From the teacher's perspective it was a matter of revisiting the need for the signal and having a classroom full of students *anxious* to respond appropriately. No threats, no punishment, no bribes—everybody was getting with the plan.

The high school teacher took a different approach—though the signal word would have worked as well, as long as it is not overused and is reinforced. In her case, however, the plan was to talk more softly. High school students are old enough to understand that there is appropriate behavior and inappropriate behavior, and that there are expectations of self-responsibility. So when the teacher started talking softer, they understood that they were missing something that they would be held responsible for getting. In this case, she could still come up with a signal of some sort upon which the class has agreed because there might be times when the class is not talking unacceptably loud (during some activity), but she will still need everybody's attention. The lower voice level, however, provided a message to the students that did not punish them or impugn their character.

Once the signal is chosen, take a few moments to actually practice it. Let the class talk, perhaps even move around in the classroom if that is something appropriate for your situation. Then give the signal and get everybody's attention. Note: *Do not move on until you have everybody's attention.* If you do, it will become obvious that it isn't really a signal for the entire class. Practice a few times. Challenge them to respond more quickly. Reinforce success. And certainly, in a few days—or whenever you see it is necessary—practice it again.

Inform

Now that you have a means for getting their attention in a way that is nonthreatening to them and nonstressful to you, it's time to inform them of the plan that will be used in your classroom.

Begin with the rules. As we've discussed previously, you may want to write your own set of rules or involve the students in the writing of the rules. In the first case it means that you know what the rules are going to be. Depending on your situation you may want to make a copy of the rules for each student, write them on a poster for display in the class, or put them in a PowerPoint® presentation that you can use while addressing the class. If none of these suit your situation, you may want to get to the classroom early enough tomorrow to copy them onto the chalkboard or whiteboard before the students arrive. You will be much better off if your students can see the rules as well as hear you discuss them.

If, on the other hand, rule writing is going to be a class activity, then you should nonetheless be going into the classroom with a solid set of rules in mind. Your task is going to be to let the students discuss possible rules as you deftly guide them to the rules you have identified as necessary for *your* classroom. As we have said, if they come up with a couple of extra ones that actually sound good to you, include them as well. Have some way of displaying the rules.

> *Even if you intend to allow the students to take part in writing the rules, go into that process with a solid idea of what rules you require for the classroom you will manage.*

> *If you fail to enforce your rules, then your plan will fail as well.*

With the rules identified, clearly explain the consequences for following the rules and the consequences for failing to follow the rules. You may be barraged with a flurry of "what if" questions, but stay with your plan. If you have identified appropriate consequences (particularly for not following the rules) then it needs to be made clear that these *are* the consequences and they will be enforced. During this stage, of course, demonstrating your resolute attitude about enforcing the rules will be a bit difficult. However—and we cannot make this any plainer—if you fail to enforce your rules, then your plan will fail as well. This is why it is so important to have reasonable rules and consequences that you can reasonably enforce.

Presentation of the rules and consequences is Part 1. Part 2 is to discuss the classroom procedures. Only discuss those procedures that need to be addressed immediately. Your list of procedures (and routines, of course, though on the first day nothing has gotten to the point of being routine yet) is likely extensive. Trying to explain them all would be overwhelming to anyone. So choose those that the students need to know right away. For example, procedures for entering the classroom, for getting supplies, for asking questions, for sharpening pencils, for heading papers, and for leaving the classroom would be high on the list. In the younger grades you may need to discuss the procedures for walking in the hallway or for being in the lunchroom. Introduce other procedures as they come up over the next several weeks. And do yourself a favor by writing out each of these procedures (again, not all at once—that would be overwhelming to you!) and putting a copy of the procedures in your management notebook. In the middle to upper grades you may want to have a notebook available to the students that has a page for each procedure.

It is necessary while teaching these procedures that you emphasize the fact that these procedures represent things that students are responsible for doing. Remind them that there are *rules* for how the class behaves as a group, but procedures are not rules; they are explanations for how to get things accomplished. And some of those procedures, no matter what age you are working with, will become routines that you expect them to accomplish without direction from you. This is all about helping students develop self-responsibility. By assisting them in this task and reinforcing their success, students will ultimately realize the intrinsic reward in terms of their self-esteem.

Practice

As you introduce the rules and procedures, take some time for your class to practice each of them. Yes, start everyone talking and then use your signal to bring their attention to you. Have everybody demonstrate the behaviors that your rules require and reinforce them positively for doing so appropriately. Have them get up and walk down the hall as a class, or walk into the classroom as you desire, or sharpen pencils/get supplies as you have directed. These are observable behaviors with identified outcomes. It is not likely that your students will gather together to practice these things after school. It is *your* responsibility to provide them with guided practice in each of these behaviors. Each student should experience the correct performance. If, for whatever reason, you decide to forego this step of practicing the behaviors you have identified, then do not be at all surprised when the students fail to do these things. Athletes, musicians, artists, writers, and *teachers* all practice the things they do—and many of them do so for a lifetime! It is not asking too much of your students to practice those things that you have identified as instrumental to having a well-running learning environment.

> *It is not asking too much of your students to have them practice those things that you have identified as instrumental to having a well-running learning environment.*

Reinforce

We've mentioned it enough for you to know this already, but just in case you've started reading right here, you must reinforce appropriate behavior if you want to increase the probability of that behavior continuing. No, we are not saying to lavish praise on your students for every little thing they do. However, in this classroom-management plan you have developed a number of things you expect your students to do so that you can have an effective classroom, so be sure to bring it to their attention that you appreciate their actions.

Three typical types of reinforcement that one often hears of with regard to behavior are direct, vicarious, and self-reinforcement. Your goal is to have your students following your rules and accomplish their procedures and routines because they find it personally gratifying to do so. That's what we refer to as

self-reinforcement. The good news with this is that you have specifically put into place a system of behaviors and expectations that are intended to benefit your students. That makes getting to the self-reinforcement level a lot easier.

Along the way to self-reinforcement, however, your students need a little assistance. That's where direct and vicarious reinforcement come into play. It is really not necessary that everything in a child's educational life have to be a matter of treats and trinkets. When students come to expect these things it is only because they have been *taught* to expect them (behavioral psychologists would say "conditioned"). You, as the professional educator, do not need to resort to external rewards. Rather, the appropriate use of direct and vicarious reinforcement to individuals and the group as a whole will bring you the behavior you want and the learning environment that you need, and will put your students on a path to building greater self-esteem.

Direct reinforcement is when you tell an individual or the entire group that a particular behavior was good or well done, or much appreciated or impressive. **Vicarious reinforcement** is when you single out an individual or perhaps a small group and make an overt comment meant to be heard by the others, saying that he is doing something appropriately. The intent is that others hear the praise that someone else is receiving and so modify their own behavior to get some of that same recognition. This may sound simplistic, but it is far more powerful than you may think.

When using either direct or vicarious reinforcement in an educational situation it is important that you (a) acknowledge the appropriate behavior (and, if using vicarious reinforcement, acknowledge the appropriate behavior of others as it is demonstrated) and (b) from time to time bring it to the students' attention that their behavior in following the rules and procedures is paying off for them in other ways as well. That is, indicate that the range of topics you have discussed in class is impressive, or that their test scores have been getting better, or that other people have commented on how well this group works as a class. You must keep in mind that tying these two things together—appropriate behavior and the benefits of it—are something that *you* must do as part of the overall program of managing, and teaching, this class. These sorts of things are what make you a professional educator.

Three typical types of reinforcement with regard to behavior are direct, vicarious, and self-reinforcement. Your goal is to have your students following your rules and accomplishing their procedures and routines because they find it personally gratifying to do so.

The final thought in this section about implementing your program is to never be afraid of practicing anything that needs to be practiced again. When you see behavior starting to slide or a particular rule being abused, bring other matters to a stop and spend some time reestablishing the behaviors that you require. You will lose far less time rehearsing rules and procedures to tone them up again than you will if you allow "rusty skills" to constantly interrupt your instructional agenda.

FINALLY: ASSESSING YOUR ■ CLASSROOM-MANAGEMENT PLAN

You've put your plan in place. OK, there may have been a glitch or two in the process, perhaps you needed to work a little more closely with several students to get them on board with the program. It may even have been the case that it took a little longer than you expected to get an entire class up and running, particularly if you are trying to turn around a group that has not had the benefit of a real plan of action up until now. That's OK. Don't get the idea that changing group behavior will happen just because one day you said so. It takes time. You, however, have the knowledge during that time that you are putting a program in place and making it work. Establish your expectations, stick to your rules, and impose your identified consequences. Be consistent.

With that said, it now becomes important to consider that final phase of the classroom-management plan that you have compiled: *assessing the plan.* Remember, this is not a matter of assessing how well the students are following the plan. Instead, this is when you take some time to consider whether the plan is accomplishing what you want it to accomplish.

You should already have determined when this is going to happen (if you filled out a complete plan in the previous section), but if you haven't, let's figure that your first assessment will occur after the first day that you present your plan to the students. So, now that the time has arrived and you are all comfortable in a safe and secure location, let's consider some of the questions that you might want to ask yourself. Table II.2 (see page 97) organizes this assessment task into several categories: planning, implementation, and effectiveness. There may be more categories that you want to consider, but these should help you get started. It may be helpful to make a copy of Table II.2 that could be added to your management notebook. If you do so, for each Management Plan Assessment (MPA) add in another page and write the date on it just to give some structure to your review. Also, be sure to make use of those pages labeled *Keep*, *Change*, and *Throw Away* that you included at the end of your management notebook.

Take a look at the items on the MPA table. For each question, if things are OK as they are, check the box in the "OK" column. If you have a nice little comment to make such as, "It actually went better than I'd expected!" go ahead and write that in on the "Comments" line. On the other hand, if there is an issue with one of the items, put an asterisk in the box so that it will be easy for you to notice it. Then in the "Comments" section note your concern and your intended action. We know it's not a lot of space, but this table is just for your record. Use those pages in the back of your notebook to work out the details, and then add or revise pages in the appropriate section(s) of your plan as you refine your program.

This is really a much more important activity than you may be thinking it is right now. You will find that if you do get comfortable and then take just a few minutes to specifically consider what is happening in your classroom in terms of the management program you have designed, it won't take long to make adjustments. In fact, you may start to use this approach in other aspects of your work! So, don't be one of those folks who throw a plan out there and then just wait to see what happens. Instead, decide right now when your MPA time will be (you won't need more than half an hour each time) and schedule several of them throughout the semester or year.

Well, if you have followed through with this whole unit, you have come a long way. Keep your management notebook somewhere that is readily accessible. Don't be afraid to add pages that allow you to use it as a management "diary" if that suits your style. Having some place to jot down successes, failures (let's just call them "setbacks"), new ideas, and insights will help you to keep this aspect of your work dynamic and at hand without becoming a bookkeeping burden. It is an unfortunate circumstance that no matter how much pleading we do, many teachers will learn classroom management as a trial by fire. You can avoid that and find the time to enjoy quality teaching experiences with your students if you'll just invest some time in planning for classroom behavior now. And once you have that program up and running, every so often, while your students are working away, take a moment to pat yourself on the back for the program you have put in place and for your ability to run that program. You *and* your students are the beneficiaries!

Unit II Appendix

Table II.2   Management Plan Assessment

Planning	OK	Comments
Did I compile a complete plan?		
All elements clearly articulated?		
Comfortable with all elements?		
Anything else I should include?		
Implementation		
Explained clearly to students?		
Any problem areas show up?		
Need more/less time to get going?		
Pleased with initial results?		
Effectiveness		
Is it working well?		
Changes needed?		
Reinforcements appropriate?		

UNIT III
Instruction

INSTRUCTION

■ UNIT III CONCEPT MAP

Unit III

1 the curriculum
- four types
- perspectives of curriculum
- purpose of curriculum
- defining curriculum

2 the student
- reading ability and learning styles
- students with exceptionalities
- visual and auditory challenges
- social influences on diversity
- cultural influences and ethnicity

3 conceptualizing your role
- bringing the world to your students
- instructional techniques
- monitoring and flexibility

4 putting it all together
- modeling
- questioning
- listening
- demonstrating, directing, and orchestrating

5 this is a people profession
- enjoying your profession
- preparation, preparation, preparation

UNIT III PEP TALK ■

The next time you sit in class or are attending a faculty meeting, watch your professor or administrator as she walks into the room. It is likely that she enters with some information that she wants you to know before you leave. However, the information itself is just one aspect of the dynamic event that is about to take place. In addition to information, this individual likely has a strategy for teaching the course or conducting the meeting. That strategy includes a number of components such as techniques for teaching, methods for monitoring what happens, ideas for activities to enrich understanding, and of course, a means for assessing whether the information has been acquired (Deshler, Ellis, & Lenz, 1996; Tomlinson, 2000). Lecture or otherwise, information is just part of the strategy that a presenter brings to each class session.

So, we are talking about instruction from a strategic perspective. **Strategy** refers to the art of planning some course of action *and* coordinating the implementation of that plan. It represents a broader view of the overall goal. The strategic nature of teaching requires an understanding of the bigger picture of what is to occur during the year (curriculum) with a particular group of students, and as a function of individual lessons (instruction). For example, the syllabus for a course represents a plan for the semester. That syllabus probably stays pretty much the same from semester to semester or class to class. However, it may be the case that different combinations of students move along at different rates or respond better to different teaching styles. In such a case a professor may adjust her *strategy* for reaching the goal even though the basic plan (syllabus) remains the same.

> *Strategy refers to the art of planning some course of action and coordinating the implementation of that plan.*

As a strategist you are responsible for combining content (subject matter), technique, and resources to provide an effective learning experience. This responsibility is what makes you a professional rather than a technician or a teacher's aide. In essence, an educational strategy must

- identify what we want to accomplish,
- determine with whom,
- account for the means (either in terms of the teacher's capabilities or other resources) for putting the plan into action, and
- indicate how to assess the results.

We will discuss the assessment aspect in Unit IV, but the other topics are what this unit is all about!

FIRST: THE CURRICULUM ■

Does it seem as if you've been in school all your life? Given that, you probably think of what goes on in school not only as the norm, the way it is, but also as if it's always been that way. The reality is that curriculum is constantly evolving. As we will see in this unit, many influences affect a school's curriculum.

There is considerable discussion these days about requiring public-school children to wear uniforms to school or to prohibit the wearing of clothing that displays "culturally offensive" messages. Are these rules part of the curriculum? Did the high school *you* attended have a dress code? Was that part of the curriculum? How about the food served in the cafeteria? Many schools today are removing soda machines and no longer offering sugary beverages for sale because they are not considered to have nutritional value. And what of the offering of "ethnic" foods? Is this part of the curriculum? How about the teaching, or not teaching, of evolution as a topic in science classes, or the removal of books considered to represent "new age" philosophy from the library bookshelves? Which of these issues enter into determining what constitutes curriculum—the message of the school? Issues such as these can be divisive in communities, states, and the nation. Since you will one day be in the middle of the debate, you should have an appreciation of what curriculum is and how it is developed.

Defining "Curriculum"

Curriculum refers to the means and materials with which students will interact for the purpose of achieving identified educational outcomes. Arising in medieval Europe was the *trivium*, an educational curriculum based upon the study of grammar, rhetoric, and logic. The later *quadrivium* (referring to four subjects rather than three as represented by the trivium) emphasized the study of arithmetic, geometry, music, and astronomy. These seven liberal arts should sound a lot like what you experienced during your formal education.

The emphasis on single subjects persists even today. Very likely you moved from classroom to classroom, particularly throughout your secondary education, studying a different subject with each teacher. Yet there was more to your education. Perhaps you participated in athletics, or the band, or clubs, or student government, or made the choice *not* to participate in any extracurricular activities. All of these (including the option not to participate) are part of what we might call the contemporary curriculum. But there is more.

Some educators would say that the curriculum consists of all the *planned experiences* that the school offers as part of its educational responsibility. Then there are those who contend that the curriculum includes not only the planned, but also the *unplanned experiences* as well. For example, incidents of violence that have occurred at a number of schools across the nation are hardly a planned component of the curriculum. However, the manner in which violence is addressed before, during, and after the actual event sends a very definite message about how people in our culture interact and how the laws of our nation are applied.

Another perspective suggests that curriculum involves *organized* rather than planned experiences because any event must flow of its own accord, the outcome not being certain beforehand. For instance, competitions, whether academic or athletic, can be organized, but the outcomes will depend on a myriad of factors that cannot be planned.

Which brings us to the notion of emphasizing *outcomes* versus *experiences*. This shift to the notion of outcomes is very much in keeping with the current movement toward **accountability** in the public schools, that is, the perspective that there are indeed specific things that the schools are supposed to accomplish with children. District personnel, school administrators, and you as one of many teachers are to be held accountable by the public/taxpayers for ensuring that those objectives are met.

Curriculum, it turns out, is indeed much more than the idea of specific subjects as represented by the trivium or the quadrivium. And, as we will see in the next section, it can be characterized not only by what it *does* include but also by what it intentionally *excludes.*

A key concept to keep in mind is that the curriculum is only that part of the plan that *directly affects* students. Anything in the plan that does not reach the students constitutes an educational wish, but not a curriculum. Half a century ago Bruner (1960) wrote, "Many curricula are originally planned with a guiding idea . . . But as curricula are actually executed, as they grow and change, they often lose their original form and suffer a relapse into a certain shapelessness" (p. 54). Curriculum—however grand the plans may be—can only be that portion of the plan that actually reaches the student. Planning that keeps that point in focus can be expected to result in a more focused curriculum.

> *Curriculum—however grand the plans may be—can only be that portion of the plan that actually reaches the student.*

The Purpose of Curriculum

We have suggested that curriculum refers to the means and materials with which the student interacts. To determine what will constitute those means and materials, we must decide what we want the curriculum to yield. What will constitute the "educated" individual in our society? In other words, what purpose does the curriculum serve?

The things that teachers teach represent what the larger society wants children to learn. However, beyond teaching reading and writing, what *are* the necessary things that they should be taught? Is it really necessary to teach science? Does teaching mathematics really lead to logical thinking, or does it just provide students with some basic computational skills that may or may not come in handy at some future time? You may feel that answering such questions is not something a teacher has to be able to do, but rest assured that at some point a parent will ask you questions like these. As a teacher, you will be the representative of "the curriculum" to whom parents and students turn for answers. The purpose of the curriculum is to prepare the student to thrive within the society as it is—and that includes *the capacity for positive change and growth.*

> *The purpose of the curriculum is to prepare the student to thrive within the society as it is—and that includes the capacity for positive change and growth.*

You Actually Have Four Curriculums

There are essentially four curriculums at work in most educational settings: the explicit, implicit, null, and extra-, or cocurriculum. You are probably familiar with the notions of explicit curriculum and extracurricular activities. The real *intrigue* of curriculum debate and design comes into play with the implicit and null curriculums.

There are four curriculums:

Explicit curriculum: subjects that will be taught, the identified "mission" of the school, and the knowledge and skills that the school expects successful students to acquire

Implicit curriculum: lessons that arise from the culture of the school and the behaviors, attitudes, and expectations that characterize that culture

Null curriculum: topics or perspectives that are specifically excluded from the curriculum

Extra curriculum: school-sponsored programs that are intended to supplement the academic aspect of the school experience

The Explicit Curriculum

Explicit means "obvious" or "apparent," and that's just what the **explicit curriculum** is all about: the subjects that will be taught, the identified "mission" of the school, and the knowledge and skills that the school expects successful students to acquire. If you speak with an administrator at your school or where you do your observations or practicum work, ask about the curriculum; it is this publicly announced (and publicly sanctioned) explanation of the message of school that will be explained to you. The explicit curriculum can be discussed in terms of time on task, contact hours, or Carnegie units (high school credit courses). It can be qualified in terms of specific observable, measurable learning objectives.

The Implicit Curriculum

Sometimes referred to as the *hidden curriculum*, the **implicit curriculum** refers to the lessons that arise from the culture of the school and the behaviors, attitudes, and expectations that characterize that culture. While good citizenship may be part of the explicit curriculum, a particular ethos that promotes, for example, multiethnic acceptance and cooperation may also characterize a particular school. This is not to say that parents, teachers, and administrators sat around a table and said, "Hey, let's promote acceptance of diverse ethnic values in the context of the American experience." That would be nice, of course, but then it tends to fall into the category of the explicit curriculum. By virtue of a high multiethnic enrollment, a particular school may have a culture of multiethnic cooperation. Another school, isolated in that its enrollment is primarily that of one ethnic group, would develop a different sort of culture.

INSTRUCTION

Individual schools within a district, or even classrooms within a school that share a common *explicit* curriculum, can differ greatly with regard to the *implicit* curriculum. This is not an altogether bad situation, but to a great degree the implicit curriculum is subjected to less scrutiny than is the explicit curriculum.

There are other aspects to the implicit curriculum, and interestingly enough it is the students who pick up on these messages. Notice how the classrooms and common areas are decorated. These decorations will demonstrate what the implicit curriculum of the school values. Watch the children to see how they interact with each other within the class and throughout the building. Does the school display student work throughout the building? Is there an unwritten rule that children are to be seen and not heard? All of these contribute to a very particular message sent to students about expectations, demands, and codes of conduct.

If you want to investigate the notion of the implicit curriculum further, speak with some elementary school students. Ask them what is required to get good grades or the approval of the teacher. Don't be surprised when rather than telling you about studying for an hour every night or completing homework correctly, they tell you things like "sit up straight" or "be quiet in class" or "be on time." The implicit curriculum, difficult as it is to identify and articulate, is something that students understand very quickly. When young children explain the expectations for a student in school, it will likely be the implicit curriculum that they discuss.

The Null Curriculum

Just as compelling as the notion of the implicit curriculum is Eisner's (1994) concept of the **null curriculum**. This aspect of curriculum refers to "the options students are not afforded, the perspectives they may never know about, much less be able to use, the concepts and skills that are not a part of their intellectual repertoire" (p. 106–107). The teaching of evolution provides an example. For more than seventy-five years this topic has been an issue of debate. The decision by individual states or school districts within states *not* to include this topic within its explicit curriculum places it in the category of the *null curriculum*. In other words, the decision to exclude particular topics or subjects from a curriculum nonetheless affects the curriculum by its very omission.

Another example would be the topic of sex education. Sex education has long been an issue with regard to the degree to which it should be included in the school curriculum, but the newer issues of gender orientation, alternative lifestyles, and alternative family configurations—just to mention a few—exemplify how exclusion from the explicit or implicit curriculum, and thus inclusion in the null curriculum, affects the overall educational experience.

It is an interesting paradox that ours is a country that to a great degree has succeeded based upon a spirit of innovation and risk-taking, yet these tendencies are not fostered within the curriculum to the same degree as conformity, procedure, and discipline.

Extracurricular Programs

The fourth aspect of curriculum is that of the **extracurriculum** or *cocurriculum.* This curriculum represents all of those school-sponsored programs that are intended to supplement the academic aspect of the school experience. Athletics, band, drama, student government, clubs, honor societies and student organizations, and school dances and social events all fall under the heading of extracurricular activities. Participation in these activities is purely voluntary and does not contribute to grades or credits earned toward advancement from one grade to the next or to graduation. Extracurricular activities are typically open to all, though participation often depends on skill level.

Participation in extracurricular activities is purely voluntary and does not contribute to grades or credits earned toward advancement from one grade to the next or to graduation.

Perspectives of Curriculum

Suppose you wanted to buy an automobile. You would expect the vehicle to have a chassis, an engine, four wheels (with tires, of course), the necessary controls to operate the vehicle, and that it should suffice to get you from one place to another. Those characteristics would, in general, represent what we think of as an automobile. But you know that there are millions of cars out there, and they differ in many ways. Color, power, styling, and sound systems are just some of the aspects of cars that would make *your* car unique. We are in a similar situation as we now discuss the different perspectives that can characterize a curriculum.

Two dominant perspectives of curriculum have occupied the educational spotlight, though more often than not they are embroiled in a struggle to find a common ground. One perspective is the *subject-centered curriculum*, the oldest curricular format in the Western world, dating back to classical Greece and Rome. The other is the *student-centered curriculum*, which found favor through the work of John Dewey early in the twentieth century and later enjoyed a resurgence in popularity beginning in the latter 1960s. Since any curriculum must ultimately center on the student, we are going to borrow from the results of the White House Conferences on Education that occurred in 1956 and 1964 and adopt the terms *cognitive* (which takes an objective "thinking skills" perspective) and *affective* (which adopts a subjective perspective emphasizing attitudes and personal meaning) to distinguish between the two approaches. With these two perspectives established, you will see that most versions of curricular design fall into one category or the other. Of course, there will also be those variations that attempt to reconcile the differences and find the middle ground.

The Cognitive Perspective

The **cognitive perspective** focuses on the acquisition of knowledge. To that end, curriculums are typically divided among several distinct subject-matter areas. In the elementary school the different subjects are taught at scheduled times each day, with reading and math typically scheduled in the morning when students are believed to be most alert. In the secondary curriculum, students typically move from one room to another for different subjects. In either case, each subject is taught in isolation with its own facts, skills, and lessons to be learned. Figure III.2 lists four variations on the cognitive perspective theme.

Figure III.2   Cognitive Perspective of Curriculum

(typically subject centered)	
Subject-Centered Curriculum	Emphasizes the subjects that all students should learn
Core Curriculum	Emphasizes a particular body of knowledge within the subject areas that all students should learn
Mastery Learning	Sets a standard that must be met and allows time to meet that standard
Outcome-Based Education	Establishes the specific outcomes of education that are expected

The Affective Perspective

While the cognitive domain was concerned with levels of thinking (Bloom's taxonomy begins with *knowledge* and rises to the more sophisticated levels of *synthesis* and *evaluation*), the affective domain is concerned with feeling and valuing. Using the **affective perspective** should not only present information to students but should also help them see the value of that information and to concern themselves with matters more "human" than the mere acquisition of facts (see Figure III.3 on page 108).

The notion of **child-centered education** uses subject matter as the context around which student growth and development will be facilitated. That, of course, entails at least two considerations: what subjects will be taught to foster that development, and what we, as a society, want to develop in our children. Dewey tried to balance these two considerations by couching education in terms of the child's life and the society's needs. A key observation in understanding Dewey's perspective is his idea that school does not *prepare* one for life; it *is* life. Thus, if we want children to learn to function in a democratic society, we must offer them opportunities to exercise democratic policies (were you on the student council in high school?). If we can identify prosocial behaviors that we wish to develop in children, we must then put children in situations that provide opportunities for them to act in desired ways.

Figure III.3   Affective Perspective of Curriculum

(typically student centered)	
Student-Centered Curriculum	Emphasizes the natural interests and curiosity of the child
Humanistic Education	Seeks to bring elements of value and meaning to education
Cooperative Learning	Establishes academically heterogeneous groups of students and downplays competition
Broad-Fields Curriculum	Integrates the subject areas to find the broader meaning
Problem Solving and Inquiry	Makes the curriculum more relevant to the student by providing real problems to solve and topics to investigate
Activity Curriculum	Designs a particular curriculum for a particular child at a particular time. Problematic for working with the millions of students enrolled in the public school system

You will likely find elements of several curriculums at work in your school. As we mentioned previously, tinkering with curriculums over the years has resulted in eclectic versions that try to please many constituencies. Unfortunately, such a situation makes it very difficult to clearly articulate the purpose of a given curriculum.

■ SECOND: THE STUDENT

Have you ever found anyone who was exactly like you? Of course not. Even though there may be some people who are a little like you or even a lot like you, the fact remains that you are unique. A set of special qualities and characteristics is what makes each of us special and makes the world a richer place.

As a teacher you will encounter diversity in the classroom. One of your most important challenges will be in coming face-to-face with the many ways in which students differ. To illustrate, in a report titled *The Schools We Have: The Schools We Want*, James Nehring (1992) summarizes, "We assume . . . that all kids are the same . . . We force all kids through the same mold. If there is one thing on which both research and common sense agree, it is that kids are not the same" (p. 156).

Culture and ethnicity are just a few of many factors that will make each of your students unique. However, appreciating and accommodating differences are particularly important within our multiethnic American culture.

Cultural Influences, Ethnicity, and Personality

Culture represents the values, attitudes, and beliefs that influence the behavior and the traditions of a people. Notice that these are social, not biological, dimensions. Though people often label others according to physical features, culture is actually a matter of commonly held ideas. A chief purpose of schooling has been passing on the traditions of the society. Education has been the means by which people came to understand their heritage and the attitudes, behaviors, and beliefs the society valued.

In most communities in the United States, however, many cultures are represented and, as a result, diversity is also considered in terms of **ethnicity**. James Banks (1994) defines ethnicity as a sense of common identity based upon common ancestral background and the sharing of common values and beliefs. That sounds a lot like culture, though ancestral background implies another dimension. In discussing ethnic minorities, Banks (1997) qualifies the definition to say that ethnicity involves "unique physical and/or cultural characteristics that enable individuals who belong to other ethnic groups to identify its members easily, often for discriminatory purposes" (p. 66).

Seen in a broader perspective, these definitions show that while a culture might be characterized by a particular ethnicity, one culture (such as the American culture) could actually include people from many ethnicities. The result is a culture that has been evolving since the United States was founded.

Religion

Religion is not just a part of culture; it is a very powerful part. As recently as 2003 an Alabama Supreme Court Chief Justice, Judge Roy Moore, was removed from the bench because he refused to have a stone sculpture depicting the Ten Commandments removed from the courthouse lobby. Even with a strong and sincere effort to make school a more culturally friendly place, religion (in the sense of practicing a religion, not in the sense of discussing one) typically is not a part of the curriculum. Yet as a classroom teacher you must consider the impact of religious beliefs on the classroom. For example, some parents do not allow their children to take part in any celebrations at school. This includes not only events with a religious overtone (for instance, a Christmas party), but also birthday celebrations. You may also have students who dress in accordance with their religious beliefs, students who miss class in observance of religious holidays (and you will have to provide a way for such students to make up work missed), and students whose religious beliefs may be in opposition to particular subject area content.

You cannot be aware of every nuance of religious belief that might be represented in the classroom. However, as a teacher you must not devalue a student's religious beliefs or observations because they differ from your own or from the mainstream in your community. As a teacher your role will never include passing judgment on a religious perspective, or implying that your own convictions are superior, but instead your role is to demonstrate that in your community of learners, tolerance and considering other perspectives are of value.

Gender

Of all the categories of student diversity, gender is likely the most enigmatic. In sorting this out we will consider the difference between gender and sex, sexual stereotyping, and cognitive differences between the sexes.

Gender refers to the social aspect of sexuality, that is, behaviors that are considered masculine or feminine. The social forces that teach gender-specific behaviors and expectations are prevalent from birth. Names given to boys and girls have a social context that implies gender. The way children are dressed implies gender. Activities in which boys engage versus those in which girls engage, even the way that they are taught to interact with other people, are all gender bound. We say gender bound because none of these examples has any biological basis.

However, when people speak of the different physical and cognitive abilities of boys and girls in school, gender is not the issue. The issue is **sex**, the biological distinctions of male or female. For example, do males and females learn differently as a function of being male or female? For our discussion, the focus is on how these distinctions and expectations are treated in the classroom.

Gender and sexuality have been an issue throughout our country's history. It is not resolved at this point, and the increased visibility of alternative lifestyles and sexual orientations ensures that it will continue as an issue. In the meantime, it would be appropriate for classroom teachers to

- avoid imposing sexual stereotyping,
- promote collaboration between boys and girls,
- make all subjects equally accessible to both sexes.

Language

Language differences across and within cultures can influence student diversity. You will notice significant differences in language usage even among your students for whom English is their native language. At one end of the spectrum are youngsters who have neither traveled beyond their local communities nor developed an awareness of the structures and interrelationships of their immediate surroundings. Such students possess impoverished or different vocabularies (street language, for instance), poor formal learning skills, and inadequate and inaccurate academic concepts. Poverty rather than culture or ethnicity is the predominant connection with low levels of achievement (Jencks & Phillips, 1998; Payne, 1998).

On the other hand, some students may possess a rather sophisticated grammar and vocabulary. These students typically speak in complete standard-language sentences and verbally communicate with their peers and adults on a variety of topics. It is likely that their parents read and talk to them and introduce them to a variety of cultural experiences, both vicarious and direct.

English as a Second Language (ESL) and Limited English Proficiency (LEP)

ESL, *English as a second language*, refers to English being taught to native speakers of other languages. ESOL is another term that you will hear used, which stands for *English for speakers of other languages*. TESOL refers to *teaching English to speakers of other languages*, and ELL or simply EL refers to *English-language learners*. The referent in each case is a person (in our case, a student) whose first language is something other than English.

You will also hear of LEP, or *limited English proficiency*. A student identified as LEP can be someone who speaks no English at all or a student who knows a few words of "playground language" but not the complex English that characterizes texts and other formal print materials.

With regard to instruction that is provided for students for whom English is (or will become) a second language, there are several concepts you should know. With language **immersion**, all instruction is in English. The idea is that students need to be immersed in English all day long, much as they would if they visited (another) foreign country. Another approach is to provide a pullout program during which English-language learners receive separate instruction, often in basic skills. Another approach is to provide initial instruction in the students' native language, thus delaying the introduction of English instruction.

An alternative concept is **bilingual education**, in which instruction is provided daily in both English and the student's native tongue. The topic of immersion or delayed English or bilingual education has been, and probably will continue to be, controversial (Gilroy, 2001; Shannon & Milian, 2002).

Motivation

Students vary greatly in their degree of **motivation**, which is an intrinsic desire to accomplish some task. That is, motivation comes from within. As a teacher, you can provide students with a reason to do something (a grade, aversive consequences, as a personal favor), but that student determines whether or not he or she is motivated by the reason that you create. What motivates one child is not necessarily a motivator for another child. The art of teaching comes into play as you try to find the reasons that ignite an intrinsic desire toward growth and achievement.

Academic Self-Concept

One of the most overlooked differences in people is that of **academic self-concept**. Much of what children learn or fail to learn may be influenced by their academic self-concepts. Students who have become accustomed to succeeding and who feel academically competent are generally successful in a variety of scholastic activities. Those who become accustomed to failure and who feel academically inferior tend to continually fail in scholastic endeavors. Interestingly, these children are likely to perform as they have in the past and, what may be more significant, they tend to accept their performances as inevitable.

People typically reflect the academic concepts others have of them. When teachers and classmates consider a child in a positive manner, he or she tends to develop self-confidence and react as the group seems to expect. Conversely, when teachers and fellow classmates consider a pupil in a negative manner, the student begins to mirror their prejudices and react in the way they expect. Thus we have the spiral that is often referred to as a self-fulfilling prophecy.

Temperament

"She's got a great personality." "He's so friendly." What do you mean when you make those statements about the wide range of **temperaments** that children can exhibit? Like economic, intellectual, and social characteristics, factors related to the development of personality are clearly interrelated. Emotional differences are inextricably intertwined with other aspects of student development. Anger, happiness, sadness, confidence, introversion or extroversion, appreciation of or apprehension about novelty (things being different or changing often), and competitiveness are factors regarding temperament that you may notice in different students. Clearly, you may need to tailor your interactions with different personalities to accommodate individual students' needs.

Reading Ability and Learning Styles

It is interesting to note that in 1900, the ability to write one's name identified the person as literate. By the mid-1930s, a literate person was one who had attended at least three years of school. In 1947, the Census Bureau set the bar at fifth grade, and in 1970 the U.S. Office of Education adjusted the bar to ninth grade. Today the bar is high school completion (Gordon & Gordon, 2003).

Regardless of the grade you teach, your students will have a wide range of individual differences in reading ability. Riley (1996) notes that in kindergarten it is common to find a *five-year* range in children's literacy-related capabilities. While some children enter school able to sing or recite the alphabet and read a few words or simple books or, on occasion, more complex texts (Jackson, 1991), others arrive without possessing the basic skills, concepts, attitudes, and strategies essential for successfully encountering a multitude of learning tasks.

A popular perspective on student diversity and learning is that of **learning styles**. Though there is some debate about this topic, especially in regard to how it relates to instruction, publications by Dunn (1995, 2001), Dunn et al. (1995), Carbo (1996), and Barbe and Swassing (1988) argue that teachers should take account of students' various learning preferences.

You may already be familiar with the basic categories of learning preferences:

Visual: These students prefer to see things (maps, charts, a problem written out).

Auditory: For these students, processing is facilitated by hearing things and through discussion.

Tactile/Kinesthetic: For these students, movement is very important (writing, actually going through the movements of an activity, manipulating materials).

Vocalic: This refers to talking oneself through something (counting out loud, repeating a phone number aloud, verbalizing the steps in some process or procedure).

Most people indicate a preference for some combination of these styles rather than just one. As you continue your professional growth as a teacher, you will learn to design lessons that address multiple learning styles. If you are taking courses now, it is likely that your professor lectures to the class or engages the class in dialogue (auditory and vocalic) while also writing key points on the board or projecting them on a screen (visual), during which time you take notes (tactile/kinesthetic). In this way, multiple learning styles are being accessed.

Students With Exceptionalities

The contemporary perspective toward students with exceptionalities is to bring them fully into the educational experience, for "exceptional education" embraces a broad range of capabilities and literally millions of children. The old philosophy of separating these children for instruction has been replaced with a philosophy of **inclusion** that seeks to bring such children into the general education program at every opportunity. Even more important is the attitude of providing positive support—an emphasis on a child's abilities rather than on a child's disabilities—which affirms the child's rightful place as a member of the general education population.

Learning Disabilities

The term **learning disability** as defined by the Individuals with Disabilities Education Act (IDEA), which was reauthorized by the U.S. Congress in 2004, refers to "a disorder in one or more of the basic psychological processes involved in understanding or in using language, either spoken or written, which manifests itself in imperfect ability to listen, think, speak, read, write, spell, or do mathematical calculations" (20 U.S.C., Sec. 1400). A study based on two surveys conducted by the U.S. Department of Education (Coutinho, Oswald, & Best, 2002) found that students classified as learning disabled were most likely to live in poverty, be minorities, or be males. Indeed, boys are three to five times as likely as girls to be diagnosed as learning disabled (Young & Brozo, 2001). The disorders include conditions such as perceptual disabilities, brain injury, minimal brain dysfunction, dyslexia, and developmental aphasia. They do *not* include a learning problem that is primarily the result of visual, hearing, or motor disabilities, of mental retardation, of emotional disturbance, or of environmental, cultural, or economic disadvantage (Turnbull & Cilley, 1999). The conditions that eliminate a person's impairment from consideration are visual, hearing, and motor disabilities, which are special conditions but are not learning disabilities. Most states and school districts require that students meet three criteria to be classified as learning disabled (Mercer, Jordan, Allsop, & Mercer, 1996):

1. **Inclusionary criterion**: There must exist a severe discrepancy between the student's perceived potential and actual achievement as measured by appropriate assessment instruments.

2. **Exclusionary criterion**: The learning disability cannot result primarily from a visual or hearing impairment, mental retardation, serious emotional disturbance, or cultural differences.

3. **Need criterion**: There is a demonstrated need for special education services without which the student's learning will be compromised.

You must be cautious in your approach to possible learning disability situations. Teachers are not certified or qualified to diagnose such conditions. Thus, you should avoid telling parents that a student has a particular impairment. Your professional role is to make keen observations, document them, reflect on alternative possible causes, and then, if the situation demands it, refer the student to the appropriate personnel in your school (school guidance counselor, school psychologist) without labeling the student. By law, only an interdisciplinary team (on which you may participate) can make such a determination. The process is lengthy and is spelled out in the federal statutes.

A second point to keep in mind is that a specific learning disability is not to be confused with mental impairments. In general, a person with a specific learning disability possesses at least average ability. Based on some intelligence tests administered to determine the cognitive functioning of a student, the average range is 85–115. Thus, students with learning disabilities are presumed to be at least average in ability. The presence of a specific learning disability neither presumes below average intellectual function nor precludes functioning on a gifted level.

Attention Deficit/Hyperactivity Disorder

It is likely that as a classroom teacher you will have one or two students in your class who just can't seem to focus on what's going on or, alternatively, who just can't seem to settle down long enough to find out what's going on. Before losing your temper and becoming upset with the students, consider that such behaviors may fall into the category of **Attention Deficit/Hyperactivity Disorder (AD/HD)**. According to the American Psychiatric Association (2000), approximately 3 to 7 percent of the school-age population has some form of AD/HD. Notice that unlike statistics we have presented for other disorders, this is not 3 to 7 percent of students with some sort of cognitive disorder; this is 3 to 7 percent of the entire school-age population. Of these students, the prevalence of AD/HD in boys to girls is about 3 to 1 (American Academy of Pediatrics, 2000).

For a student to be diagnosed with AD/HD, the symptoms must be manifested before the age of seven, continue for at least six months, and occur in at least two social settings, such as at school and at home. Of course, not all students classified as AD/HD are hyperactive and attention deficit. Some students may be *hypoactive*, that is, very slow to respond.

As a classroom teacher you should be aware that these behaviors can interfere with learning development and social experiences. Your first task will be to see the student apart from the behavior and so avoid becoming frustrated over behaviors the child is struggling to control. Next, it will be important for you to coach, model, and role-play appropriate behaviors with the child and to reinforce appropriate behaviors (Roan, 1994). With regard to academics, Shank (2002) recommends keeping these seven words in mind: relevance, novelty, variety, choices, activity, challenge, and feedback. Orienting your planning around these terms can involve everything from the timing of lessons to the writing of behavior contracts and the recognition of appropriate achievement.

Emotional and Behavioral Disorders

Of all the cognitive differences we have discussed so far, the category of **emotional/behavioral disorders** is perhaps the most difficult to pin down. There are some 477,000 students with emotional or behavioral disorders in the United States (National Center for Education Statistics, 2008a). That represents approximately 1 percent of the entire school-age population, or 1 out of every 100 students.

The IDEA definition for this disorder, which qualifies an individual to receive services under the Act, is as follows:

1. The term emotional disturbance refers to a condition exhibiting one or more of the following characteristics over a long time and to a marked degree that adversely affects a student's educational performance:

    A. An inability to learn that cannot be explained by intellectual, sensory, or other health factors.

    B. An inability to build or maintain satisfactory interpersonal relationships with peers and teachers.

    C. Inappropriate types of behavior or feelings under normal circumstances.

    D. A general pervasive mood of unhappiness or depression.

    E. A tendency to develop physical symptoms or fears associated with personal or school problems.

        (i) The term includes schizophrenia.

        (ii) The term does not apply to children who are socially maladjusted unless it is determined that they have an emotional disturbance (34 C.F.R., sec 300.7 [c][4] [1999]).

A key distinction between this definition and the broader view lies in the reference to "socially maladjusted" and its cause. For instance, a youngster may join a gang because of peer pressure. This would be considered an environmental influence and not entitle the child to services as part of the act. However, IDEA would provide services if, by contrast, the child chose gang membership as a result of an emotional disorder. The quandary is that in the latter case, the child receives special educational services, whereas in the former case (the example being gang membership as the result of peer pressure), the child is considered as a delinquent to be punished.

Behavioral disorders are often thought of in terms of externalizing behaviors and internalizing behaviors. In the classroom, externalizing behaviors are those such as acting out and not complying with instructions. You have likely witnessed this on more than one occasion throughout your own school experiences. Internalizing behaviors may be a little more difficult to spot. They include depression, withdrawal, anxiety, obsessions, and compulsions. Because these behaviors typically do not interfere with the overall functioning of the classroom, they are more likely to be overlooked or to fade into the background.

An important theme that has developed in addressing the needs of students identified with emotional or behavioral disorders is that of strength-based interventions (Brendtro, Long, & Brown, 2000). This approach seeks to assist students by building on their strengths rather than emphasizing their problems. Teachers are advised to provide learning environments that are structured and predictable and to provide positive interactions with the students. The building of skills in self-management, problem solving, and conflict resolution will be of significant value to these students.

Visual and Auditory Challenges

Physical impairments can have a pronounced effect on learning, and a number of conditions are classified in this category. Among the most common are visual sensory disability, auditory sensory disability, and physical and health impairments (National Center for Education Statistics, 2008a).

Visual Sensory Disability

The diagnosis and reporting of visual disorders varies considerably from state to state, and even among local educational agencies. In the 2000–2001 school year approximately 25,000 children received special education services as a result of visual disorders (National Center for Education Statistics, 2003). However, it is estimated that one out of four school-age children have undiagnosed vision problems significant enough to affect their performance in school and in life. Keep in mind as you read this section that (1) the visual disorders discussed here do not refer to simple matters of visual acuity that are accommodated with corrective lenses, and (2) a student with visual impairment would need substantial assistance to read the words you are reading now.

The definition of visual impairment in IDEA is "an impairment in vision that, even with correction, adversely affects a child's educational performance. The term includes both partial sight and blindness" (34 C.F.R., sec. 300.7 [13]). The key element of this definition is that the impairment interferes with learning. Within the category of visual impairment, individuals can be further classified with regard to their ability to use their vision and their reliance on tactile means (for example, the use of Braille materials) for learning (Lewis & Allman, 2000):

Low vision students can read print though they may require optical aids.

Functionally blind students may be able to navigate their environment with their vision but rely on Braille materials for printed communication.

Totally blind students do not receive visual input. They rely on auditory and tactile means to interact with their environment.

Visual impairments do not determine what a child can learn, but instead how the child will learn. As a classroom teacher you will likely find yourself to be a member of a collaborative team that augments instruction and instructional materials to meet the needs of these students.

Auditory Sensory Disability

In the school year 2000–2001, approximately 1.1 percent of children receiving special education services were those with hearing impairments. That represents approximately 70,000 children (National Center for Education Statistics, 2003). The actual number of children with some degree of hearing loss may be greater, because many children with hearing impairments may be classified under other disability categories.

Deafness can dramatically remove one from the surrounding environment. You would likely be surprised by how difficult communication becomes and, in particular, how difficult the learning of language becomes in the absence of sound.

Hearing loss is typically graded as follows:

Normal   No impact on communication.

Slight   Faint speech is difficult to understand in noisy environments.

Mild   Classroom discussions are difficult to follow. Faint or distant speech is difficult to understand.

Moderate   Conversational speech can be heard only at close distances.

Moderate   Only loud and clear conversational speech can be heard.

Severe   Conversational speech cannot be heard unless very loud. Speech is not always intelligible.

Profound   Conversational speech cannot be heard. Speech may not be developed at all. (Turnbull, Turnbull, Shank, & Smith, 2004, p. 428)

A child in your classroom who appears to have difficulty hearing may benefit by being moved closer to the source of conversation. However, working with children with deafness or hearing loss will likely require substantial adaptive measures. The next time you go to class, consider how much of what is said is offhand or dependent upon auditory clues for interpretation (i.e., vocal inflections or perhaps a contrived whisper as if something is secret). Students with hearing impairments would find it very difficult to keep up with such cues.

Social Influences on Diversity

We now look at a different aspect of student diversity, one that does involve the choices that people make. Children do not choose to have a learning disability or giftedness any more than they choose a particular ethnicity. Our concern is with social issues and socializing influences that are either imposed upon children (e.g., child neglect or homelessness) or are choices made by children (e.g., drug or alcohol abuse, or violence).

When discussing social issues it is necessary to keep in mind that there is an incredible amount of overlap, and there are exceptions. Though we look at topics such as child abuse and neglect, homelessness, and alternative family structures, combinations of these conditions can all be influencing the life of a particular child. They do not typically stand in isolation from one another. It is also true that statistics tell us about trends in populations, which means that specific aspects will be true for some people but not for others. For instance, a child from a single-parent home is not necessarily at risk for failure in school, but statistically the chances are greater than for a child from a traditional two-parent home.

Family Structure

One common way to classify family structures is to divide them into nuclear and extended groups. A **nuclear family** consists of one or more parents or guardians or foster parents and may include one or more children. Although it is tempting to say that the nuclear family is the traditional model in the United States, such is not necessarily the case. Historically, families representing more than two generations have often lived in the same household. The presence of several generations is referred to as an **extended family**, which can include aunts and uncles or other relatives as well as grandparents. In some situations, one or more grandparents may be rearing the child.

Single-Parent Families

With approximately one-third of all marriages ending in divorce, the number of children living in households headed by a single parent or in a home with a stepparent has increased dramatically in the past fifty years. According to the *Family and Living Arrangements: 2007* study, 68 percent of children live with both married parents, 26 percent live with one parent, 3 percent live with two unmarried parents, and 3 percent live with someone other than a parent (U.S. Census Bureau News, 2008).

When the mother (usually but not always the parent with primary custody of the child) is the wage earner, children often return from school to an empty house. These **latchkey children** (so called because they carry a house or apartment key) have little or no supervision and are subject to dangers imposed by others and by poor choices they may make. For instance, older adolescents who don't live with both biological parents manifest far more problem behaviors (e.g., selling and using drugs, being involved in gangs, engaging in vandalism and assaults) than do their peers who live with both parents (Mayer & Leone, 2007). About 22 percent of students in Grades 4–8 care for themselves regularly after school (Federal Interagency Forum on Child and Family Statistics, 2008).

Some latchkey children come from affluent homes, but their parents are busy with their jobs, community activities, and social lives. These children are, at best, provided day care; at worst they are often left to their own devices. Thus, they have financial security but not family stability. Today, two-wage-earner families are the norm, and researchers look to other adaptive influences to explain the difficulties and successes in these families.

Divorce often results in lowering the economic status of children due to changes in family income, and it causes other problems as well. Among them are believing that the divorce was caused by something the child did, negotiating the tension between two angry separated parents, or losing contact with a parent (and sometimes both parents when for economic or other reasons a child or children must go to live with other relatives). In fact, in single-parent households resulting from divorce, children are more negatively affected by the family conflict preceding the divorce than by living with one parent (Amato, 2001; Amato & Keith, 1991).

The single-parent family dynamic has several other variations. For example, children in single-parent homes due to loss (the death of a father or mother), as opposed to divorce, may not experience the psychological stress of interparental conflict, but they may suffer the economic difficulties that such a loss might impose. Their emotional needs may tend toward overcoming the loss rather than overcoming any imagined guilt.

Another single-parent possibility is the situation in which there never were two parents in the home, whether because the mother and father did not marry or live together or because the mother became a parent without a partner via artificial insemination or adoption. Children in the first subcategory have experienced a greater disadvantage academically than children of divorced or separated mothers (Korenman, Kaestner, & Joyce, 2001). There is little information thus far, however, with regard to children in the second subcategory, which is a small but growing segment.

Alternative Family Structures

When both partners (whether married or not) bring children to the relationship, we have what is called a **blended family**. Thus, the children may be his, hers, and theirs. This family structure causes unique social relationships that must be addressed. According to work done by Beller and Chung (1992), the chances of dropping out of school or pursuing opportunities to attend college are much the same for children from blended families as for those from single-parent families.

Another alternative family structure is that of children in households with gay or lesbian parents. Without doubt, your exposure to this emerging family structure will be affected by the region in which you teach, because support for same-sex partnerships varies widely across the country. Typically, couples in such relationships do not receive the same sort of social support as couples in heterosexual marriages (Oswald, 2002). As a result, keywords in an analysis of families in same-sex relationships are *resiliency*, the processes that facilitate family survival under difficult social conditions (McCubbin, Thompson, Thompson, & Futrell, 1999), and *intentionality*, which refers to actions taken by partners to validate themselves as family members and to strengthen their network of support (Oswald, 2002).

Gay or lesbian households do, however, present an interesting version of the alternative family structure. From one perspective we can expect that such families may encounter significant obstacles in terms of achieving social legitimacy and support under the law (Oswald, 2002). On the other hand, support networks with members from all sexual orientations can provide children in these families with a broad range of influences.

"At-Risk" Students

At-risk students are those who, for a variety of reasons, statistically have a high probability for dropping out of school or failing to acquire the competence needed to function in the larger society. Based on a Census Bureau survey of 50,000 U.S. households, the following risk factors were identified for students between the ages of five and seventeen: (1) lack of English proficiency, (2) the presence of a personal disability, (3) school retention, (4) absence of either or both parents in the home, (5) at least one foreign-born parent of recent immigration, (6) an unemployed parent or guardian, and (7) low family income (Kominski, Jamieson, & Martinez, 2001).

Students with low achievement test scores are also at risk, especially in school districts that tie promotion or graduation to student performance on high-stakes tests. Since achievement tests are constructed in such a way that one-half of the students score at or above grade level (i.e., passing) and the other one-half score below grade level (i.e., below passing), a typical school will always have large numbers of students who are unable to keep up with their peers. Surprisingly, some students are at risk even though they make good grades. This phenomenon occurs when students compile a good grade point average for the wrong reasons: they may do better than most of their classmates and therefore get the "good" grades; they may be well behaved, have a pleasing personality, and have nice manners; they may have a parent or guardian who is actively involved, either as a supportive adult or as one who is quick to assume a confrontational role in parent–teacher contacts; they (or their parents or guardians) may do extra-credit projects to pull up low grades; they may depend on open-book tests, multiple-choice exams, cooperative group grades, and take-home tests; and they may engage in cheating, which is also a common practice, even among high achievers. Indeed, studies indicate that most high school graduates have cheated but have not been caught (Cizek, 2002–2003). As a result, students receive grades for which no corresponding amount of learning has been acquired.

Poverty

Poverty has a pervasive influence with clear ramifications for social development. You have probably noticed that some people in your schools wore designer clothes while others had very few outfits, and those may have been out of style. In the United States, approximately 8 million children between the ages of five and seventeen are living in poverty (National Center for Education Statistics, 2008a).

Poverty is more likely to be at the heart of a school's challenge than is race or ethnicity. You will see its effects every day in many ways. Poor students may move often, and the effect of frequent mobility on student achievement is clear. One study indicates that a student who moves more than three times in six years can lose a full year of academic growth (Vail, 2003). Although there is no stereotypical situation, students living in poverty may be subjected to more violence and more family instability. They may have less access to books and computers and watch television more than their more affluent peers. They often live in substandard housing and have less space at home, encountering more noise and more harmful secondhand tobacco smoke (Evans, 2004). In terms of school, poor students feel left out because of the condition of their clothing. Poor students cannot bring their teacher a present or pay for a field trip; cannot see the latest movies or have transportation to the town or city library; cannot participate in the band because they don't have the money for an instrument; have parents who cannot afford to hire a needed tutor; and have parents who hold several jobs and thus cannot attend parent–teacher conferences. In working with your students you must remember the debilitating influence of poverty and be sure your classroom does not become an impediment to children living in poverty.

Homelessness

When you look at the children in a classroom, you might be surprised to find that some of those children are among the homeless. They may live on the street, in an abandoned house, in a shelter, in a motel, or perhaps in a car. They may live with their parents or guardians or, less frequently, wander from place to place for protection and the fulfillment of basic human needs like food and clothing. As with poverty, homelessness is a condition that befalls families and can turn concerns such as education into a luxury item.

There are some estimates that up to 2 million adults and 1 million children are homeless. Others say the figure is considerably higher. As you can imagine, it is virtually impossible to make an accurate count because these families often move from place to place. Families with children constitute about 40 percent of people who become homeless. And this is not a problem confined to urban areas; approximately one-quarter of those living in shelters for the homeless are in rural areas.

Homeless students often have difficulty in making friends or communicating with adults. Many feel insecure and often demonstrate low self-esteem. They may find cooperative activities with other students challenging. Fagan (2001) notes that they are often shy, keep to themselves, and feel stressed or over-whelmed when asked to participate in front of the class. Koblinsky, Gordon, and Anderson (2000) found that homeless students had significantly more behavioral problems in school than did their housed peers.

If you have homeless children in your classroom, you can be sure that they will look to you for understanding, support, and acceptance. Unlike situations of child abuse or neglect, families experiencing poverty and homelessness are more often characterized by desperation, a focus on basic survival, and issues of poor self-esteem that can make succeeding in schools difficult. Children may be physically dirty because they have no regular access to shower or tub facilities and are poorly clothed. They may be teased by other children. Your compassion must come into play as you foster their intellectual, emotional, and social growth.

Child Abuse and Neglect

Child abuse and neglect, as well as their variations, are likely far more prevalent than you suspect. Even more tragic, it is often the case that children suffering abuse or neglect see their environment as normal, as if all children live in the same situation. Golden (2000) reports that more than 2.8 million cases of maltreatment were investigated in 1998, with approximately 903,000 cases yielding evidence of maltreatment. The U.S. Department of Health and Human Services (2008) estimated that 1,530 children died of abuse or neglect in 2006. Parents were the cause in 76 percent of the deaths. About 78 percent of the deaths were children younger than four, with 12 percent involving children between the ages of four and seven, and 5 percent each for children in age groups eight to eleven and twelve to seventeen. Estimates are that one out of every eight boys and one out of four girls will be sexually abused before reaching adulthood (Chauvin, 2006).

In 1974 Congress enacted a Child Abuse Prevention and Treatment Act (CAPTA), which defined child abuse and neglect as the physical or mental injury, sexual abuse, negligent treatment, or maltreatment of a child under the age of eighteen by a person who is responsible for the child's welfare under circumstances that indicate that the child's health or welfare is harmed or threatened thereby. Today, child maltreatment is classified into four categories: (1) physical abuse, (2) neglect, (3) sexual abuse, and (4) emotional maltreatment. The 1996 version of the CAPTA provides this definition for child abuse and neglect: the term "child abuse and neglect" means, at a minimum, any recent act or failure to act on the part of a parent or caretaker that results in death, serious physical or emotional harm, sexual abuse, or exploitation, or an act or failure to act that presents an imminent risk of serious harm (Section 111[2]).

The reasons that parents or other caregivers might abuse a child are many, but of equal concern is the trend indicating that patterns of abuse are passed on from one generation to the next. English and Papalia (1988) reported that 90 percent of all violent criminals and 97 percent of hard-core juvenile offenders had been abused as children. But it is also true that abuse is not always violent in nature (e.g., emotional abuse), nor does it necessarily indicate an ongoing pattern of behavior. Parents under psychological stress or extreme financial pressure or whose expectations of the child are unrealistic may also become abusers. In such cases the abuse a child suffers may be the result of a moment of rage. Far from excusing the behavior, you can see that a single action—or failure to act—constitutes maltreatment. Even the teacher whose temper is lost and refers to a student as stupid or who demeans a child can be accused of emotional abuse.

Since poor school performance and poor behavior in school are common problems associated with child abuse, it may fall to you as a classroom teacher to report possible cases of mistreatment. You may notice that a child becomes withdrawn or demonstrates very low self-esteem. You may notice a significant change in the student's academic performance or social behavior. You may even observe bruises, burns, or cuts on a child. Most states require that you report your concerns. You will have to check with your school district for the proper reporting procedures. In some instances reports may go to school personnel. In other situations, you may be required to report the concern to your state's agency for social services. IMPORTANT: Teachers are typically considered to be **mandated reporters**, that is, required by law to report suspected child abuse to state authorities and protected by law in so doing. Your local principal may want to keep everything "in house," but you should determine whether state law *requires* you to report suspected child abuse to state authorities rather than just to your local school district personnel.

Issues Facing Children and Adolescents

A child does not choose to be homeless or to live in one family circumstance or another. Society must provide services to help children overcome these disadvantages, and teachers need to bring their compassion to the task of working with such children. Though services and compassion are also necessary to address this next set of challenges, the context has changed, and we will discuss inappropriate or detrimental behaviors in which children and youth choose to engage.

Substance Abuse

As children become older, issues involving negative peer influences become supreme. Of course, even young children are aware of drug and alcohol use by adults, even if only in its social context. By middle school, however, experimenting with drugs and alcohol may begin, and they may have friends who are users. The desire to be a part of the group often overcomes common sense and consideration of consequences. School-age substance abuse most commonly involves alcohol, tobacco, and marijuana. Increasing accessibility and use of more potent drugs is also an ongoing concern.

Children from one generation to the next have been exposed to mixed messages about alcohol and tobacco use through advertising, attractive portrayals in the media, and familiar adult social behavior. The 2007 *National Survey on Drug Use and Health* found that of students twelve to seventeen years of age, 15.9 percent had used alcohol in the previous thirty days. The use of tobacco products by students aged twelve to seventeen has decreased from 15.2 percent to 12.4 percent, with almost identical percentages of girls and boys smoking cigarettes (Substance Abuse and Mental Health Services Administration, 2008).

School Violence, Vandalism, and Bullying

School violence refers to aggressive acts against people. **School vandalism** refers to aggressive or destructive acts toward school property. Violence and lack of discipline consistently rank among the general public's most frequently cited problems with public education. During the 2005–2006 school year, over 628,200 incidents of school violence were reported (National Center for Education Statistics, 2008b). Vandalism alone accounted for nearly 100,000 of those incidents, and the National Parent–Teacher Association has estimated that the resulting cost exceeds $600 million, a figure greater than the national budget for textbooks. Some estimates suggest that reported incidents represent just a small percentage of the actual total.

The prevalence of school violence is difficult to pin down because (a) not all incidents are reported and (b) there is no consensus as to what constitutes "violence." For instance, Willert and Lenhardt (2003) suggest,

> To define violence simply by its aftereffects—a theft, a fight, a murder—rather than by the behaviors that expose its roots—such as teasing, verbal taunting, and exclusion—is to ignore the sources of violence that can be effectively addressed through joint school and community action. (p. 111)

You are probably familiar with the bullying that may go on in different ways in a school but have not considered it as violence. Yet by varying degrees—teasing, verbal put-downs, shoving, and so forth—are not only the precursors to violent behavior but can also be the impetus to violent revenge behavior from victims who otherwise would not have been violent. Since they have been well publicized, you may be aware of reports of incidents that escalated to tragic proportions; the ones you read about are just the tip of the iceberg. Many potentially serious incidents are either prevented when peers share concerns with adults or when perceptive and compassionate teachers prevent peer problems through establishing a community of learners.

You never know until it is too late whether the hazing or "just teasing" or shunning of a student results in intolerable social conditions, not only for the victims but also for the perpetrators. But here's one wakeup call: 71 percent of the elementary teachers in one survey admitted they avoided becoming involved when students engaged in teasing or bullying behavior (Schroeder, 1999). Stemming the tide of violence and vandalism is not solely the responsibility of the teacher. Teachers are, however, stakeholders in the community that shares the task of prevention and intervention. Prevention is the appropriate first step. Druck and Kaplowitz (2005) offer the following advice:

- Do not tolerate bullying.
- Set classroom behavior rules.
- Learn and teach conflict-resolution and anger-management skills.
- Learn the warning signs.
- Enforce school policies.
- Help implement a safe school plan.
- Report safety threats.
- Encourage and sponsor student-led antiviolence activities.
- Talk to parents.
- Cultivate a supportive classroom atmosphere.

Teen Pregnancy

Though in 2005 there were 414,593 babies born to teenage females between the ages of fifteen to nineteen, over the past several decades the birthrate among teenage girls has declined (Kids Count Data Book, 2008). This is good, for babies born to teenage mothers are typically less likely to receive proper prenatal and postnatal care and are more likely to have low birth weights and problems such as cerebral palsy, chronic respiratory problems, retardation and mental illness, blindness and deafness, and learning problems (Black, 1998). Even with the decline in birth rates, the incidence of children born to children is far greater in the United States than in other industrialized nations. It is also true that the decline in births does not correlate to a decline in sexual activity among young people. Rather, with the availability of contraceptive devices, the percentage of teenagers engaging in sexual activity has actually increased.

Children receive mixed messages with regard to sexual activity. Though schools have provided sex education programs for decades, the society at large bombards children with sexually charged messages through media such as TV and movies.

Lest we end this section acting as if these teenage girls somehow had a baby by themselves, we should report that figures from 1994 indicated that 51 percent of births in that year to girls seventeen and under were fathered by men twenty and older (Kids Count Data Book, 1997). With regard to teenage fathers, or potential fathers, programs such as *Baby Think It Over*® (Jurmaine, 1994) are provided to the boys as well.

Adolescent Suicide

After motor vehicle accidents and homicides, suicide is the third leading cause of death among people aged fifteen to twenty-four. According to the Centers for Disease Control and Prevention (CDC), adolescent suicide rates increased from 6.7 percent in 2003 to 9.4 percent in 2007 (O'Connor, 2008). Also of great concern is the report of the CDC that in 2007, 14.5 percent of high school students admitted that they seriously considered attempting suicide within the previous year and that 7 percent actually tried to do so during that period. At-risk factors include depression or substance abuse of the student or a family member, behavior problems, a previous suicide attempt, a recent traumatic event (e.g., breaking up with a friend, death of a loved one), and the availability of a gun, with suicides five times more likely in a house in which there is a gun (O'Connor, 2008). Notice how many of these factors reflect a loss of hope, an aspect that teachers should recognize and attempt to address (possibly in conjunction with other school personnel and human services agencies).

We do not want to suggest that as a classroom teacher you will be able to recognize all of the nuances of your students' behavior and thus be able to prevent something as tragic as a suicide. However, there are some signs that might give you reason to take a closer look. If you see these signs, report them to the appropriate personnel in accordance with the policy of your school district. One thing that can help in your interactions with the student is to be positive and affirming of the child's self-esteem.

NOW: CONCEPTUALIZING YOUR ROLE ■

Now that the foundation work of understanding curriculum and student characteristics is behind us, it is time to consider what you will actually *do* in the classroom. The challenge for you is to accumulate a set of tools (both conceptual and physical) that when properly implemented will contribute to an overall strategy for teaching the identified content. We have discussed these tools, the elements of a strategy, in terms of (a) providing opportunities for student experiences, (b) instructional techniques, and (c) monitoring the classroom and being flexible. You may have noticed that we haven't included subject matter as one of the tools. This is because what the teacher does is to use the tools, or elements of a strategy, to bring subject matter and students together in an experience that facilitates learning. Therefore, subject matter is not a tool, per se, but more like the material from which the experience is fashioned, much like a carpenter uses tools to work with the wood that eventually becomes a house. If we take the perspective that learning is something that occurs *within* a child or, from Vygotsky's (1978) perspective, *between* children and adults, then the role of a teacher is to facilitate that process. The teacher arranges the setting and materials in a manner that will *enable* a student to have an educative experience and learn a particular lesson.

Bringing the World to Your Students

The essence of teaching is arranging opportunities for experiences from which students can learn. Though a lecture may seem a rather dry and passive approach to some, it nonetheless can be an experience that a teacher decided would be the most appropriate means of conveying information in that particular situation. Another teacher may choose to use DVDs (CD-ROMs, Document Cameras, electronic presentation boards, PowerPoint, etc.) to present information. Yet another teacher favors some approach that more actively engages the students. There are merits to each, but all are a matter of the teacher trying to engage students in learning situations.

> The essence of teaching is arranging opportunities for experiences from which students can learn.

The section that follows will discuss four broad categories of experiences: classroom lessons, multi-media, guest speakers, and field trips (see Figure III.4 on page 129).

As you consider each category notice the progression from the specialized atmosphere of the typical classroom, which metaphorically brings the world to the students, all the way to the opportunities for experiences provided in a real-world context, in essence taking the students to the world.

Classroom Lessons

Classroom lessons are those experiences most typically associated with teaching school. As states and school districts struggle to bring class sizes to a manageable level, a typical classroom today will have twenty to thirty students. Depending on the district's policy with regard to ability grouping, it could be the case that all students in your classroom are classified on the same grade level (which does not mean the same thing as being *on* the same grade level academically). Some districts use regrouping plans that bring students from other grade levels to your room for instruction in particular subjects such as reading or math. In any case, classroom lessons represent a format in which teachers bring information, culture, and the world at large to the students. The contributions of scientists, mathematicians, authors, composers, artists, and all the rest are represented as passages in books, class discussions, activities, and discrete assignments to be completed. It is no wonder that students, elementary students in particular, think of their teachers as knowing everything. There is a certain mystique associated with being the individual who brings new ideas to the classroom day in and day out. That, of course, is the romantic aspect of being a teacher. The responsibilities that come along with this are formidable.

Everything that will be necessary for the presentation of a lesson must be accounted for by the teacher. If special skills are required for any aspect of the presentation (e.g., working with hazardous materials in a science demonstration or operating electronic equipment), they are skills that the teacher needs to possess. The autonomy of working with your own classroom can be empowering, and the sense of accomplishment for completing a well-presented lesson is what leads to pride in a job well done. However, even the best teacher can become tired of hauling the world (let alone the universe!) into class every day, and so there are other ways that teachers can augment some of these classroom lessons.

Multimedia Presentations

Technology is a ubiquitous term in our new millennium. Increasingly there are **multimedia presentations** available that make use of a wide range of electronic media. Books and encyclopedias on CD-ROM allow whole-text searching of documents and files. Television (broadcast, satellite, and closed-circuit), VCRs, DVDs, and the Internet not only bring high quality presentations into the classroom but also allow students to engage in interactive projects that can collect information from all around the world. Even so, the teacher remains as the ringmaster.

A key difference between high tech of today and high tech of days gone by is the heavy reliance on computer-based systems. While this brings with it the requirement that teachers be better versed than ever in the use of technology in the classroom, it is also the case that most students, and first-year teachers, come to the classroom with a significant amount of computer literacy. To avail yourself of the benefits of educational technology, you may simply have to move from the basic skills of word processing to computer-based record keeping, spreadsheets, interactive investigations, recording grades, and so forth.

The effective use of multimedia allows the teacher to bring a more accurate representation of the real world to the classroom setting. It also allows students to interact with the sights and sounds of historic events, scientific inquiry, and self-expression in matters academic or artistic.

Guest Speakers

In terms of the continuum moving from representations of the real world to the real world itself, next on the scale would be bringing **guest speakers** to the classroom. Having a real person in the classroom is bringing life outside of the school inside. However, guest speakers don't come with all of the bells and whistles that a slick multimedia presentation typically has. Nonetheless, it is valuable in our increasingly electronic and interactive age that children have the opportunity to speak with people.

Many guest speakers are well versed in the requirements of being teacher for a day and come prepared to inform and dazzle. Others may be flattered by your request to address the class and are full of good intentions, but are understandably lacking in what is required to seize and hold the attention of a classroom full of students. They may need your assistance to carry off the presentation successfully. In either case, a teacher wants to seek out organizations and individuals who can offer significant insights about a topic under consideration in the class. Note, however, that it will *always* be a good idea to have something else planned for when the speaker finishes early or at the last minute calls to say he just can't be there. Being prepared for that contingency is part of the strategy. And it is just as important to prepare your students for the guest who will be speaking with them. Your students should understand why this person is in the room and how it relates to what you have been teaching. Requiring older students to take notes or to listen for particular information will also increase attentiveness.

Field Trips

There comes a time when no amount of pushing and shoving will fit the real world into a classroom. At this point, the only alternative if the experience is to occur, is to take the students to the world. **Field trips** to a museum, an assembly plant, nature study areas, or other specialized environments can provide students with rich experiences that simply could not be duplicated in the classroom.

Field trips have fallen into disfavor in recent years. This is not because of the efficacy of the experience but rather is due to the logistics, expense, and liability involved when moving large numbers of students away from the relatively safe confines of the school. Such concerns have given rise to the explosion of multimedia presentations available to educators. Those multimedia products can also serve a role in making field trips more plausible by preparing students for what is going to occur.

There is another perspective to be taken, however. That is, the real world is not far away. In fact, it waits just beyond the classroom door. This might not do much for you if what you want is to have your students sit down in front of the local philharmonic orchestra, but keep in mind that sometimes the "field" you need is just outside the building. That is, try to overcome the feeling that all things educational must happen within the walls of your classroom. Science, art, mathematics, and even history can be found just outside of the school building, and still on school grounds, in the "real world."

As a teacher conceptualizes a lesson, it tends to emerge as one form or another of the four situations just described (classroom lesson, multimedia presentation, guest speaker, field trip). It is interesting to note the inverse relationship between the frequency of each type of experience and exposure to the real world. Thinking back over your own classroom situations, you will find that the vast majority of your educational experiences were presented in terms of classroom lessons. To a lesser degree your teachers incorporated various multimedia presentations and activities to enhance the experience. To an even lesser degree, people from the community and specialized services were brought in to speak with you. And you can probably count the number of field trips that you ever took. Since school is all about preparing students for the world in which they will live, it is an intriguing paradox that the most basic practice within organized education (classroom lessons) is the furthest removed from that world. Many factors play into this, not the least of which are matters of efficiency and economy. That is what makes this a very specialized challenge of the classroom teacher: arranging opportunities for educational experiences within the classroom that students can find relevant outside of the classroom.

INSTRUCTION

Sometimes, the "field" you need is just outside the building!

Figure III.4 The General Categories of Instructional Experiences

Classroom Lessons	Bring experiences and knowledge to the students
Multimedia Presentations	Bring depictions of people and events to the classroom: can also provide instructional experiences
Guest Speakers	Bring expertise, knowledge, and insight from people who represent particular skills, abilities, and responsibilities (e.g., local political figures)
Field Trips	Take students to the real-world experience in its natural environment (i.e., away from the classroom)

Instructional Techniques

Having decided which of the basic formats a lesson will involve, you must next decide which of many instructional techniques would be most appropriate for the particular situation. Issues such as the developmental level of the students, the instructional venue (indoors, outdoors, individual desks, tables and chairs for group work, etc.), and the subject matter to be presented must be considered. Generally speaking, there are eight categories of techniques from which a teacher might choose. As has previously been the case, the teacher may well determine that a combination of techniques would be most appropriate. You will find the instructional techniques summarized in Figure III.6 on page 136.

As you read through the techniques, consider that we have arranged them in terms of increasing sophistication of the thinking required of students. This is not to say that any one of the techniques is inappropriate for particular ages. After all, you can probably remember being lectured to by your parents at one time or another in your life, and you likely discovered some things on your own even as a young child. However, when planning for educational experiences, teachers need to identify the level of cognitive processing they want to engage and select the technique that best encourages that level of thinking (Lasley, Matczynski, & Rowley, 2002). Our list of techniques parallels Bloom's Taxonomy, the *Taxonomy of Educational Objectives Handbook I: Cognitive Domain* (Bloom, Englehart, Furst, Hill, & Krathwohl, 1956). The taxonomy begins with the least sophisticated level of processing, that being the recall of knowledge and facts, and progresses to the highest level, thinking that involves evaluative processes (see Figure III.5, below).

Figure III.5   The Taxonomy of Educational Objectives: Cognitive Domain

Cognitive Skill	Verbs that characterize the skill
Knowledge	Label, list, match, recall, select, state, underline
Comprehension	Describe, explain, interpret, summarize, paraphrase
Application	Complete, organize, solve, calculate, compute, use
Analysis	Categorize, classify, find patterns and relationships, compare
Synthesis	Compose, create, formulate, hypothesize, write
Evaluation	Judge based on criteria, support, conclude

Direct Instruction

We list **direct instruction** in the teaching of skills as the lowest level of our taxonomy of instructional techniques because in this case the teacher decides what is important for the students to know and specifically explains or demonstrates a skill, and the student attempts to replicate it. There is very little abstraction involved here, though that is by no means intended to imply that the task is a simple one. As children struggle to reproduce the letters of the alphabet, they need all the concentration and control they can muster. Similarly, the high school student performing the steps of an experiment can be very focused and intent. Nonetheless, the demands for deep understanding and recombining of information on the part of the student are minimal in a direct instruction format. The emphasis is clearly on the acquiring of information or procedural skills.

Drill and Practice

One level up from direct instruction is **drill and practice**. Though it might seem that this technique is even more rote in nature than direct instruction, the implication is that something has already been learned, or at the very least been presented, and now the emphasis is on repetition to hone the skill or provide a strong link to the information to improve remembering it.

With this particular technique there is not a great emphasis on abstraction or on the synthesis of new understanding. Your own experience with multiplication tables would be an example of drill and practice. There was not much mathematical theory being taught when you were required to memorize those products.

Lecture

The mainstay of a traditional college education, the **lecture**, shows up third in our instructional technique hierarchy. What does that tell you about the thinking that lectures require of a student? We are by no means denigrating the lecture approach, but the simple fact is that lectures in their pure form serve only to offer information from one person to another in a one-way verbal transaction.

It needs to be mentioned that many times teachers will follow up a lecture with some sort of discussion session. However, lectures can be, and often are, presented without any opportunity for an intellectual exchange between student and teacher. Its strength is that a large amount of information can be conveyed to a large group of people in a short amount of time with a concomitant personal touch.

Question and Answer

At this point we begin considering techniques that actually require *reflection* on the part of the student and thus involve evaluation and the synthesis of new information, the two highest levels of Bloom's Taxonomy. Reflection requires that a student receive information and then consider it with regard to his or her own experiences and interpretations. The **question-and-answer** technique supposes that to one degree or another the teacher and the student share a common body of knowledge. This does not mean that the student has the same depth of knowledge or understanding, but there are sufficient elements to the common core that allow the student and teacher to make consideration of the topic a two-way exchange.

There are several approaches to using the question-and-answer technique. In one approach, the students may question the teacher. The teacher needs to be sufficiently knowledgeable of the subject matter to provide appropriate responses without knowing the questions in advance or having the opportunity to look things up. A teacher cannot have all of the answers, but *being prepared to deal with the unexpected is part of being a teacher*, not something that happens once in awhile. Children come to school thinking about the same questions that they have heard their parents discuss at home. They may not always understand those questions, but the idea of asking the teacher for an answer is typically considered to be a good one.

Being prepared to deal with the unexpected is part of being a teacher.

The other side of question and answer is the situation in which the teacher asks questions of the students. You are certainly familiar with this approach! However, our concern now is with the reason for those questions. One purpose would be for giving the students practice with the recall (and perhaps application) of particular information. Another would be for assessing the students' acquisition of particular information. In either of these cases, techniques such as providing think-time (Gambrell, 1983) and challenging initial responses will be valuable skills to improve the use of question-and-answer sessions. Indeed, in her classic study of the effects of wait time, Mary Budd Rowe (1978) found that providing students additional time to think increased the number and quality of responses and decreased discipline situations.

Yet a third purpose for the use of this instructional technique is to stimulate thought and encourage *divergent thinking* (as opposed to the *convergent thinking* of the previous two examples). In this situation the teacher is challenging students to apply prior knowledge and then use that as a basis for synthesizing new knowledge. The challenge presented to the teacher is that when such questions are asked, a wide range of answers is possible. The teacher must be prepared for whatever might come along, and this involves finding ways to identify merit in virtually any response. If a teacher is willing to open up the classroom to divergent thinking and the opinions of the students, then he or she must be ready to help students formulate and reformulate their ideas without diminishing the value of the original idea. Asking students for their opinions and then telling them they are wrong is one of the surest ways to bring original thinking in the classroom to a halt. The amount of innovative and creative thinking that a teacher can initiate, in virtually any subject area, is empowering both for students and teachers.

Discussion

A step higher on our taxonomy of instructional techniques is **discussion**. This differs from the previous level in that neither the teacher nor the student holds the upper hand. In this situation the teacher is concerned with a very different treatment of information than possible using the previous methods. Discussions involve the exchange of ideas. With this approach a teacher hopes to develop greater depth of thinking and perhaps to foster the manipulation of information for solving problems rather than just the acquisition of knowledge.

Some might argue that discussion is not the most appropriate term for what teachers wish to accomplish. In fact, discussion does refer more to the arguing of points of view whereas *dialogue* refers to an exchange of ideas. In either case, the instructional intent is to take students beyond "just the facts" and to engage them in a more poignant treatment of the subject matter.

Mental Modeling

Mental Modeling (Culyer, 1987) and a variation of it, the "I wonder . . ." model (Bentley, Ebert, & Ebert, 2000), are techniques specifically intended to enhance students' ability to direct their own learning by modeling the use of cognitive processes in the solving of some problem. This might sound "elementary" at first, and it is quite effective when working with young children, but it is a process that you may well have been exposed to in your secondary and now higher education experiences.

For example, during an elementary school lesson about using maps a teacher might say,

> I'd like to find my way to Sarah's house. I know the address, but I don't know how to get there from the school. I think I'll use the map of our city to find the way there. First I'll check the street index to find out where to look on the map. Then I'll use the numbers from the index to find the street.

In this way a teacher demonstrates how to sequence steps and put information to work in solving a problem. Students are then able to practice the same procedure.

The "I wonder . . ." model uses the same approach, though in the context of science education. Bentley, Ebert, and Ebert (2000) consider this to be one of the best ways of initiating the information-seeking process. An otherwise unobservable process, this technique attempts to *verbalize* the thinking that goes on. Here's an example from *The Natural Investigator* that a teacher might use with elementary level children:

> This morning I looked outside and noticed that it wasn't very sunny. I observed lots of gray clouds. I wondered if it was going to rain today. I could have just carried an umbrella in case it did rain and not thought about it anymore. However, I was planning to wear my new shoes, and I really didn't want to get them wet and dirty the first time I wore them. So I checked the newspaper and the weather channel. The paper predicted . . . (p. 127)

In this scenario, the children are exposed to the steps of listing observations, formulating a question, and identifying possible sources of information. These steps are not confined to elementary instruction. For instance, in college-level science courses you are encouraged to go through the same three steps. Your chemistry professor probably will talk you through conducting an experiment to prepare you for what might occur.

Mental modeling is a powerful technique that is on a high cognitive level. Precisely for that reason, it is something that you should try to use with your students at every opportunity. But practice first! The keys to using this technique are modeling thinking that your students can understand and then providing them with immediate opportunities to apply what they have learned. Having your students explain their own mental models or "I wonder . . ." models aloud will help clarify the process for them and allow you to assess their understanding.

Discovery Learning

Discovery learning is an approach to instruction that focuses on students' personal experiences as the foundation for conceptual development. It is unlikely that children will walk into your classroom with all of the necessary experiences that relate to the concepts you want to teach, so the challenge is to *provide* your students with the opportunities for experiences they need in the context of discovery. That is, allowing students to find the information for themselves by virtue of some activity you have provided. The students in your class will then share a common experience that you can develop as it relates to the concept under consideration. In essence, we are cheating just a bit because, from an instructional perspective the idea is to have children discover what we *want* them to discover. It's new to them, of course, but it is all part of the strategy for the teacher.

Discovery learning channels the natural inquisitiveness of children (and the natural inquisitiveness that remains in adults) by providing structure to the experience without imposing unnecessary structure on the *thinking*. That is, unlike the science experiments that you did in high school that were "wrong" if they didn't come out the way the book said they should, discovery learning encourages children to engage in the activity and document what does happen.

Even with structured activities in the classroom, twenty students will experience the activity in twenty different ways. Because of that, for discovery learning to be pedagogically sound it must be accompanied by a structure that goes beyond the discovery phase of the exercise. Such a structure, or framework, is intended to clarify the experience in terms of the concept being taught. The four-phase learning cycle (from Atkins & Karplus, 1962), a simpler version of the 7E Learning Cycle discussed in Unit I, offers one such framework.

FOUR-PHASE LEARNING CYCLE

1. **Introduction:** a question, challenge, or interesting event that captures the students' curiosity.

2. **Exploration:** the opportunity for students to manipulate materials, to explore, and to gather information.

3. **Concept Development:** With a common experience to relate to, terminology is introduced and concepts developed in class discussion.

4. **Application:** This could take the form of an enrichment activity, an opportunity to apply what has been learned, or a test to assess learning.

An example might be packaging an egg to withstand being dropped from a height of ten feet or so. After posing the question to the students about how this might be done (Introduction), students are provided time to devise various packaging strategies (Exploration). Instruction about packaging is not provided before the egg is dropped; the students are on their own at this stage. Discussions of forces, mass, acceleration, and so forth do not yet enter into the picture. It is only after the eggs have been packaged, dropped, and checked for survival that the lesson moves to a discussion of what has been found. With the common experience of this trial-and-error activity, students are prepared to have a meaningful lesson about the topics relating to forces and motion (Concept

Development). Finally, the students might be challenged to package another egg (or something else) to apply what they have learned (Application). You can see that this entire lesson, though arranged by the teacher, is centered on the students' thinking. In fact, the students' thinking will drive the lesson as the teacher assesses and accommodates the various perspectives that the students will have.

Inquiry

We have placed **inquiry** at the highest level of our taxonomy not only because it involves the use of prior knowledge and the discovery of new knowledge, but because it also involves *generating the question* to be answered. It is no coincidence that the tendency to ask questions is characteristic of children as well as of adults at the top of their professions. Scientists, professors, writers, politicians, and others are people who frame questions and then go about finding solutions. Children, with their natural curiosity, are compelled to ask questions and take delight in finding answers. The task for professional educators is to channel that inquisitiveness in ways that are beneficial to the individual and perhaps even to the world at large. Suddenly our discussion has come a very long way from rudimentary direct instruction. Teaching changes lives, and it changes the world!

The teacher who uses an inquiry approach has a considerable amount of preparation to do and also must be prepared to teach the students how to use inquiry. Foremost among the concerns would be helping the student frame a question in a manner that can be investigated. For example, what would your response be if a child were to ask, "Why do birds fly?" Would you say that birds fly because it's faster than walking? Because they enjoy being in the air? Just *because*? *Why* birds fly is a legitimate question, but likely one to be addressed by theologians or philosophers. A more appropriate question might be "How do birds fly?" This is a question that can be investigated in the context of school. Students could even investigate what factors allow one type of bird to fly faster or higher than another or, in the case of ostriches and chickens, not at all. Helping to frame an appropriate question, without diminishing the validity of the initial question, is a primary challenge the teacher faces.

A chief strength of the inquiry approach is that it can integrate the curriculum by involving many disciplines in meaningful ways. Children can read, write, calculate, engage in scientific investigations, address social concerns, and use the arts, all in the context of answering their own questions. While the amount of lecturing that a teacher does is significantly reduced, the intellectual challenge for a teacher preparing and conducting such activities is considerable, and considerably rewarding.

A teacher may use combinations of all of the techniques we have discussed in the course of a single lesson. A lesson plan may begin with a question-and-answer session that stimulates student interest and thinking and then proceed to a discovery-learning experience that will be followed by a discussion of what was learned. It is important for you to understand that teaching is a task that requires considerable instructional flexibility, and we still have not even considered the topic of knowing the subject matter!

INSTRUCTION

Figure III.6 The Taxonomy of Instructional Techniques

	Teacher Focused
Direct Instruction	Teacher explains or demonstrates
Drill and Practice	Repetition to hone a skill or memorize information
Lecture	Teacher provides information to students in a one-way verbal presentation
	Dialogue Oriented
Question and Answer	Requires reflection as information is exchanged in response to a question
Discussion	An exchange of opinions and perspectives
	Student Focused
Mental Modeling	Assists students in managing their own learning by modeling a problem-solving technique
Discovery Learning	Uses students' personal experiences as the foundation for building concepts
Inquiry	Allows students to generate the questions that they will then investigate and answer

If you were an astute observer of the nature of each technique that we have discussed, you may have already noticed that the first three levels represent approaches in which the teacher does the most talking or directing of student activity. The middle two levels transition to a dialogic approach in which the teacher and student share more of a partnership. The teacher continues to direct the activity, if only by virtue of having planned the whole experience, but the exchange of ideas is of central concern with these levels.

But notice what happens as we move to mental modeling and the levels beyond. See how the emphasis changes now to the thinking that students will do? At these levels students are not only investigating academic topics but ultimately are also asking their own questions and finding ways to seek answers and solve problems. You have probably heard that education is a process that seeks to develop lifelong learners. The teacher who uses all levels of the taxonomy with an eye toward leading students to these highest levels and allowing them to develop their critical and creative thinking abilities will be the teacher whose students develop that love of learning that we all wish to impart.

Monitoring and Flexibility

Deciding on a format for presenting opportunities for educational experiences and selecting the most appropriate technique(s) for presenting the lesson constitute the foundation work that any teacher must do to present a lesson. In the course of your own educational experiences you have been in classes with teachers who have prepared this foundation to greater or lesser degrees, and no doubt you have been able to tell the difference. We would suggest to you that a key to developing expertise as an effective teacher will be your ability to make the concerns we have discussed here a part of your typical routine for planning for educational experiences.

It would be foolish for us to suggest, however, that you can put together a plan that simply could not fail. There's no way to deny the fact that teaching is an interpersonal concern, and you simply cannot know for certain the attitudes, moods, and recent experiences that your students will bring to the classroom on any given day. Therefore, as you implement the plan that you've developed, it will also be necessary to *monitor* the progress of that lesson. Is it going smoothly? Are the students receptive? Does learning appear to be occurring? Is this experience appropriate? Is this technique working? Are there student needs that you did not account for adequately? And all of this, of course, is something you do while also teaching the lesson.

Whether or not the monitoring you do is effective will be represented in terms of the adjustments *you* make. Flexibility is a virtue that all effective teachers have cultivated to a high degree. For example, if you get into a car and turn the key, only to be met by that dreaded silence of a dead battery, no amount of turning the key will overcome the basic facts. You'll have to do something else to start the car, or find alternative transportation, or cancel your plans. So too with teaching. If the information you receive from monitoring indicates that changes need to be made, it is imperative that (a) you are willing to make them and (b) you are capable of making them. A lesson that isn't working is lost time. It's that simple.

Flexibility is what saves the day. You may even find yourself in a situation in which discontinuing the lesson and moving on to something else will be an appropriate course of action. Put that instructional time to efficient use and then devise another strategy for teaching the lesson that just couldn't take off. Monitoring and flexibility are the tools a teacher uses to maintain the momentum of learning.

TOMORROW: PUTTING IT ALL TOGETHER ■

Now that you have conceptualized a plan, a strategy for the presentation of lessons, let's discuss what happens when you walk into the classroom tomorrow. Our peek into the future (tomorrow) considers modeling, questioning, listening, and demonstrating, directing, and orchestrating. Doesn't this sound more descriptive of what teachers actually do rather than to just say "first tell the students to open their books, have everybody turn to page . . . blah, blah, blah"? Instead, these four teacher behaviors describe what teachers really do in the classroom. Let's begin with modeling.

Modeling

Modeling? How does that figure into a strategy for teaching? Well, that's a good question. Think back for a moment to one or two of your best teachers.

Did you ever notice that they never seemed to have a bad day? Their dogs never died. Stress was not a problem. They never had sour milk in their breakfast cereal. And though you may have come to class a time or two with tales of woe explaining why your homework wasn't done, you got the feeling that those calamities never seemed to befall those teachers. Well, it just wasn't true. Teachers are people, and they have the same problems that other people have. However, as with folks in show business, when it's time for class to begin, personal problems, concerns, sadnesses (and sometimes gladnesses) are left outside. The class must go on!

Are Teachers Role Models?

What is really happening here involves an undeniable aspect of teaching: teachers are **role models**. At the very least they model an attitude toward learning that includes the joy of discovery as well as an understanding of how difficult discovery can be. They model the idea that learning is worthwhile. Your best teachers made dull subjects (were there any dull subjects?) come alive by virtue of their own enthusiasm for what they were doing. It is likely that very few, if any, of your really good teachers modeled despair, discontent, and disinterest. And that left an impression on you, didn't it? You will teach lessons to students simply as a function of who you are. Students, to varying degrees, will want to be like you. Those desires will be based on the model that you provide every time you interact with them in school or away from the classroom.

Your actions as a teacher, beliefs, sense of humor, self-discipline, bearing, and demeanor are all lessons that are presented to students throughout the educational experience. Albert Bandura's (1986) landmark work with social learning theory places great emphasis on the impact of observing and imitating a model in the development of behaviors. We can expect that children will imitate and internalize those behaviors that they observe as being valued and rewarded.

As a teacher in a public or private school, you can anticipate that the school will expect you to model behaviors such as self-control, good grooming, a good work ethic (valuing work, punctuality, preparedness, following the rules, etc.), and placing a value on learning. But you may also expect that the school wants you to model ideologies such as being prodemocracy, accepting of cultural diversity, and maintaining a high moral standard. Whether or not explicitly stated within the curriculum, these are lessons that schools bring to the students. The teacher who encourages students not to recite the Pledge of Allegiance, albeit on defensible grounds, will likely be at odds with the district and the community. The teacher who habitually arrives late for work probably will not have a contract renewed. Teachers are not expected to be surrogate parents, but they are—without question—role models of one sort or another to their students.

Are Teachers Role Models Away From School?

There is another compelling side to the role-model issue: Are teachers role models *away* from school? Based on what has been presented thus far, the obvious answer is "yes." Students—and this applies to students anywhere along the educational continuum—delight in seeing their teachers away from school. Their expectations, however, remain the same. Seeing the teacher who is always neatly dressed at school now loading bags of mulch into the car at the local gardening shop will be a cognitive stretch for the child. Since gardening is not something on the list of improper behaviors in a child's mind, the experience will likely just require a cognitive assimilation. This could actually be a good expansion of the child's view of the world.

However, seeing their teacher purchase alcoholic beverages at the local grocery store or appearing somewhat inebriated at a community function will leave a very different impression. The question, therefore, is whether teachers are *responsible* for modeling particular behaviors even when away from school? Is this a fair expectation?

Whether or not it is fair, you will find that the expectation is widely held. This is a delicate issue that involves one's personal rights as well as the concerns of a community (society) that has entrusted its children to the influence of the teachers it has hired. Keep in mind, as you consider this issue, that children typically do not get involved in the philosophical and political aspects of these deliberations. The teacher is "the teacher."

No matter where you may see your students, you will still be "the teacher."

Questioning

Just as teachers are role models for learning, they are role models for asking questions. Think of it this way: Statements, with that period right at the end, bring thinking to a halt. Questions, on the other hand, are what initiate and encourage thinking. And that, of course, is what teachers are trying to do. Imagine how many questions a teacher asks in just one day. The questions range from "How are you?" or "How was the [game, performance, play, concert, etc.] last night?" to "Who will show us how to balance this equation?" At times you may hear questions related to safety and the learning environment, such as "Does everyone understand why you should wash your hands with soap?" or "Do you need to move so you can see the SMART Board?" Typically you hear lots of questions about the application of concepts that are the focus for the day's lessons, such as "What is the answer to the third problem?" or

> Statements, with a period at the end, typically bring thinking to a halt. Questions, on the other hand, with that thought-provoking question mark at the end, initiate and foster thinking. Which do you suppose is the powerful tool for teachers?

"What is the next word in the sequence?" or "Which strategy did you use to solve the problem?" Occasionally there are reflective or philosophical questions, such as "What did you learn today that surprised you, or that interested you, that you want to talk about when you get home?" While these reflective questions are the least often asked, they may be the most important. What kind of questions do you frequently ask? As we have said, it is the asking of questions—of ourselves or as teachers—that initiates thinking.

Lower-Level and Higher-Level Questions

There are various ways of classifying questions, with the two most frequent ones being in terms of Bloom's Taxonomy and convergent vs. divergent thinking. As we have seen, Bloom's taxonomy has six distinct levels and questions can be made to match those levels quite easily. For example,

1. **Knowledge**   What is the word for a group of turkeys?

2. **Comprehension** What is the purpose of a topic sentence when writing paragraphs?

3. **Application**   Using our numerical code rather than the alphabet, how would you write your name?

4. **Analysis**   In what ways are deciduous trees and evergreen trees similar?

5. **Synthesis**   How could you use a barometer to determine the height of a building?

6. **Evaluation**   What do you think will be the most significant change that individuals can make to offset global warming? Why?

Perhaps more frequently, questions are classified into two subdivisions of the taxonomy: higher-level thinking questions (often referred to as *higher-order thinking*, or H.O.T.) and lower-level thinking questions. Lower-level questions are those on the Knowledge level. Using this system it is easier because identifying questions for specific higher-level questions, especially application and analysis, sometimes depends on the context or setting. For example: What is the nutritional value of mushrooms? For this question the level of thinking depends on the situation. Did the lesson on nutrition state the value of mushrooms? If so, the answer would require recall. If the lesson provided a list of foods but did not include mushrooms, the thinking involved in answering the question would be more challenging. The following are other examples of low-level vs. high-level thinking questions:

Lower Level

What is photosynthesis?

What is the name of the main character in the story?

$9 \times 3 = \rightarrow$?

Higher Level

How is the formula for photosynthesis similar to respiration?

Who is your favorite character in the story? Why?

How could you simplify this equation: $9x + 27y = 153$?

Convergent and Divergent Questions

Convergent questions are those that typically have one correct answer, while **divergent questions**, also called open-ended questions, are used to encourage many answers and generate greater participation of students. Besides engaging students' memory through recall, convergent questions can be used to guide students' observations, perhaps during a demonstration. Divergent questions, on the other hand, stimulate student creative or critical thinking, encouraging students to be better observers. These open-ended questions can guide students as they discover information for themselves, analyze data, make inferences, and identify relationships.

Examples of convergent questions:

- How many of the pilgrims who sailed on the Mayflower survived the first winter?
- Which is smaller, 5/16 or 3/8?
- Is saltwater denser than freshwater?

Examples of divergent questions:

- What do you predict will happen?
- What can you tell me about shadows?
- What sacrifices made by settlers traveling west by covered wagon would be most difficult for you?
- What different strategies can we use to solve the problem?

Questions That Can Derail Thinking

Teachers typically ask many more convergent questions, perhaps 85 percent of the time. A more balanced frequency will assure a value of and an emphasis on student thinking. By making audio recordings of your instructional time, you can determine the level and frequency of your question types.

Sometime teachers ask the *wrong* question. For instance, does a teacher really want to know the answer to the question, "Who can tell me how a sundial works?" "My dad" is probably not the answer the teacher was expecting. What about questions such as this: "Using information in the data table, can you construct a graph comparing the size of the fish in the aquarium?" There is great potential for H.O.T., but the way the question is worded, the answer is either "yes" or "no." In each case, however, there is potentially a good question that will encourage students to think.

Another category of questions that you will want to use sparingly includes those that employ guesswork. For example,

1. Only women have femoral arteries.   True or False

2. The average number of times college students change majors is _____.

   a) 2 times   b) 4 times   c) 6 times

There is a 50 percent chance of guessing the answer to the first question, and a 1:3 chance with the second one. If the students' answers are correct, *you are not going to know whether they guessed correctly or actually knew the information.*

Of course, there are times when you, as teacher, must ask convergent questions. They are an appropriate part of the curriculum as long as you avoid limiting your questions to convergent ones.

> There are times when you, as teacher, must ask convergent questions. They are an appropriate part of the curriculum as long as you avoid limiting your questions to convergent ones.

Why? Questions

The "why?" question is a wonderful question. It can stimulate one's thinking, encourage creative and critical thinking, and open up a whole realm of possibilities. It is a question that typifies four-year-olds but engages adolescents and adults as well. Why does thunder have to be so loud? Why don't I understand algebra? Such questions are asking for explanations (inferences) from someone perceived to be wise or at least more experienced, or are pointing the way toward further understanding.

But why stop there? Yes, four-year-olds ask those questions that sometimes challenge adults to really think about something. Rather than stifling the questions of young people as they continue their efforts to understand the world around them, teachers can capitalize on their natural curiosity. By encouraging children to develop their own questions related to the topic of study, the search for answers becomes a great motivation for meaningful learning. Ultimately, the teacher can help the student to change those "why?"

questions into questions more suited for investigation: What causes thunder to be so loud? What is preventing me from understanding algebra?

Taking their cue from the teacher, students place value on the types of questions asked most frequently or those questions that dominate the lessons. If you want to value a particular level of thinking, consider the amount of time or frequency with which you encourage that level.

Listening

Good communication depends on three essential components: (1) someone willing to share, (2) someone willing to receive, and (3) a common language. Sometimes teachers listen for what they want to hear. For example, if the question is asking for students to recall the three types of rock and a student says, "Igneous, sedimentary, and metamorphosis," the teacher may respond, "Yes, igneous, sedimentary, and metamorphic" and proceed to the next question. What happens when the answer is, "sedimentary, metamorphic, and granite"? In this situation, the teacher may say, "Yes, sedimentary, metamorphic and granite is an example of igneous." In both cases, the teacher was listening for the three important words and accepting the answers without giving thought to the reasons behind the actual responses given and clarifying the misunderstandings. The emphasis was on recalling information at the expense of comprehension.

Good communication requires three elements:

1. A willing sender of information

2. A willing recipient of information

3. A common language between sender and receiver

In some situations there are multiple answers to a question, but in the given context the teacher has one answer in mind. For example, when a geometry teacher asks, "How can you determine the height of a tree?" At the end of a lesson she most likely is expecting an answer that uses the information about determining the sides of a right triangle. However, students may respond with other ways that would be useful in determining the height of a tree. What would you do as a teacher when a student says to chop it down and then measure it?

A student teacher, a few years ago, reported that during a third-grade science lesson on plants, she asked the question, "Where do seeds come from?" With confidence and sincerity a little girl said, "From Walmart!" As a teacher how would you respond to that child? That is, would you simply dismiss this answer as incorrect (from the perspective you were pursuing) or would you give it merit—which values her thinking—and *then* redirect your students to the idea you were trying to develop? One approach fails to "hear" the student and the other

Good listening skills will help you avoid talking at your students and focus on talking with your students.

one empowers the student as a thinker. Talking *with* students, rather than *at* them, requires good listening on the part of the teacher.

Suggestions for Improving Your Listening Skills

There are several things you can do, and do right away, to begin improving your listening skills. With each of the following suggestions you will see that there are two parts: listening to what is said and then handling what has been said. Let's take a look.

A Correct Response Is Not a Stopping Point

Teachers are sometimes so focused on identifying the correct answer that little attention is given to the thinking on the part of the student. For example, a teacher assigns math questions that require students to apply the new problem-solving strategy just presented. The teacher then calls on individuals for answers. When a student gives a correct answer, the teacher asks another individual to answer the next question. When a student responds incorrectly, the teacher asks others to respond until the response is correct. In both cases, it appears that the answer is important.

What would happen, however, if you ask a question and, when a student provides a correct answer, you *don't* stop there? Ask follow-up questions such as, "How did you get that answer?" or "How do you know that is correct?" How will the students react? Well, the first time you do that the student is going to think that the answer was incorrect. After all, what is the purpose of talking about the answer?

Try Writing Down the Students' Answers Verbatim

By using a marker board or a projected computer screen, write students' responses, being as careful as possible not to change the wording. If the teacher is listening for the correct answer or proper use of terminology, the temptation will be to reword the answer to fit. Instead, by listening carefully and writing down the exact words used by the students, you advance two important outcomes of teaching. First, it sends a message saying you value the individual and the thoughts that student has to share. That is an important step in empowering the thinking of students. And second, as you listen to several students' responses or explanations and you capture their words on the board, you will actually be able to hear the diversity of understanding within your class.

Try Providing Time to Think

This is popularly referred to as allowing wait-time. Before calling on a student to respond to the question, allow some silent time for thinking. Most often, teachers wait only 0.6 second before calling on someone to answer. If the question is "Who's hungry?" perhaps 0.6 second is plenty of time. However, if the purpose of the question is to have students apply something learned in class to situations outside of school, it will take time. The typical recommendation is to allow three to five seconds of thinking time before taking responses.

There is another dimension to this that most any classroom teacher is familiar with. Some students, for whatever reason, cannot wait three to five seconds before responding. Rather than sending students to the principal day in and day out (and likely the same students) simply due to wait-time violations, consider what we refer to as *dynamic wait-time.*

> Dynamic wait-time, asking students if they agree or if there is another possibility, extends thinking time even when a student blurts out an answer.

In this case, when a student blurts out an answer, correct or otherwise, don't look dismayed because the surprise has been spoiled. And certainly don't accept the answer right away and move on. Instead, ask something like, "Does everybody agree with that?" or "Is that the answer the rest of you found?" Notice that in this situation several things are occurring. First, you have not told the student that the initial answer is incorrect. Second, you have put everyone on notice that they are still expected to compose a response. And third, rather than asking the answering student to consider the response further (which is not a bad idea), you are allowing the rest of the class to continue considering the question with the additional information provided by the student. Very dynamic, it extends thinking time and includes no hidden costs or fees.

Always Provide Feedback

The encouragement and confidence that comes from hearing a teacher say things like "Great idea!" or "Very well organized" makes students want to try harder . . . *unless it is overdone.* Have you been in classrooms where teachers say "yes," "good," or "nice answer" time after time? Teachers will sometimes automatically say positive responses without really listening to the students. On more than one occasion, we have seen preservice teachers walking around the room monitoring student work and making positive, encouraging remarks without actually reading the answers carefully. The feedback was meant to compliment the child for completing as many of the items on the page in a short amount of time. In one case, if the teacher actually looked at the answers, it would have been seen that the responses to the first two questions were reversed.

Demonstrating, Directing, and Orchestrating

Demonstrating is an active instructional approach to teaching that is strongly teacher oriented. The teacher is the one who touches the materials and manipulates the objects while students observe the demonstration. Because it is so strongly teacher oriented, the number of times demonstrating is the preferred approach are few. However, there are three circumstances in which demonstrating is a necessary instructional strategy:

1. When the activity involves special precautions or working with hazardous materials, ensure the safety of everyone by conducting the activity.

2. When expensive pieces of equipment are involved, a demonstration may be warranted. Under these circumstances, provide special directions and demonstrate the appropriate use of such equipment before students use it (e.g., the first time microscopes are used).

3. Sometimes things happen so quickly or subtly that students would miss key observations unless the teacher did the demonstration. You can facilitate those observations by conducting the demonstration and stopping when appropriate to ask pertinent questions or tell students what to look for.

Directing is an instructional approach that is more student oriented than demonstrating. The teacher may present a new concept, provide examples on the board, direct students to read in the appropriate book, and then have students participate in an activity that clarifies the concept or reinforces understanding. For example, you might plan a lesson that involves introducing a new method for determining the volume of irregular shapes. You write examples on the board, and your students are then directed to work with math manipulatives to achieve a better understanding of the concept for the day. Being able to provide clear, meaningful directions either orally or in writing is essential to this instructional approach. The success of activities depends on students following directions.

While designing activities, make sure everybody has something to do at all times. Classroom management becomes a problem when children don't know what to do or they think that they don't have something to do. When your students work in small groups, provide directions that assign specific roles for each student. For example, there might be

- a procurement officer who collects and distributes materials needed to complete assignments,
- a spokesperson (aka reporter) who is the first person from the small group to share the group's findings or report results,
- an encourager who provides positive feedback when others are working well and encourages teammates when there is a lull in activity,
- a worrier who makes sure everyone on the team knows the answers to questions or solutions to problems, or has collected and recorded appropriate information.

The ones we mention here are merely examples. Your imagination can generate other roles and responsibilities throughout the year. Keep in mind that directions are key to this instructional approach. If you provide the information, making sure the students know what to do and how to do it, the students are quite likely to be successful.

Orchestrating is the most student-centered instructional approach. Students are not only actively engaged in the learning; they are encouraged to assume responsibility for their own learning. In this situation the teacher is not determining the questions and making decisions about seeking answers to the questions. The students start with their own curiosity to pose a problem or identify the initial questions and determine the ways to solve the problem or answer the questions. Much as the orchestral leader relates to the musicians, the teacher is there to facilitate the learning of the many individuals involved in the activity. Just because the students have more responsibility for the learning, the teacher does not have less work. More anticipation and preparation are involved not only before the lesson begins but also throughout the unit of study as it evolves.

FINALLY: THIS IS A PEOPLE PROFESSION ■

Everything involved in the work of a teacher is all about people. You will work with students, parents, other teachers, administrators, the community at large, and then there's . . . you. The needs of all of these constituencies (you included) are to be met through the work you do. So as we conclude this unit on instruction, let's consider two people-oriented topics: preparation and taking time to enjoy your work.

Preparation, Preparation, Preparation

In real estate it's location, location, location. In higher education, we once heard a professor say, "At Cornell it's all about three things: research, research, and research." Well, for the classroom teacher it comes down to preparation, preparation, preparation. This will be the key to a successful lesson.

Understand Your Constituents

You will work with many constituencies. Each one needs a different sort of preparation. Your students come to you to learn the identified curriculum (OK, they don't look at it that way, but that's what is happening). Administrators, however, are concerned with the degree of success you are having in presenting that curriculum. Parents are concerned with the performance, and happiness, of their particular children. And *you* need to be able to meet the needs of all of these folks while preserving your mental health and enjoying the work you do.

Life as a professional educator can be both overwhelming and deeply gratifying. Preparing appropriately for each constituency is what will breed confidence and success through your career as an educator. Do not take any constituency for granted! They each have their specific needs.

Understand the Curriculum You Enact

The specific curriculum where you teach is what you now need to study. Read the background information. Review the textbooks and instructional materials that your school has adopted. Be as prepared for *planning* a lesson as you wish to be for presenting a lesson. Really, would you feel comfortable sitting in an examination room at a medical office knowing that the physician was in the next room studying up before seeing you? Of course not; you expect that person to know what they are talking about before they come in to assist with whatever ails you.

You need to know what you will be teaching. Think about the questions provided in the textbook or teacher's edition of the curriculum materials. Do you want to use any of the questions or add your own questions? Try to anticipate questions your students might ask. If you are going to do a demonstration or have the students do an activity, practice ahead of time. If something can go wrong, you don't want that to happen during the lesson. Practice is a necessary part of learning.

Make Learning Relevant

With all this preparation and understanding of teaching, it is to be hoped that the children see connections between lessons in school and the world in which they live. Though you will find various ways to help make learning relevant for students, keep in mind that the student is the only one who can actually establish relevancy. The teacher can create opportunities and design experiences that are more likely to be seen by the students as relevant through connections to the world in which they live.

Homework typically has been used to provide students with opportunities to practice newly acquired concepts, principles, skills, and vocabulary. Most homework assignments involve contrived situations that do not make direct connections to the world outside of school. This approach to practice perpetuates what Moravcsik (1981) calls the sterile manipulation of a set of rules. Instead, you might conceptualize homework as the academic bridge between the lessons at school and the relevance of those lessons to the world of the student. With a little bit of effort, you can create assignments having students apply their new learning within the context of their own environments. You will find great satisfaction in hearing a student explain how he or she used what had been done in class or recognized in a nonschool activity something that had been discussed in class.

Take Time to Enjoy Your Profession

And finally, take time to enjoy your work. It will be far too easy to let the paperwork, planning, and preparation occupy all of your concern. It is the interaction with children, and with colleagues, that has brought you to this profession. If you follow the suggestions presented in this unit so that you understand what you are going to do and plan well to do it, then get in there and have fun! Your enthusiasm, particularly during the presentation of difficult topics, will influence the performance of your students as well.

Reflective teaching is a term you will hear quite a bit these days. This means to take time to consider what works, what didn't work so well, and how you might make changes. But you don't always have to wait until it's a rainy Saturday afternoon to do this reflecting. As you work with your students, consider what is happening and whether you need to change pace or direction. And certainly ask yourself whether you are smiling enough. If the answer is "no," then take a breath, adjust your perspective a bit, and remember that *you* are the one who is controlling the attitude, the atmosphere, in your classroom. That alone is an empowering statement for the work of a professional educator.

> Remember that you are the one who is controlling the attitude, the atmosphere, in your classroom. That alone is an empowering statement for the work of a professional educator.

UNIT IV
Assessment

■ UNIT IV CONCEPT MAP

1 the basics of assessment
- basic terms
- standardization and classroom assessment

2 making assessment a part of instruction
- foundation ideas
- questions to ask of any test

3 writing tests
- the table of specifications
- guide for writing test items
- summary

4 analyzing the results of your assessment
- summary
- item analysis
- reviewing the summary statistics

5 assessment and the high stakes environment
- teaching, but not to the test
- how classroom assessment makes your life easier

Unit IV

UNIT IV PEP TALK ■

Assessment—you probably hated it when *you* were in school, and now here you are having to do it to someone else! Actually, assessment has gotten a bad rap. The problem is not so much with the *assessing* of performance; it's in what we do with that information. But even there we can go a long way toward making the evaluation component fairer, more relevant, and less painful.

So much time is put into the planning and preparation of a lesson, followed by the actual presentation, that assessment is often thought of as something that just happens at the end. It is much more than that, and abandoning the "assessment comes at the end" misconception will be the first step to take.

Assessment is something that happens at the *beginning* to inform your own preparation to teach, continues *during* instruction so that you can adapt appropriately to the students' progress, and then shows up *at the end* to find a defensible evaluation of student achievement. So you see, there are three *assessment zones* to any lesson or unit of study. The good news is that we just need two perspectives of assessment to cover all three: formative assessments (used at the beginning and during instruction) and summative assessments (used when it is time to assign grades). We will discuss both in detail.

And there's even better news! When it comes to classroom assessments (as opposed to standardized assessments that we will discuss shortly) you have complete control over the whole show.

> *There are three assessment zones for any unit or lesson: before, during, and after instruction.*

FIRST: THE BASICS OF ASSESSMENT ■

Assessment instruments on any level serve at least one of two purposes. One purpose can be to give an *individual* some indication of actual *achievement.* The other purpose is to identify trends among *groups.* The information compiled from standardized tests tells districts how their students are doing in comparison to students in similar situations around the state or nation. From this information, districts can make decisions about the delivery of their educational program. In the classroom, assessments can inform the teacher about the progress of students as a lesson proceeds and of their achievement when instruction has concluded. In all cases, it boils down to gathering information for making decisions. Simple. There's nothing mystical or magical about this, though it seems that assessment folks often try to make it so. Just read carefully and you'll see how it all works.

The Basic Terms

Assessment and evaluation are two completely separate activities. So let's make a clear distinction between them. We cannot ensure that you won't see them used interchangeably elsewhere, but our hope is that you will have a broader perspective of this important instructional tool. We will further break this down into two types of assessments: formative and summative.

ASSESSMENT

Assessment

Assessment, whether your version in the classroom or those districtwide high-stakes standardized versions, is *the means by which information is gathered to make a variety of decisions.* For example, a house may be assessed in terms of size, building materials, location, and number of bedrooms and bathrooms. In the classroom you might assess a student's skill, knowledge, reasoning, or dispositions. When information about the characteristics or qualities of something or someone is gathered, that constitutes an *assessment*.

> Assessment is not synonymous with evaluation.

In school, and in your particular classroom, assessment is part of an effective educational strategy because it comes at the beginning (finding out what your students already know) *and* at the end of instruction (determining what has been learned as a result of the learning experience). In your work as a teacher, there will be times when you need information for purposes of *making instructional decisions* and other times when you will need to *place an academic value* on the information gathered. In either case, good assessment is the basis for all that follows.

Evaluation

Since assessment is just the gathering of information, that's not the part that really bothers test takers. Rather, it's the next step when the assessment information (data) is compared to some *value structure*. **Evaluation** is when *value* is placed on accumulated assessment data. When a teacher places a value (a grade) on test results, or a tax assessor places value (in dollars) on the assessment of a house, then evaluation has occurred. So you can see that *all evaluations include assessments, but not all assessments necessarily include evaluations.*

So, *assessing* and *evaluating* are two different activities with different guidelines. For assessment the key point is to gather the appropriate data for the decision that needs to be made. For evaluation the key point is in establishing an appropriate value structure to represent the data.

> The keys to good evaluation of your students' progress:
>
> 1. Gather the appropriate data (assessment)
>
> 2. Establish an appropriate value structure to represent the results (evaluation)

Formative and Summative Assessments:
Two of the Most Important Tools in the Box

Though we will also discuss standardized testing, our emphasis is going to be on classroom assessments that a teacher uses. Rather than shifting back and forth between assessment and evaluation, we will make a useful distinction between two types of assessments: formative and summative.

Formative assessments are those data collection activities that a teacher uses *to make instructional decisions.* Don't let the "form" in formative confuse this with

> **Formative assessments:** data-collection activities used to make instructional decisions
>
> **Summative assessments:** intended specifically for the purpose of assigning a grade

meaning a "formal" test (whatever that is). In this case we are using data to help formulate our course of instruction. This could be as structured as a lengthy written test given before a lesson or unit begins to find out what your students know. It could be that same test given to the students midway through the lesson to see how things are going—or even at the end but before the final test just to see whether the students have progressed as you desired. But it could also be a pop test here and there or even just the questions that you ask in class to see how things are going with the lesson. It could also be the case that you use a checklist as you monitor student work. In all of these cases you are using the information to make decisions about what *you* need to do. No grades are assigned, no stickers distributed, no smiley faces or frowns on the student's lab report. Formative assessments are the means you use to find out how things are going so that you can decide how to proceed. The robust use of formative assessments, if you pay attention to the data you collect, will be the key to providing effective learning experiences for your students.

The robust use of formative assessments, if you pay attention to the data you collect, will be the key to providing effective learning experiences for your students.

So, an important aspect of the assessment component of an effective teacher's strategy will be the consistent use of formative assessments. Rather than plowing through some unit of study and simply having a test (summative assessment) at the end, a teacher who uses formative assessments throughout instruction can monitor the progress of the students and *adjust instruction accordingly*. This is the purpose of formative assessments.

It is important for you to understand that assessment techniques represent *skills* that a teacher must develop. Simply asking a class, "Does everybody understand?" will not suffice for a viable formative assessment. Students who do understand will likely answer affirmatively while students who don't understand may prefer not to make that point known. No one likes to look foolish in front of one's peers; thus formative assessments must be conducted in a manner that protects the student's self-concept.

A teacher might conduct formative assessments by asking open-ended questions and watching to see who responds and who does not. One might direct questions at individual students but ask for opinions or rephrasing. The teacher could also ask a question and, upon receiving no response, rephrase the question as if the difficulty had been in the original phrasing. Paper-and-pencil tests, quizzes, checklists, and other exercises that are *ungraded* protect the self-esteem of a student among classmates but provide the teacher with assessment data that can clarify the instructional route to pursue either with the group or with individuals.

Summative assessment, which we might typically think of as evaluation, is intended specifically for the purpose of assigning a grade. There is no plan to reteach the topic based upon the assessment results, but instead the teacher considers the instruction for the particular topic to be complete: students will be assessed and evaluated for their mastery of the material, and then the class will move on to the next topic.

When constructing summative assessments, Stiggins (2001) recommends that teachers keep the perspective that the real users of assessment data are the students themselves. Merely receiving a letter or numerical grade advises a student of the value placed on the work, but it does not do anything to clarify the learning that has—or has not—taken place. That is, what questions were answered correctly? Which were incorrect? Assuming that the information was taught because it bears some importance, what does the student still need to learn? Keeping the focus on students and learning as assessments are designed represents the first step toward high-quality assessments. So, while formative assessments are specifically intended to inform the teacher, summative assessments must also communicate effectively with the test taker. And this is true as well if the assessment is one that the teacher completes rather than the student. That is, if the teacher—perhaps in a kindergarten setting—uses checklists or anecdotal notes to assess students as they work, the student still ultimately needs to know whether they are making progress, doing things correctly, or have mastered the lesson. The bottom line? Don't keep the results a secret from the people who really need to know the results—the students.

Formative and summative assessments are indispensable aspects of effective instruction, but clearly the aims are different. The former is used to modify or plan instruction, the latter for recognizing the level of academic achievement a student has reached. And as you will see in upcoming sections of this unit, assessments are not necessarily a matter of responding in writing to questions on a page. There are many formats that we can use, and it will always be the case that we want to choose a format that is suited to the task at hand and developmentally appropriate for the student.

Figure IV.2   Formative and Summative Assessment

Formative Assessment	Summative Assessment
Teacher might ask questions, use observations, or a written test	Teacher might ask questions, use observations, or a written test
Responses tell the teacher whether students are ready to move on or if students need more instruction	Responses used to assign a grade; there will be no reteaching

Standardized and Classroom Assessment

Before we get to work on writing tests to use in the classroom, let's do a primer on standardized testing since these are major influences in the contemporary classroom.

Standardized testing refers to a system of assessment that is typically administered to a broad population of students. This could be districtwide, statewide, nationally, or even a test used internationally. Elementary and secondary schools may use such a test to measure student achievement in various subject areas. It could, however, be a test administered to an individual student (such as with tests of intelligence or cognitive ability) but the scoring of which is based on the performance of a broad population.

With regard to the academic progress of your students, standardized tests are usually administered to all test takers in the same manner and under conditions and restrictions that are kept as consistent as possible. The results your students obtain are reported as compared to the scores that were received for a group of similar test takers who were identified as being representative of the population that would be using the test. The scores for that group, the **norm group**, were used to set the *standard* for the test.

> *Criterion referencing and group referencing are both based on the data collected from a norm group. The question is, how do we want to use the assessment data?*

There are two practices for setting the standard for the test based on the results from the norm group: criterion referencing and group referencing. This gets a little confusing at times because group referencing is sometimes referred to as *norm referencing*. The fact is that *all* standardized tests rely on the results of some group of test takers who represent the normal population for whom the test is intended. So in both cases, criterion and group referencing, some norm group is involved. And it is also true that for any set of scores it is possible to take a criterion-referencing approach to the assessment results or a group-referencing approach. It is not a function of the assessment instrument; it's a matter of deciding how we want to use the test data.

Criterion referencing is an approach in which the norm group is assessed and the results are compiled. Then, in its most basic form, the results (often referred to as the *baseline data*) are examined, and some group of folks determines what the passing grade will be for future test takers based on the how the norm group performed. Most tests of skills (whether it is reading, math, or how to fly an airplane) will be criterion referenced because the concern is whether or not the individual possesses the skills he or she is required to possess.

This is really much the same as what you've been exposed to throughout your academic career. For the most part, your tests, projects, and papers were graded on a 100-point scale (or some variation of it), and accumulating so many points along the scale related to a letter grade. Oftentimes it would be something like 70–79 was a C, 80–89 was a B, and 90–100 was an A. The numerical score you needed for a particular grade was the *criterion* that had to be met to receive that grade—thus, it was a criterion-referenced test.

The big question, and especially so when it comes to a standardized criterion-referenced test, is, how do we decide what the criteria will be? Is there really something special about getting 80 points rather than 79 that makes one grade a B and the other a C? Who set the criteria and why did they set it where they did? Because the vast majority of tests that you write will be criterion referenced, we will need to revisit this question of setting the criteria when we discuss classroom assessments.

Group referencing takes a different approach. We still have some group of test takers who represent the students for whom the test is intended. The difference, however, is that rather than establishing some criteria for passing the test, scores are reported in terms of how the test taker compares to the test takers who set the standard. And there's a very important consideration made in how we go about making that comparison. It's based on the *normal curve.*

Standardized testing from first grade through high school has embraced a statistical model, the **normal curve** (also called the *bell curve*), that anticipates a particular distribution of test scores. According to the model, if enough people are tested we can expect a distribution of students' scores to have a certain percentage of grades in the high range, a similar percentage in the low range, and the majority of scores (approximately two-thirds) to be distributed just above and below the average. The bottom-line assumption is that most people are average.

When you look at the normal curve in Figure IV.3 you will see that its highest point represents the average score *and* that more people achieved that score than any other. So, rather than reporting a score in terms of whether it meets a particular criterion (or, more typically, how close it comes to a perfect score), *group referencing reports how much a test taker's score differs from the average score*—the idea being that since most people are average, that should be our reference point.

Figure IV.3   Normal Curve With z Scores, T Scores, and Percentiles

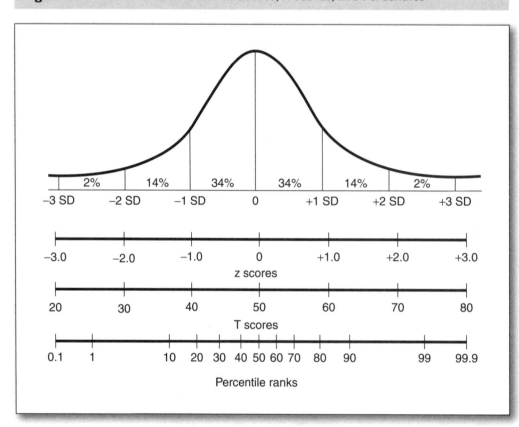

Across the broad spectrum the concept of the normal curve seems to make sense. If the performances of enough people are measured on any characteristic, scores do seem to distribute themselves "normally" with most people scoring at or just around the average. If you watch the distribution of scores from your own teaching over the years, you will likely see a normal distribution. Keep in mind that even if the grades are consistently high, those high grades will distribute themselves as the few that are really high, those that are low-high (so to speak), and a majority of grades in the mid-high range. This distribution occurs if your assessment instruments are well designed. If not, you may have scores of 100 on a 100-point scale year in and year out. But in this case it is more likely that the *assessment instrument* was not as fine an indicator of the differences among students as it could have been.

Classroom assessment is probably of more immediate importance to you as a teacher because it comes into play every day as you work with students. We refer now to the tests you will use to assess students on what has been specifically presented in class. Even here it can be anticipated that the principal in your building will expect your grading to reflect the normal curve over time.

You probably don't like this idea of being *expected* to assign low grades to some of your students. However, you can overcome such expectations and bring a greater number of your students to a level of excellence as long as your assessment program effectively documents that your students have achieved at a higher level. Writing a test that everyone aces or one that everyone fails is neither difficult nor worthwhile. Writing a test that appropriately identifies the strengths and weaknesses of your students is your target. If everybody achieves to a high level and blows the normal curve out of the water, there is no problem if it can be demonstrated that your assessment instrument (test) was well constructed and did what it was supposed to do.

Understanding Standard Scores

Standardized scores, which often include all sorts of statistical manipulations and strange-sounding names (e.g., z scores and T scores), also include some numbers that you are probably quite familiar with already. They are known as the *measures of central tendency*, and that would be a good place to start.

Measures of Central Tendency

The measures of central tendency are the mode, median, and mean. You've probably known of these for years. Their definitions, as they apply to academic assessment, are as follows:

- **Mode**: the score that occurs most often in a distribution of scores
- **Median**: the score that falls in the very middle of the distribution when the scores are arranged in sequence
- **Mean**: the arithmetic middle of a distribution, also known as the average of the scores. In mathematical shorthand a score is represented as X and the mean is represented as $\bar{X}$.

Standardized scores often include all sorts of statistical manipulations and strange sounding names, but it's really not that mysterious.

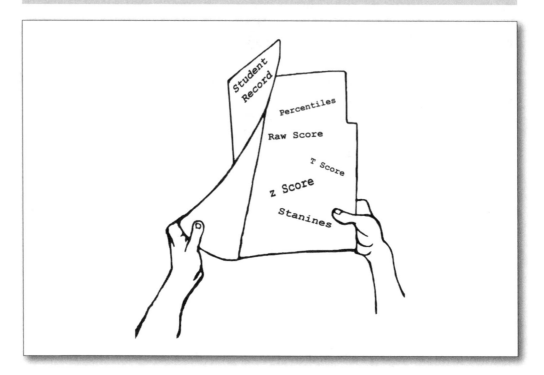

As familiar as you may be with mode, median, and mean, questions that you may not have answered are, why are they called *measures of central tendency* and what makes them important? Well, let's begin with the first question.

As we discussed in a previous section, when scores are represented on the normal curve most scores are just below, right at, or just above whatever the average happens to be. Technically, *on a normal curve*, there are more scores (the mode) right at the average (the mean) than anywhere else, and the number that would be smack dab in the middle of the distribution (the median) would be the same as the mode and the mean. In addition, a full two-thirds of the population would fall just below, right at, or just above the score that represents the mode, the median, and the mean. What this says to us is that when comparing students to a particular standard (as set by a norm group) *most* scores are going to fall somewhere around the *center* of the distribution, and so we make our comparisons in terms of how much a student differs from the average. That might seem a little strange to you since throughout your academic life the emphasis has been on how close you were to the highest possible grade. Well, that high grade does fall somewhere on the normal curve, but since most people are right around the average, we use the middle of the distribution as our reference point. And so the measures of central tendency describe the "middle" of the distribution of grades.

> *The measures of central tendency are used to describe the middle of a distribution of scores because, theoretically, that is where most scores are expected to fall.*

Understanding Students' Test Scores Based on the Normal Curve

Many calculators these days have a standard-deviation key on them. Just punch in each score, and it does the rest for you. But let's take a moment to explain five versions of standardized scores that you might see on a student's record or test report.

First and foremost you need to keep in mind that each of these represents just a different way of expressing the exact same score: raw score, z score, T score, percentile, and stanines. Look at it this way. Suppose you know someone named Robert. You could call him Robert, or Bob, or Rob, or Robby, or maybe even Bert. But in all cases, they are just *different names for the same person.* When we talk about scores based on the normal curve we are simply talking about different ways of stating an individual's score. Placement along the curve doesn't change from one version to another, just what we call it.

Raw scores, z scores, T scores, percentiles, and stanines are just different ways of representing the exact same score.

Raw Score

The **raw score** is the person's actual result on the test. For instance, on a test in your classroom the raw score might be something between 0 and 100. On an intelligence test it would (usually) be between about 70 and 140. On the SAT a raw score might be 1500. Based on whatever scoring system is used for the particular test, the raw score represents how that individual did on that test. No comparisons are being made. For this number to be meaningful, you would need to know how many points were available on the test, something you might not know when looking at a student's file.

z Score

When looking at standard scores on student records you may be faced with a student's score but not know anything else about the points available on the test. That's where the **z score** (and its derivative, the T score) come into play.

The z score translates the raw score into units of standard deviation. In that form, you don't need to know how many points were available for a particular test because the z score tells you exactly how far from the mean (which, as a z score, has a value of zero) a score lies. Positive numbers (e.g., +1.1) would be above the mean, while negative values (e.g., –2.3) would be below. A student with a z score of zero would have a raw score that was the average for the norm group. It would be a zero because it did not differ at all from the average. For someone who understands units of standard deviation based on the normal curve, the z score is the most informative representation of a raw score.

A student with a *z score* of zero would have a *raw score* that was the *average* for the norm group.

T Score

You may have noticed already that there's one bothersome little aspect to the z score. While the z gives us, as professional educators, a very precise statement about the student's score relative to the norm group, it can be awfully difficult to tell a parent that their child had a zero on the standardized test. Now we both know that the zero actually means that the child received the average score, but still, it just doesn't come across too well—let alone having to tell a parent that the child's score was a *negative* number (even though a –0.1 is barely below the average). What to do? The **T score** gets us around this dilemma by placing the entire curve on a 100-point scale.

Since 50 points would be the middle of the 100-point distribution, it lines up right under the 0 of the z score scale. Thus, if a student had a z score of 0, the T score would be 50. Remember, it's still the same raw score, in the same place, but if we use a z score we'd call it 0 and if we use a T score we'd call it 50.

Moving along, each unit of standard deviation represents ten more points on the T score scale (see Figure IV.3). The formula for converting the z score to a T score is very simple: $T = (10z) + 50$. Done!

Using this approach, there are no zeroes and there are no negative numbers to report. Same score, same placement along the curve, but it sounds better than telling a parent that the child has a zero (which is not bad) or negative number for the test result.

The T score places the entire curve on a 100-point scale. This eliminates negative numbers as test scores, and the average score becomes a 50 rather than a 0 (as with the z score).

Percentile

Another likely representation of a score is that of a **percentile**. The percentile refers to the percentage of scores *from the norm group* that fall *at or below* the particular score. Notice that this does not say that a particular percentage of scores was below the score in question. Instead, it includes those scores that were below *and* those that were the same as the score. It is a subtle point, but statistically important.

It is worth taking the time to see the curious picture of percentiles when they are stretched out beneath the normal curve. Take a look back at the percentile scale in Figure IV.3. What do you notice about it relative to either the z score or T score scale? Go ahead, take a look.

Isn't that interesting? While the z score and T score scales are evenly distributed in terms of their intervals, the percentile scale comes along and is all stretched out on either end but bunched together in the middle. Why would that be? The reason is that approximately two-thirds of the population is clustered between –1 and +1 units of standard deviation, and that still has to be true when we speak in terms of percentiles. Unless you memorize the distribution of scores along the percentile scale in Figure IV.3, just seeing a student's score represented as a percentile will probably not tell you which population group it falls in along the normal curve. It will tell you, without a doubt, the percentage of test takers *in the norm group* who had that same score or below.

The percentile refers to the percentage of scores *from the norm group* that fall *at or below* the particular score.

Stanines

One other way of representing scores on the normal curve is in terms of **stanines**. The stanine scale was developed by the U.S. military around the middle of the twentieth century. It uses the same normal curve but divides it into nine equal segments, thus a *st*andard *nine*-point *s*cale (stanines). If you take a look at Figure IV.4 you will note that the fifth stanine (which is the one in the middle) straddles the mean rather than being placed right on the mean. Figure IV.4 gives the percentage of the population that is expected to fall into each stanine. You'll notice that the distribution is symmetrical on either side of the fifth stanine (where about 20 percent of the population would be expected to score).

Generally speaking (no reference to the military intended there) Stanines 4–6 would represent "average." Below average would be Stanines 2 and 3 with the first stanine as well below average. Similarly, Stanines 7 and 8 would be considered above average with the ninth stanine representing a well-above-average score.

FORMATS FOR REPORTING STANDARDIZED SCORES

Raw Score	The test taker's actual score (you have to know the possible points available for it to be meaningful)
z Score	A raw score converted to units of standard deviation (tells you precisely where the score lies with regard to the results from the norm group)
T Score	A kinder, friendlier version of the z score (it does not change a score's position along the curve, but reports all scores as positive numbers)
Percentile	Percentage of scores from the norm group that fall at or below the given score
Stanines	Reports a given score in terms of which of the nine units of the scale into which it would fall

---

OK, maybe standard scores and the computations of them are not the most exciting thing in the world, but assessments and the data they generate are a

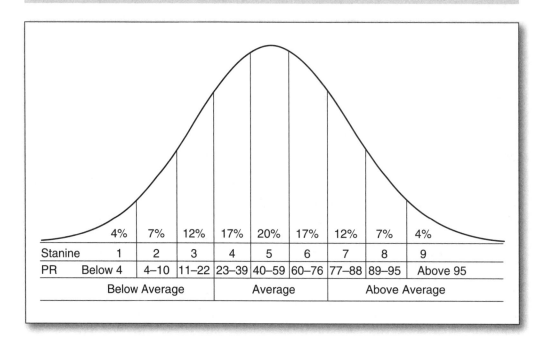

Figure IV.4 Normal Curve With Stanines and Percentages

	4%	7%	12%	17%	20%	17%	12%	7%	4%
Stanine	1	2	3	4	5	6	7	8	9
PR	Below 4	4–10	11–22	23–39	40–59	60–76	77–88	89–95	Above 95
	Below Average				Average			Above Average	

fact of any professional educator's life. Knowing how those scores are derived and what they tell someone about the student or the group is something that should be expected of teachers. You now have the background. Use that knowledge to broaden, heighten, and continually raise the level of your teaching. That's not such a bad thing, is it?

■ SECOND: MAKING ASSESSMENT A PART OF INSTRUCTION

The previous section provided the foundation for carrying on a discussion about the assessment of students. Now it is time to consider some of the important ideas behind the process.

Decisions regarding the selection and administration of standardized tests are usually made at district and state levels and thus are out of the hands of the classroom teacher. *Classroom assessments*, however, are a different matter. Many writers, such as Stiggins (2001), suggest that it is classroom assessment that paints the true picture of a student's academic achievement. After all, the assessments that are provided in the classroom are designed for those students in particular and are based on what has actually been done in class. This assumes, of course, that the assessment instruments used are of a high quality.

ASSESSMENT

Ensuring quality is a responsibility of the classroom teacher. Curricular materials are often provided from the publisher along with test banks, quizzes, and worksheets. The presumption that these materials are of high quality is dangerous on several counts. First, using the prepackaged assessments assumes that everything in the chapter has actually been taught. Second, it assumes that the assessments were prepared using best assessment design practice. The fact could be that individuals other than the authors have prepared the test materials. Even the authors may lack expertise in test design. After all, their strong suit is the content that they write about rather than writing test questions.

However, a teacher with a solid understanding of test design is well equipped to construct, administer, and evaluate assessment instruments and the data they collect for any topic that has been taught. *The bottom line is that no one other than the classroom teacher actually knows the students in that classroom, knows what experiences those students bring to the class each day, and knows what instructional experiences were provided in class.* Because *you* are the only one who knows all of these things for your class, *you* are the most informed person around when it comes time to put together a test.

> Ensuring that instruments used for classroom assessments are of high quality is the responsibility of the classroom teacher. It is part of being a professional.

> No one other than the classroom teacher actually knows the students in that classroom, knows what experiences those students bring to the class each day, and knows what instructional experiences were provided in class.

The Foundation Ideas

There are four major ideas to keep in mind about assessing your students. We have already discussed one of them: the classroom teacher knows his or her students best. Second of these big ideas is one that is a little tough to understand at first because it sounds somewhat counterintuitive. The idea is this: Good assessments discriminate. That's not a bad sort of discriminating among students. Instead, the notion is that a really strong assessment will tell the teacher the strengths and weaknesses of individual students so that the most appropriate instructional experiences can be designed to meet their individual needs.

The third major idea to use as a foundation for your assessment program is that good assessments (that includes formative and summative) are the key to making *instructional decisions* (what and how to teach), *meaningful evaluations* (because you ask the right questions and value the responses appropriately), and *effective learning* (because the student is informed of strengths to build upon and weaknesses to address).

Finally, it is important that you recognize and accept that as a professional educator the quality of the assessment program in your classroom rests squarely with you. Teachers have little impact on the design, administration, scoring, or interpreting of standardized tests. In the classroom, however, you must accept responsibility for the quality of the assessments you use and the manner in which the results of those assessments are put to use. This is a statement of teacher empowerment that we hope you will take to heart.

Figure IV.5 The Foundation Ideas

- The classroom teacher knows the students and what experiences were provided better than anyone else.
- Good assessments discriminate between students, indicating their strengths and weaknesses, thus allowing the teacher to design appropriate instruction.
- Assessment is the teacher's key to making good instructional decisions, constructing meaningful evaluations, and fostering effective learning as a result.
- The quality of a classroom assessment rests with the teacher.

Questions to Ask of Any Test

Whether you are about to take a test or build one, there are three questions to keep in mind. However, note that at this point we are considering *the test as an information-gathering instrument*—we are not talking about the test results just yet.

Formative or Summative

The first question to ask is whether the test is to be formative or summative. Why does that matter? Certainly it matters to you as a student, right? And it would similarly matter to *your* students because formative tests do not carry that "evaluative" weight of summative tests. But as a test *designer* it is a particularly important question to ask. As we have already seen, formative and summative tests serve different purposes, and so it is important that you know just what you are trying to accomplish with the test you are about to write. Is it to get information for designing instruction or are you trying to determine your students' level of achievement so that you can assign a grade? Clearly, the answer to this question of formative or summative has implications for what happens after the test.

Internal Consistency

The next question concerns what is called the **internal consistency** of the test. That is, it refers to matters about the integrity of the instrument (the test) for doing what it is supposed to do. Internal consistency is addressed in terms of validity and reliability.

THE QUESTIONS OF INTERNAL CONSISTENCY

Validity: Does the test measure what it is supposed to measure?

Reliability: Does the test yield consistent results?

Validity

Validity, quite simply, is a matter of whether the test measures what it is supposed to measure. If you are going to write a test for what you taught in science but include a few questions from social studies "just to see whether they were paying attention," then the test is not valid. If you want to write a test about that same science lesson but decide to include something that wasn't, for instance, from the chapter the class actually studied—or was content from the chapter that you didn't get to—then the test is not valid. You could announce that whether or not you discussed it in class *anything* from the chapter could be on the test, but then you would have to ask yourself whether the teacher is really necessary or whether we should just assign readings and give the students a test. We don't want to seem silly about this, but you and a classmate have very likely walked away from taking a test and complained that something was on there that you hadn't expected. Well, now that *you* are writing the test, we want to be sure that only the appropriate material is included—that is, that the test is valid. So, before giving a test you should ask yourself whether the test you have written is valid rather than waiting for your students to tell you that it isn't.

Three Types of Validity

1. *Content validity*	The test assesses knowledge and comprehension of that knowledge (this is the typical test you will write).
2. *Construct validity*	These tests assess characteristics or attributes such as intelligence, creative thinking, or musical ability.
3. *Predictive validity*	Such tests attempt to predict future performance such as the SAT or the tests used for applying to graduate schools.

Content Validity. As background, there are three basic categories of validity, though your test writing will almost always be focused on one type in particular. **Content validity** refers to a test of knowledge or comprehension of knowledge. Spelling, math, history, science—these are all content areas. Obviously, the vast majority of tests that you write will revolve around the idea of content validity. That means that you will want to be sure that the test addresses what you have actually done in class (or assigned) and nothing else.

Construct Validity. **Constructs** are areas that can't be assessed by just asking for knowledge-based responses. Musical ability is a construct. So is creative thinking. Another is intelligence. For these areas, and others like them, an assessment instrument will ask a variety of questions or perhaps require the demonstration of various skills, and from the responses we *infer* a degree of intelligence, or of creative thinking, or of whatever construct is under consideration.

Predictive Validity. Similarly, you will rarely—if ever—need to design a test based upon **predictive validity**. It could be argued that mastering the work in one grade level could predict success at the next grade level, but that would not really be accurate. Mastering work at one level provides the foundation for *attempting* the next level. So the one is not really making a prediction as much as it might just set up an expectation. The tests you may have taken to get into college, on the other hand, were designed to predict your future academic success. As we all know, the predictions are not always accurate, though that is the nature of predictions. On the whole, however, a high score on something such as the SAT or the ACT tends to correlate positively with college success.

Reliability

Supposing that we feel pretty confident that a particular test is valid, the next question is that of **reliability**, which is the question of whether or not a test gets consistent results. A test that every class aces each time it is administered is reliable. So is a test that everybody fails each time. Even one where students routinely have so-so scores may be considered reliable. Admittedly, this is a concern that is most closely related to standardized tests that will be used in their same form over and over again. If on such a test the scores from one administration to the next vary widely, the test designers would have to consider whether the reason for that variation is because of the different populations taking the test or whether it is because something about the test itself is coming across differently to different groups. It would not be good assessment practice to attach a particular score to a student's performance— something that could have significant implications for that child's further academic work—only to decide some years later that the test was flawed. Reliability becomes a very important consideration.

During your teacher-education program you likely had a course in tests and measurement. At that time you may have addressed several methods of determining the reliability of a test such as test–retest, split-half, and alternate forms. With that in mind, and considering that this book is not intended as a course in assessment, we are going to briefly consider those three approaches in a nonstatistical manner.

Test–Retest Reliability. The **test–retest** approach to checking the reliability of an assessment is *not* the same as a pretest/posttest situation. In the latter, you may be giving your students a test about some topic *before* you teach the topic (that's the pretest). Your intent is to find out what they already know (or don't know) so that you can design appropriate instructional experiences. Following your teaching you will again test the students (the posttest) to see what progress they have made. The key element here is that instruction on the topic occurs *between* the pretest and the posttest.

In a test–retest consideration of reliability the key element is that *no* instruction (on that particular topic) occurs between the test and the retest. Having finished a particular lesson or unit you may decide to test your students. You put together a nice valid test of the content taught and let the students have at it. Then you let some time go by. Could be that everybody goes home for a holiday vacation or you continue on with some other topics to be presented. In either case, after a week or so you give the same test to the students. They, of course, will be wondering why they are taking the same test again. You will know that the reason you have readministered the test is not actually to check the students but instead to check the reliability of the test.

There probably aren't many teachers who really want to see how the students do a week or two later (expecting the scores to drop precipitously), but keep two things in mind: First, if the scores are relatively parallel in terms of their distribution (even if, e.g., they are ten points lower across the board), then you probably have a reliable test that you can feel comfortable using again—as long as the instructional experiences you provide to the next set of students is consistent. Second, it's that second set of scores that will really tell you what your students learned. And that could be very worthwhile to know.

If the scores fluctuate substantially, however, you may want to take a look at the test to see whether there is something about the wording or the tasks involved that is coming across differently to students the second time through. In terms of a paradigm, test–retest uses one test, administered to one group, two times.

Split-Half Reliability. Don't want to take the time to test them twice? Well, there are other options. If you are writing a test for a subject in which multiple questions could be asked that are parallel in what they assess (e.g., a math test that could have twenty or thirty variations of two-digit by three-digit multiplication problems) then the **split-half** approach would give you an idea of the reliability of the test. Let's use the example of two-digit by three-digit multiplication problems. Write out perhaps twenty problems, all of which follow the same two-digit by three-digit format. However, when you score the tests, score Items 1–10 and write out a result for each student (5/10, 7/10, etc.) and then score Items 11–20 separately. If the scores are fairly similar, then chances are good that the collection of problems you have assembled is a reliable test for that topic. Hold on to it and keep using it instead of staying up late every year coming up with a new test.

If the scores seem significantly different, then you need to look over the problems to see whether there was a pattern of what problems were missed. Keep in mind, just as we said about test–retest, that you're interest here is in the test instrument more so than in student achievement. You are in the process of designing a good, strong test for that particular topic. A paradigm for this approach: one test, given to one group, one time.

Alternate Forms Reliability. The third approach is a little more labor intensive. On the upside, it can leave you with two or more good tests to use so that throughout the day (if you are teaching middle school or high school), or year-to-year (for you elementary school teachers), students are not tipping off other students about the upcoming test. What we are talking about is the **alternate forms** approach to checking test reliability.

Alternate forms reliability can work well with subject areas that require responding to questions (as opposed to solving problems). Let's suppose you are writing a test for a social studies lesson and will use a short-answer format. This approach to checking for reliability will require that you write out two (or more) separate tests. On both tests you will ask questions about the same topic but in slightly different ways. The questions need to be roughly parallel, that is, both tests should ask about the same items rather than covering some items on one test and others on the second version. Give some of your students Form A and some Form B. When you compare the results, scores should be essentially equivalent on both forms. If that is not the case, examine the two tests to find out where there seemed to be a disparity. For some reason, those particular questions are not coming across to the students as you had intended.

As you can probably see, there is a real advantage to doing this. Once you have constructed two tests that yield equivalent results, you could use both at the same time (alternating from one student's desk to another) and eliminate cheating during the test—at least once you've pointed out that the students all around them have different tests. This was likely the case when *you* took standardized tests. The test designers have many forms of those tests, and even if they use just one during your particular test session, the one they use for the next test session is likely different. The paradigm for alternate forms: two tests, given to one group, one time.

PARADIGMS FOR CHECKING TEST RELIABILITY		
Test–Retest	1 test, given to 1 group, 2 times	
Split-Half	1 test, given to 1 group, 1 time	
Alternate Forms	2 (or more) tests, given to 1 group, 1 time	

A test that is valid may not necessarily be reliable. Similarly, a reliable test may not be valid. These are two different concerns for the test designer.

Validity and reliability are important considerations for test designers. Even if we are talking about the tests that you write just for one time use with a single class—or even for one student—ensuring that the test you write is assessing what it is supposed to assess and that it is a reliable assessment instrument are part of your responsibilities as a professional educator.

Statistical Referents

The third question that should be asked is a matter of how the results will be referenced. This question addresses several concerns. That is, will students have to reach a particular score to receive a particular grade, no matter how the other students do on the test (criterion referencing), or will each student's score be determined by the overall performance of the group taking the test, sometimes known as grading on the curve in the classroom setting (group referencing)? The overwhelming majority of tests that you write will be *criterion referenced*. For example, the test is worth 100 points and students must reach 93 or above to receive an A. Though an interesting mix of criterion-referenced and group-referenced tests are used in the schools, the classroom tends to emphasize an individual's performance against an announced standard rather than comparing students to each other.

Also of concern to you, particularly as a test giver rather than as a test taker, will be the summary statistics (the measures of central tendency and the standard deviation) that we spoke of in a previous section of this unit, *Understanding Standard Scores*. A look at the summary statistics will help determine whether you need to make some adjustments in your teaching or test preparation. In other cases you may find that the test simply was a good detector of student strengths and weaknesses. And that, by the way, is the kind of test we want to use.

Without a doubt you will probably calculate the mean for the distribution of scores to give you a sense for how the class as a whole fared on the test. But you should also take the time to look at the mode and the median as well. Recall from our previous discussion that if all three measures of central tendency are the same value, then you likely have a symmetrical distribution of scores. That is an indication that the test itself may have been a good assessment instrument. On the other hand, means that are above or below the mode will start pointing you in the direction of considering whether the test was simply too difficult or too easy. *Note: We are not suggesting that you write tests where only a few students do well and everybody else is average!* We are simply saying that you should verify that the results of the test you are using truly reflect academic achievement rather than simply being a test that was not well prepared.

NOW: WRITING TESTS ■

Enough of theory, let's get to writing tests! In particular, we want to consider three topics: ensuring the quality of a test that you write, formulating a plan, and then applying the appropriate method appropriately, so to speak.

As Figure IV.6 indicates, there are five key considerations for designing high-quality assessments that we should keep in mind. The first three items are concerned with the questions of *what*, *why*, and *how*. The implication is that if the test designer cannot answer these questions clearly, the assessment instrument that follows will likely be of poor quality. For example, think of it in terms of designing a building. If the architect does not know what the building will be used for, why the client wants it built, and how best to build given the circumstances, it will be difficult to design an appropriate building.

Figure IV.6   Keys to Quality Assessment

What	What is the teacher trying to assess? This is a question of the specific content or skill.
Why	Why is the assessment being conducted? For example, is this assessment to be formative or summative?
How	How should the student be assessed? Should the assessment be multiple choice? Essay? Performance? What is the best way to assess the target?
How Much	Of all the content taught, or all the skills taught, how much does the student have to demonstrate so that the teacher is confident of the student's achievement?
Clarity	How can the teacher be certain that the test items are clear to the test taker?

With those three concerns addressed the teacher must now turn to the final two considerations: how best to sample the material that has been taught and how to ensure that the testing materials clearly present the academic challenge. With regard to the first of these two, one typically can't ask about *everything* discussed in class and the accompanying materials, so the designer must decide how much to include on a test to safely infer a student's level of achievement. With regard to the final concern, the test designer must be sure that the test items do not impede assessment by having errors or obstacles within the questions themselves. For instance, questions written at a reading level that is higher than that of the test taker or in a language that the test taker does not understand fluently will affect performance for reasons other than the student's understanding of the material taught.

Test design is a skill. You can begin to develop these skills by paying close attention to the techniques your teachers use(d). Listen for questions that fall into the category of formative assessment during a lesson. And by all means, look closely at the summative-assessment instruments that are presented to you. Ask yourself (and, if you dare, your professor) whether you can find evidence of each of the five keys to quality assessment within the instrument. For now, let's move on with designing a test.

The Table of Specifications: The Most Important Lesson

As with any construction project, it is best to begin by writing a plan. Doing so will help to address the first of our keys to sound assessments. The **table of specifications** (TOS) that we describe next is perhaps the most important lesson to learn as you begin a career of assessing student achievement. It is one of those things that takes much more time to explain than it does to actually design, but it will require some practice. In a sense, you are already familiar with this idea. Remember how your teachers kept pushing you to write an outline before writing a paper or an essay? And do you remember how you hated to do that? Well, the TOS is the outline, the blueprint, for the test you are about to design. We are confident that if you adopt this idea and practice it a few times, you will find that writing a TOS is neither difficult nor time-consuming, *and it will make a significant difference in the quality of tests that you design.* Table IV.1 (see page 196) shows you the general layout for such a table.

Writing a Table of Specifications is neither difficult nor time-consuming, and it will make a significant difference in the quality of tests that you design!

All by itself it doesn't look so impressive, does it? By the time you fill it out, it will become a most valuable source of guidance that makes writing the test much easier. Here are some things to keep in mind:

> *By far, skill in the writing of a TOS can be the most powerful tool in your test-design toolbox!*

- *There is nothing sacred about the number of rows or columns.* We have printed one version here, but your TOS may have more or fewer rows or columns. It all pertains to the particular test you are writing.
- *Once designed, the TOS represents your plan.* Plans can change, however, so if you find that something has been left out or was weighted inappropriately or is just not working, you are allowed to change the plan. It is your TOS, so finagle it until it works for you.
- *You don't need a formal, formatted page each time.* As you can see, the TOS is just a table. Draw it out by hand if that's convenient. You need not find your TOS form each time you start to plan a test. (Though if you like the one in Table IV.1, feel free to make some copies.)
- *Share the plan.* This is not a secret document. If this plan represents what the test will address and how it will be organized, let your students in on the plan. It does not give them the questions or the answers, but it does show them what to expect come test day.
- We have constructed a sample TOS to accompany this explanation (see Table IV.2 on page 197). Follow along as we go through each step for the design of a test based on this unit.

Concept Categories

Take a look at the top row of Table IV.2. In the upper left-hand cell we've put the name of the test under construction: Assessment Unit Test. In the upper right-hand cell is the word "Totals." On every TOS the far-right column and the bottom row are for totals (we'll explain totals of what in a moment).

The cells between the test name and "Totals" are the **Concept Category** cells. Here you will write down the major concepts, or chapters, or topics that are the subject of the assessment. For example, for our "Assessment of Unit IV" we have listed the following topics: Aims/Basic Terms, Making Assessment Part of Instruction, Writing Tests, Analyzing the Results, and the High-Stakes Environment. You will notice that these are roughly the major headings of this unit. If we had just wanted to do a test of any one of those sections, we could have listed the subheadings from just that portion of the unit. *The important point here is that you be able to identify the specific topics that should appear on your test.* By doing so on the TOS, you ensure that you won't forget to include an important topic.

Now, drop down to the bottom row of the TOS. The bottom left-hand corner is labeled "Totals," and you will see that in Table IV.2 we have filled in the bottom right-hand cell with "100." In this case, the 100 represents the total points available for the test. Everything that gets listed in the bottom row will total 100 points, and everything listed in the right-hand column will total 100 points.

But wait! You don't have to put 100 in that cell. If your particular test is going to total to 50 points, you would put a 50 there. If it was going to total to 37.5 points (37.5?) then that's what you would put there. Or, if you want to list the number of questions on the test instead of working in terms of points, put the total number of questions there. Or, that number could represent the percentage of the test being allocated to each cell—ultimately totaling 100 percent no matter what point system you want to use. The table of specifications is a very flexible system—customize it to fit your needs. For our example, the 100 points available for the test is probably a good way to set it up.

Here comes a very important step. Take a look at the Concept Categories that you have listed (or see Table IV.2) and ask yourself how much of the test should be devoted to each category. For instance, you can see that we have placed the most points in the categories of "Making Assessment Part of Instruction" and "Writing Tests" because these are the longest sections of the unit. "Aims/Basic Terms" has just fifteen points because it is largely a section of information to be remembered (rather than skills to master). By considering the time and emphasis placed on each topic listed on the TOC you can ensure that the test will properly reflect the instruction that has been provided. What would this tell you as a test taker when you look at the total points for the remaining two Concept Categories?

Item Categories

Down the left side of the TOC, between the cell with the test name at the top and the word "Totals" at the bottom, we will add in our **Item Categories**. That is, we will indicate what sort of test items will be included in the assessment instrument. Here, as with the Concept Categories, you have considerable flexibility. You might want to list a different type of test question on each row (or just one type listed on one row if that is your preference). For example, you may intend to include some multiple-choice questions (list that on one row), some matching questions (list that on another row), and finally some essay questions (listed on the next row).

With that filled in, move over to the far-right column and list the number of points that will go with each item type. You may decide to have 50 points allocated to the multiple-choice questions, 10 for the matching, and 40 for the essays. You can, of course, distribute it any way you'd like. We will discuss the four general test formats in the next section of this unit.

You have probably noticed, however, that we did not use question formats in Table IV.2. Instead, as is our preference, we choose to conceptualize the item types in terms of the kind of thinking that we want students to use on the test. One approach may be to use a combination of the K-S-R-D item types that we often see today: knowledge, skills, reasoning, and dispositions. We prefer to use the levels of Bloom's Taxonomy (Bloom et al., 1956): knowledge, comprehension, application, analysis, synthesis, and evaluation. It is not necessary—and likely not appropriate most of the time—to use *all* of the levels, but a combination of two or more is almost always a good idea. In Figure IV.7 you will see the levels of Bloom's Taxonomy listed beside a more recent version, the New Bloom's Taxonomy (Anderson & Krathwohl, 2001). Note that perhaps the most significant difference between them is that the order of the highest two levels has been switched. On the New Bloom's Taxonomy, creating ("synthesis" on the old version) is now the highest level.

Figure IV.7   Old and New Bloom's Taxonomy

Bloom's Taxonomy (Bloom et al., 1956)	Revised Bloom's Taxonomy (Anderson & Krathwohl, 2001)
• Knowledge	• Remembering
• Comprehension	• Understanding
• Application	• Applying
• Analysis	• Analyzing
• Synthesis	• Evaluating
• Evaluation	• Creating

Using Bloom's Taxonomy to conceptualize the items on your test will go a very long way toward building a test that engages your students' higher order thinking. As you can see in Table IV.2, we allocate only 15 points out of 100 to the knowledge (lowest) level of the taxonomy. A quick look at Table IV.2 should tell you which levels of thinking are to be emphasized on this sample test.

Concept Categories	These are the major topics you want to address on the test.
Item Categories	These are the types of items you want to include (e.g., levels of thinking or question types such as essay or selected response).

At this point no test questions have been written. We have not put together a bunch of multiple-choice items with their multiple incorrect answers. Essays with several tasks have not yet been written. We haven't even broken down the point values for each cell within the table of specifications. Yet, the TOS indicates the topics to be covered, the weight given to each topic, the types of items to be included, and the points available for each item type. Before writing the individual items we already have a clear idea of how this test will go together. That's good news for you and good news for your students.

Filling In the Grid

What remains in this test-planning phase is to fill in the grid with the points going to each cell. Note that some cells will receive zero points. That's not a problem. However, every row will total to the numbers in the right-hand column and every column will total to the numbers listed across the bottom row. And keep in mind as you fill in the cells that if you find that things are not working out in a "comfortable" way, then adjust the weighting of the Concept Categories or the Item Categories. It is your design, and having a good strong design will make writing the test much easier.

Looking at Table IV.2 you will see how we allocated points on the test with regard to the different levels of thinking we want our students to use and for each concept category identified. For instance, with 8 points allocated to "Aims/Basic Terms" on the *knowledge* level, students would likely be asked to define terms such as *assessment*, *evaluation*, *formative assessment*, and *summative assessment*. On the *comprehension* level they may be asked to explain why it is important to distinguish between assessment and evaluation. On the *application* level they may be asked to indicate whether a teacher would use a formative or a summative assessment under particular conditions.

Similarly, you can see that a full 32 points is being allocated for the comprehension level under "Making Assessment Part of Instruction." This section included the topics of internal consistency, the normal curve, and standard deviation. A student could expect to see a number of questions (which would total to 32 points) requiring that they demonstrate an understanding of these topics rather than just providing definitions. And take a look at that 15 points under "Writing Tests" and on the *synthesis* level. What do you suppose a student would have to synthesize here? Perhaps the design of a test given a particular scenario?

Remember, the numbers along the bottom and along the right side of the table of specifications do not have to represent points. If you wanted to give your students a ten-question test, then you could put a "10" in that lower right-hand cell and all the numbers within the grid could total ten. The TOS would still help you distribute the number of questions to emphasize what was taught. And by the way, the numbers within the grid do not have to represent points for just one question. For instance, that 32 points on Table IV.2 could represent one 32-point question (whew!), two 16-point questions, or even thirty-two 1-point questions! That's all up to you. Your TOS just ensures that you allocate points appropriately to reflect what was done in the classroom.

As we told you, explaining the construction of a TOS takes more time than just doing one. The better news is that after just a bit of practice you will find that you can write out a TOS quickly and easily to guide your test writing. When you become comfortable with compiling a TOS, you will find that it helps you conceptualize a test in terms of what you've actually done in the classroom and that it keeps you on track while writing the test. By far, skill in the writing of a TOS can be the most powerful tool in your test-design toolbox!

Guidelines for Writing Test Items

Whether your intention is to construct a formative test or a summative test, you now have topics in mind (and expectations of your students for those topics) and you have constructed a TOS that indicates either the test formats you want to use or perhaps the levels of thinking that you want your students to bring to the assessment exercise. You have also "weighted" the test to reflect the emphasis you have given to the various topics. It is time to start writing items. And so now you need to address the third of the five key elements for a high-quality test: *how* to go about assessing the students.

A key to gathering data for formative or summative purposes is to select the most appropriate format. For instance, if you want to know whether a student can swim, a multiple-choice test (selected response) would not be the *best* approach. Instead, the best approach would be a *performance test* that has the student in the water demonstrating an ability to swim!

On the other hand, it is equally important that you select a testing method that does not impede a student's ability to demonstrate achievement. This brings us to a key point for all of the test formats: Assessing all students fairly does not necessarily mean that all students are assessed in the same manner. An obvious example would be that of a student who has poor writing skills but is sufficiently verbal to express his or her knowledge. It could be the case that you will use a personal communication format with this student while others use an essay format.

> *The testing method itself should not be an impediment to a student's demonstration of achievement. Assessing all students fairly does not necessarily mean that all students are assessed in the same manner.*

We will discuss four testing formats that should cover just about all situations that you will encounter as a classroom teacher: personal communication, performance, essay, and selected response. Table IV.3 (see page 198) provides a quick-reference matrix for selecting a format using the targets of demonstrating knowledge, reasoning, skills, or dispositions.

Personal Communication

A **personal communication** assessment is a circumstance in which you speak directly with the student. You've been through at least a few of these situations in your life. If you have ever been interviewed for admission to a program (e.g., entering the teacher-education program at your college or university) or for a job (e.g., with the principal of a school where you wanted to work) then you know firsthand what a personal communication assessment is all about. Keep in mind, however, that simply reading a test to a student (perhaps because of a language problem) that the other students read to themselves does not constitute a personal communication assessment. Rather, the personal communication technique provides the test taker and the test giver the opportunity to *pursue* answers beyond the initial response to the question asked.

Advantages and Disadvantages

A personal communication assessment is somewhat of a paradox in that it can be a quick and efficient way of assessing students, but it can also be a very time-consuming approach. If you have just a few questions to ask, a relatively small number of students, and very particular answers that you are looking for, then this is a good approach. On the other hand, if you have a lot of content to address, a large number of students, and you really want to put this approach to use by letting students elaborate on their initial responses, then time may become an issue that prevents using this technique. And keep in mind that as you speak with one student, all of the others will need some work to keep them occupied.

If writing is what you are assessing, then this would not be the most appropriate format. However, in a situation in which writing is not the target of your assessment, personal communication may very well open up an opportunity for success to a student who understands what has been taught but does not have the ability to express it in writing. Another advantage is that it allows you to attend to nonverbal responses such as those that would indicate the student has not understood the question.

Questioning Techniques

It may seem at first that this is a pretty simple approach to testing. We want to make it clear that this is very much an interpersonal dynamic and as such takes not only well-thought-out preparation but also practice in various questioning techniques. Your TOS will guide the writing of the initial prompts. Try to avoid asking questions that can be answered with a simple yes or no. If you must, be prepared to ask a follow-up question such as "Why?" or "Why not?"

When using personal communication there are a number of questioning techniques that you can use as you help students go beyond a superficial response.

Probing Questions. These questions offer the student the opportunity to provide more depth to an answer. For instance, as a follow-up to a response you might ask, "What more can you tell me about that?"

Clarification Questions. If a student's response is not clear to you, ask a clarification question that offers the opportunity for the student to more precisely phrase the answer. These questions, in particular, help to avoid misinterpreting or misunderstanding the student's meaning. For example, if the student has told you that deserts are hot and dry, you might ask, "Do you mean that they are hot and dry all the time?"

Elaboration Questions. These questions ask for more description or for bringing in more information about something. If you ask a student what she saw at the zoo and she responds by saying "birds," an elaboration question would ask for more description of the birds: "What can you tell me about the birds you saw?"

Redirection Questions. It will sometimes be obvious that the test taker has misinterpreted your question or has approached it from an inappropriate perspective. A redirection question clarifies *your* meaning or draws the student back to the appropriate topic without dismissing what they have already said. In particular, such a question would help to avoid making the test taker feel flustered because he or she missed the point. For example, you might say, "Yes, those are the *types* of clouds, but what I wanted to know was how they differ from one another?"

Supporting Questions. These questions are very much an example of that interpersonal dynamic we referred to previously. There is no anonymity during a personal communication assessment, and so personal vulnerability is very much out there on display. To maintain the flow of such an assessment when an answer is not quite correct or the student has realized that he or she is "in trouble," a supporting question provides support for what has been said but provides direction for overcoming the difficulty. For instance, a student has listed four of the six main characters in a story you have asked about, and now you see that pleading look in the eyes hoping that they've all been covered. You might say, "Those four are correct. Were there any other characters that we discussed?"

If you start paying attention to the questions that people ask you will begin to see these various formats. You will need to practice using them in your conversations with students (and others) before you can use them effectively as part of an assessment.

Establishing Scoring Criteria

Establish appropriate scoring criteria before speaking with the student. Just because this is a conversation does not mean that credit is given for an answer that "sounds good." Determine in advance what needs to be said to constitute an appropriate response for each question. If multiple elements exist, you can draw those out with the questioning techniques (that's the beauty of this approach), but only give credit when a student actually offers a correct response. As mentioned previously, this technique—far more so than the other test formats—offers you a way to avoid making inferences about what a student knows or means. Establish in advance what the scoring criteria will be and then use effective questioning to determine whether or not the student has mastered the topic.

Recording the Results

The final concern is with how you will record the assessment. If you spend a lot of time writing down what a student says in response to the questions, the student will likely start saying less and less. People simply get uneasy when the things they say are being written down. The best bet is to record the conversation. In that situation you will be able to attend to the responses rather than being preoccupied with documenting them. In some instances, however, it may be necessary to obtain appropriate permission before recording a conversation with a child. Other possibilities include either taking brief notes or having a checklist available for when you hear the elements of a correct answer.

Essay

You might think of an **essay** as the written version of the personal communication assessment. There is no back-and-forth discussion, of course, but the test taker does have the opportunity to provide a response that can include great detail and elaboration. Unfortunately, this also means that test takers have a tendency to write down *everything* they can think of in the hope that *something* will be correct. That is not an appropriate way to answer a question, and if the essay prompt has been written in a manner that allows it to happen, then the question is at fault as well. Let's take a closer look.

Things to Think About

Before charging ahead with the writing of essay questions there are a number of concerns that you should consider. First, are your test takers up to the task of writing responses that demonstrate their achievement? This may sound like a no-brainer, but keep in mind two things: (1) you don't want students' verbal ability (or lack thereof) to be an obstacle that prevents them from expressing what they know about a particular topic, and (2) not everyone in your class will be on the same level when it comes to verbal ability. For example, if you are giving a science test, then it is really science content that you are targeting rather than writing ability. A student who does not write well may still know the science content that you've taught.

Essentially going hand in hand with the question of whether your students can write well enough to complete essays is the question of their reading ability. As you prepare essay questions, write them on the lowest reading level represented in your class. Unless you are testing reading comprehension, the essay question itself should not be an obstacle to your students demonstrating their achievement.

Essay assessments are most effective when the questions are sharply focused and narrow in scope. Broadly stated questions (actually, that would be *vaguely* stated questions) that allow students to respond in a number of ways really indicate that the test designer has not identified the target of the assessment and has not established the scoring criteria for the essay prompts. So, rather than using two or three essay questions that require pages of responses, use four or five questions that call for brief and concise responses. This actually makes things easier on the test taker and on the person who has to grade the tests.

Which brings us to the next point: the number of students to be evaluated. Keep in mind that the evaluator (typically you) is human. If you sit down with a stack of twenty-five essay exams, three essays each, with broadly stated prompts that allow lots of latitude in responses, (a) it will take a very long time to grade, and (b) you will likely find that by the time you reach the seventy-fifth essay *your scoring criteria will have changed considerably.* We are not saying to just shelve the essay approach and go with selected response if you have lots of students. Rather, we are saying that whether you have many students or just a few, your life will be made much easier if you construct your essay questions well and establish clear scoring criteria that match with the structure of the prompt.

Writing Good Essay Questions

There are three key points to keep in mind when constructing essay questions:

Specify the Content. State plainly in the prompt what information the test taker is supposed to work with in constructing a response. If the question refers to discussions in class, say so in the prompt. On the other hand, if the question refers to something straight from a textbook or other source, state that in the prompt. And yes, if it addresses both of those, you can say that as well. For instance, your prompt may begin,

> With regard to our class discussions about the measures of central tendency and the normal curve . . .

We have now established that the only thing a correct response will relate to will be these two topics discussed in class.

Tell Them What to Do With the Information. You have now set the context for the response, and so it is time to tell them what to do once they've brought that information back from their long-term memory. You don't want the respondent to give you a simple definition of the measures of central tendency, right? If so, then essay is not the most appropriate approach for this topic. However, what *do* you want? Do you want an explanation, a description, an opinion, a value judgment? It will make the task of scoring the test much simpler if you tell them what sort of thinking they are supposed to bring to the task. How so? Because if you ask for an explanation and they give you a list, then the answer is incorrect. All you will need to do when scoring the response is go up to the prompt and underline the portion that said they were to explain. Simple. So, our earlier example might continue in this way:

> With regard to our class discussion about the measures of central tendency and the normal curve, explain why they are referred to as measures of central tendency and identify where they would be found on the normal curve . . .

Qualify Your Expectations. Your students now know what to discuss and how to discuss it. Add the final element to the question so that you encourage a well-rounded response, though without giving away any answers. That is, indicate what you expect an appropriate answer to include. This one step in the writing of essay questions will make them much more effective as assessment instruments. Our ongoing example may continue like this:

> With regard to our class discussion about the measures of central tendency and the normal curve, explain why they are referred to as measures of central tendency and identify where they would be found on the normal curve. *An appropriate answer will describe what each of the measures tells us, how they relate to scores distributed along a normal curve, and the underlying relationship between the measures and the curve.*

If you now list the points available for this question as 15, then a good test taker should be able to see that there are three components to a correct answer and that each component is likely worth 5 points. If you receive a response that does not include each of the components asked for, those points are deducted and in the prompt you should underline the component the student failed to address.

Because essays have become so misused over the years, both in terms of their structure and the responses that we accept from students, switching to the system we describe may take a bit of doing. However, students will quickly come to understand that they need to *read the question, answer the question that's been asked,* and *address each component that is required.* If you follow these suggestions for writing essay questions it will no longer be necessary to search through a response to see whether some aspect of the correct answer is in there somewhere. Write well-structured prompts and teach your students to respond to what is being asked of them. It shouldn't take more than one or two testing experiences to get the point across, and then life will be better for test taker and test grader alike.

Scoring Essay Questions

There are three final points to keep in mind if you are going to use an essay format for assessment. You may have encountered the opposite of the first point, but we hope you will see why it is a good idea to switch. That is, use enough sharply focused questions to address the content the students are responsible for knowing/understanding *and* have everyone respond to the same questions. No choosing two out of three or three out of five. The only rationale for that approach is to cover the test writer's failure to construct good, solid essay prompts. Obviously, if there are questions on a test that students can opt *not* to respond to, it means that particular information isn't really important. And if it's not important, why did you teach it and why is it on the test at all? What's more, if students are responding to different questions, then the results of the assessment are not giving a true picture of the performance of your class. Instead, construct well-conceived questions that appropriately span the content for which the students are being held responsible. Your TOS will help to ensure that you accomplish this.

The second point to remember is that if someone besides yourself will be scoring any of the essays, be certain that they know exactly what you expect in an answer. As is the case when students are responding to different questions, if scorers are imposing different criteria when grading the answers, it is the efficacy of the assessment that is lost.

Finally—and here's the good news—if you've followed these guidelines you will find that grading the responses is an easy task, even if you have a lot of them to read. It is the student's responsibility to answer the question(s) that you have asked, and it is your responsibility to see whether that has been done. This will be simple if you've written a good prompt that tells them what content to use, what to do with that content, and what elements should appear in a correct response. It is not your responsibility to try to find a way to give the test takers points for what they've written. Whenever you do this—and it happens all the time—you enable a pattern of poor-quality testing in terms of both the students' performance and your approach to assessment.

> *Scoring an essay should be easy. However, if you find yourself trying to infer the correctness of a response, you then enable poor test-taking performance on the part of your students and you dilute the efficacy of the assessments you administer.*

> *It is not your responsibility to find a way to give the test takers points for what they've written. Whenever you do this—and it happens all the time—you enable a pattern of poor-quality testing in terms of both the students' performance and your approach to assessment.*

Performance Assessment

A **performance assessment** may not seem like something you will need at first thought. However, such assessments occur throughout the school on a regular basis. If you are teaching music, art, or physical education this will likely be one of your primary assessment methods. And, while we're on the topic, this is what the administrators in your building use to assess *your* performance! Performance assessment is used when a product is created or a skill is demonstrated.

It may also be the case that a regular classroom teacher will use a performance assessment whenever the demonstration of a skill is required (e.g., handwriting) or the students create some sort of product (e.g., a model in science or a diorama in social studies). In the latter case, an artifact remains after the performance that can be assessed "at leisure," so to speak. In the former case, however, it may well be that once the skill has been demonstrated, the "evidence" of the demonstration is gone. For instance, if you assess a student's ability to dribble a basketball, once the dribble has been drubbled there is no longer any artifact of the event. What this means is that you will need a way of recording the event—and that could actually be doing some sort of sound or video recording so that the demonstration can be viewed again, or simply having a scoring document available so that the skill can be assessed as it is demonstrated.

Concerns to Address

In the design of a performance assessment there are three concerns to address: clarifying the performance, determining the setting, and creating a system for scoring the results.

Clarifying the Performance. The obvious first question is whether you are assessing a product that the student develops or the demonstration of a skill.

Seems like a plain enough concern, but in terms of *designing* such an assessment, this is the first step toward articulating the target to be assessed. This decision will have an impact when it is time to score the performance because, as we have already indicated, if the performance to be assessed is a skill there may be no evidence to work from after the skill is demonstrated.

Next, you need to decide the "who" of assessment. In particular, are you assessing an individual (perhaps the reciting of the Gettysburg Address) or a group (either a team effort or perhaps a cooperative group working on a project)?

And finally, you need to determine the criteria that must be met to indicate satisfactory performance. Taken together, you may wind up with an exercise such as,

> The student will demonstrate memorization of the Gettysburg Address by reciting the entire speech with no more than two errors or omissions.

In our example you can see that we have indicated that the task involves demonstration of the skill of memorization, in terms of an individual, and the criteria for an acceptable performance.

Determining the Setting. We would call this a *structured exercise* because you would be setting the conditions of the performance, such as, in class on Thursday. The other possibility with performance assessments would be *naturally occurring events* such as observing the way students interact on the playground to assess social skills.

When an administrator drops in to see you teach, that would constitute a naturally occurring event. Though you would certainly have prepared for class, you likely have not prepared to have an observer in the class. But when they announce that you will be assessed as part of the district's induction program on a particular day at a particular time, then that leans more toward the structured exercise that has a particular set of performance indicators of which you are aware and are expected to demonstrate.

Scoring and Recording Results. As we have indicated, scoring a performance assessment can be quite different than the other three approaches we discuss. There are several considerations to keep in mind as you put a scoring plan together.

First, will this be a holistic or an analytical assessment? For example, parents sitting in the auditorium will likely evaluate the choir's performance *holistically.* That is, as a whole, it sounded great! The choir director, however, may come away from the very same performance with a laundry list of concerns that will be raised with the choir during their next rehearsal. The choir director is more likely to take an *analytic* approach, assessing many discrete dimensions of the performance. One approach is not superior to the other, it is simply a matter of you determining which one is more important for the assessment you are about to conduct. In particular, this may well be a concern if you are evaluating a group project. Will all students get the same grade based upon the finished project, or will each student receive an individual grade based upon his or her particular contribution to the project?

The second item to consider is one that we also raised while discussing the scoring of essay exams: Who will be doing the rating? There are many possibilities: the teacher, the student as a peer or the student assessing his or her own performance, or perhaps another teacher or outside expert. In any case, for performance assessments to be effective it will be necessary that all raters use the same criteria for assessing the exercise. This may entail just a brief explanation of what to watch for, but it also could require a fairly extensive training/discussion session with the other raters if you have very specific criteria to meet and a detailed method of scoring.

Third, we come to the possible options for scoring results:

- Checklist: This provides a list of the key attributes of the performance that must be present.
- Rating scales: In this case you can indicate whether an attribute is present and rate it along a scale of perhaps 0–5. A zero would indicate that the attribute was not present at all, while the 1–5 could represent values from poor to outstanding.
- Anecdotal records: While observing the performance you can write down brief notes describing what you see. The benefit is that it gives more information than the checklist or rating scale. The disadvantage is that it can distract you from observing the performance.
- Mental record: We put this here only because so many people think it is a viable means of recording your assessments. In reality, it is not. Trying to remember what you observed, particularly if you are assessing a number of performances, becomes problematic and is virtually indefensible if your ratings are challenged.

Selected Response

People often think of **selected-response** assessments (i.e., those using multiple-choice, true/false, matching, and short-answer items) as a quick way of assessing a lot of information. Well, they are correct that *scoring* can be quick and easy, provided the scoring key is accurate. It is the test *design* that will occupy much more time. Unlike essays that can incorporate a number of items into one question, selected response items must be very narrowly focused so that there really is only one correct response, and that means that it takes many more items to adequately sample the topic being tested. The upside is that once the test is designed it is one that can be used repeatedly (as long as the content taught does not change) and the results can be tabulated quickly.

Selected-response items either provide the test taker with response options from which to select the correct response (multiple-choice, true/false, matching exercises) or they are structured to allow only one correct and appropriate response (fill-in-the-blank and short-answer exercises). In the case of short-answer items, the test taker is expected to provide very specific information in no more than a sentence or two. "List and define" exercises would be a good example of this format. For all of the selected-response formats there are some guidelines to consider while writing test items.

We would be remiss if we did not state a particular drawback to the use of multiple-choice test items, especially when they are not well designed. That is, multiple-choice items actually tell you more about what a student *does not* know than they do about what they *do* know. This is because for any multiple-choice item response it is impossible for you to determine whether or not the student simply guessed at an answer. If they did guess, the chance existed that they guessed correctly. So you really don't know whether they knew the answer or not. If, however, they mark an incorrect answer then you *know* that they did not recognize the correct answer. The bottom line is that giving credit for those correct answers does not necessarily reflect whether or not the student has learned what was expected of him or her.

This point about multiple-choice items is not intended to make you turn away from using such a format (though admittedly, you are literally providing the students with the answer to each question) but simply is brought up so that you will understand the importance of designing such tests carefully rather than just throwing together a batch of questions.

General Guidelines

You may recall from our discussion of designing a high-quality test that one concern was to be certain the test items were free of bias or distortion. This becomes particularly important in the writing of selected-response tests because the students are being expected to provide a very specific response *and* because as the test designer you have the luxury of knowing the question you want to ask and the answer you want to receive. What that means is that in the writing of the test item, it is very clear to you what the answer should be and that it would be the appropriate response to the question you've written. For the test taker, on the other hand, he or she is trying to *interpret* your question and find a suitable solution. For these reasons it is important to write sharply focused questions and to have someone else read them over just to be certain that they make sense from another's perspective as well. Keep these considerations in mind as general guidelines for writing any selected-response items:

- *Write clear and sharply focused items*: You don't want students trying to figure out what you *might* be talking about with the question.
- *Ask a question*: This might not always be possible, but as a general guide if you conceptualize items in the form of a question, it forces *you* to articulate exactly what you are looking for in a response.
- *Use the lowest reading level represented in your class*: Do not make the reading level of the question an obstacle to a student's opportunity to provide a correct response.
- *Eliminate clues within or between items*: Especially since selected-response assessments typically require so many items, it's easy for you to wind up with one question that serves to provide students with clues, if not outright answers, to another question.
- *Have someone else proof your test and be sure to double check the scoring key for accuracy*: You do not want to find out that there was an error with the answer key (or within questions, for that matter) while you and your students are going over the results of a test!

Specific Guidelines for Each Format

Keep those general guidelines in mind as you write items. In addition, here are some specific guidelines for each selected response format.

Multiple Choice. Let's dispel one traditional notion about the structure of multiple-choice items: There is nothing magical about the four-response-option format. Sure, all of those standardized tests use four response options, and you probably can't even think of a time when you saw a multiple-choice test with less than four options. But think about it: Such a format has students reading three incorrect answers for every correct answer on the test. In the first place, that's a lot of unnecessary reading. In the second place, it puts a lot of emphasis on incorrect responses. We would recommend that you limit the response options to three (using only two would simply make it a 50/50 proposition) and being certain that only one response is absolutely correct and that the other two options are good distracters.

If you find that you are repeating the same word in each of your response options, change the question. There is no need for your students to keep reading words or phrases over and over again when there is already a long list of questions to be answered. For example, consider this question:

In 2010, which of the following occurred?

   a. Mortgage interest rates increased.

   b. Mortgage interest rates went down.

   c. Mortgage interest rates remained constant.

A revised version could read like this:

In 2010, mortgage interest rates did which of the following?

   a. Increased

   b. Went down

   c. Remained constant

Be sure to word the response options so they are as brief as possible and so that they are grammatically parallel. That is, if the question implies an answer that will be plural, all of the response options should be plural. Similarly, write questions and response options in a manner that does not allow the syntax to point toward an answer. For example, the following item uses "a(n)" to make all possible options feasible:

Many programs require that students maintain a visual and physical record of their achievements and experiences. This document is typically referred to as a(n)

   a. dossier

   b. portfolio

   c. academic record

True/False. These items, even more so than multiple choice, leave you wondering whether a student actually knew a correct answer but knowing for certain when they did not know the correct answer. If, however, you want to go ahead and use this approach just make certain the item you write is either entirely true or count it as false. For example:

_____Deserts are hot and dry.

It would be accurate to say True for this item, but it is also the case that deserts can be very cold at night and thus False would also be correct. It is never a good idea for the teacher to have to defend the question or the answer. A better version would be:

_____During the day, deserts are typically hot and dry.

Fill-In. These questions are good examples of selected response, yet they require the student to provide the answer. When writing such items, keep several ideas in mind:

- *Ask a question and provide a space for an answer*: Again, this pushes the test designer to write a sharply focused item.
- *If using blanks embedded within the prompt, try to stick to one blank per item*: another push for keeping the item clearly focused.
- *Don't let the length of the line be a clue*: It is the student's responsibility to provide the correct answer. The length of the line as a clue (short for a short word or long for a long word) dilutes the efficacy of the assessment. And certainly, do not use one blank for each letter of a correct response.

Matching Items. Matching items are essentially a series of multiple-choice items all rolled into one. Setting this up as a process-of-elimination exercise does not really tell you what the student knows and doesn't know. So, keep these considerations in mind as you design the exercise:

- *State the matching challenge up front*: Indicate that you want students to match items from one column with the items in another column by writing the appropriate letter or number from each in a blank space provided. The "spider web" approach of drawing lines just sets things up for arguments about which lines are going to which responses. Best to avoid this.
- *Keep the list of things to be matched short*: Too many items in a matching exercise leads to confusion and overload. Keep the list down to a manageable number—perhaps no more than ten items.
- *Keep the response options grammatically parallel and homogeneous*: If using names and dates, put all of the names in one column and all the dates in the other. Similarly, if using people and events, put all the names in one column and all the events in the other. And as was the case with writing multiple-choice items, do so in a manner that does not allow grammar to eliminate or necessitate matching particular prompts and responses.

- *Include more response options than are needed and permit options to be used more than once*: This may sound just a bit sneaky, but your intent is to determine whether or not your students know the content that has been presented. Providing just a couple of extra response options or including a response option or two that can be used more than once will give you a clearer picture of what your students know. However, be sure to include a statement in the directions preceding the exercise indicating that some options *may* be used more than once.

Summary

Each of the test formats comes with strengths and weaknesses. It is up to you to determine which format will work best for the particular assessment that you need to accomplish. Each format, however, is one that you can use for designing effective assessments. Once you have selected the most appropriate method, refer to the information provided for writing strong exercises. Table IV.3 provided you with a matrix of appropriate times to use each test format. Table IV.4 (see page 199) provides a summary of the strengths and limitations for each approach.

TOMORROW: ANALYZING THE ■ RESULTS OF YOUR ASSESSMENT

If you wrote out a TOS and stayed with it, you put together a balanced and comprehensive assessment blueprint. If you considered which of the test formats was most appropriate for the content being tested and the context of your particular students, then you had a solid foundation for building test items. And if you followed the guidelines and considerations for the particular format, you wound up with an assessment instrument that could provide a fair and realistic picture of your students' achievement. Now the students have taken the test, you've graded it (and seen how simple the grading part can be), and you've got a batch of test scores staring at you and asking, "What now?"

Reviewing the Summary Statistics

At this point you could just write down a score for each student, record them, and then give the papers back to the students. However, having come so far in putting together a strong assessment instrument it only makes sense that you will spend some time to see how those scores can inform *your* instruction. Remember, test scores tell students something about their achievement *and* they tell you something about your teaching.

> *Once the assessment is over, you are not finished. Remember, test scores tell students something about their achievement and they tell you something about your teaching.*

The most immediate picture of the results will be in terms of the measures of central tendency: mode, median, mean. Arrange the scores in rank order and count up or down to the middle of the distribution to find the median. While you are at it, count up how frequently different scores appear. The one that appears most often will be the mode. Next, take out your calculator, add up all of those scores and divide by the number of scores (N). That result will be the mean.

It is very possible that the measures of central tendency will not be the same value. The most likely reason is that the number of students taking the test was simply too small. In this case you might want to take a closer look at the grade distribution to see what it tells you. If all of the scores are really high or really low, you need to consider whether the reason rests with the quality of instruction *or* the quality of the test. We will look at item analysis in the next section, but for now you need to ask whether the test was too easy or too hard.

If, in looking over the test items you've written, you decide that the items do represent appropriate expectations based on your teaching and what you told the students they would be responsible for knowing, then we look to your instruction or the instructions you gave to the students. Lots of high scores? Great, you did a fine job, unless you told the students in advance exactly what the test items would be (teaching to the test). Lots of low scores? Then there is a problem with the instruction or the instructions given to the students. Not great news, but it *does* inform your instruction for the next time around—and that's a good thing!

Item Analysis

For a number of reasons you may want to look over each of the items on the test in terms of correct and incorrect responses. Were there questions that everybody got right? Were there some that everybody got wrong? Perhaps there were some that your better students got wrong but the struggling students got right! It happens, and what it calls for is an **item analysis**. It is quick and easy and will improve the tests you write.

This topic becomes important because our aim is to develop a strong assessment instrument. You have likely heard of (or had) teachers who dropped out test questions that everybody got wrong. Well, OK, if that's what they want to do. But by the same token they should drop out any question that everybody got right, though you probably don't recall that happening. In either one of these cases the question has failed to *discriminate* between students' strengths and weaknesses. Begin by asking yourself whether this is a question that simply must be on the test, and if it is, look to see how it can be revised in keeping with the guidelines we have provided so that it is a stronger item. If it really should not have been on the test, then whether everybody got it right or everybody got it wrong, go ahead and drop it. This is not a game of how to find points for people—it is an assessment of achievement that yields valuable information for all concerned.

For all of those other questions it is a simple matter to test them for *discrimination* and *difficulty*. Begin by identifying the top 27 percent of scores in your distribution:

1. Multiply the number of students taking the test by 0.27.

2. Round off to the nearest "whole" student. For example, in a class with 20 students: $20 \times 0.27 = 5.4$ rounded off is 5.

3. Identify the top 5 scores and the bottom 5 scores.

We will refer to the high group as HG and the low group as LG. For our discussion, let's suppose that there are 5 scores in *each* of these groups.

Discrimination. This calculation is used to determine whether a test item is discriminating between the higher-scoring students and the lower-scoring students. We look for a value of 0.3 or higher as an indicator that the item is a good discriminator. Let's say that on a particular question we had 4 out of 5 students in the HG and 2 out of 5 in the LG get the item correct. Here's the calculation:

Discrimination = (HG correct – LG correct) / Number of scores in one group

Discrimination = (4 – 2) / 5

Discrimination = 0.4

So, we would determine that this particular question did discriminate between students appropriately. But let's suppose that 3 out of 5 students in the HG and 4 out of 5 in the LG happened to get this one correct. Then we would have:

Discrimination = (3 – 4) / 5

Discrimination = –0.2

As you can see, discrimination values can be negative numbers. When this happens, it tells you that something about the wording of the question was likely throwing off your better students (essentially, they wound up overthinking it) while your weaker students breezed right past it. The wording of the question needs to be revised.

Difficulty. This calculation gives you an idea as to whether the question is appropriately challenging. As we mentioned previously, it could be the case that a question that everybody gets right (a difficulty value of 1.0) or everybody gets wrong (a difficulty value of 0.0) simply must be included on the test. If that's the case, that's the way it goes. But for most questions, we want to find a difficulty range of between 0.3 and 0.7. Let's use the same numbers from the first example. There's a slight change or two in this formula from the one we used for discrimination, so pay attention.

Difficulty = (HG correct + LG correct) / Number of scores in both groups combined

Difficulty = (4 + 2) / 10

Difficulty = 0.6

We would consider this in the appropriate range for difficulty. Let's just take a moment to look at difficulty using the numbers from our second example under discrimination:

Difficulty = (3 + 4) / 10

Difficulty = 0.7

We are at the upper limit for difficulty, but still within the range. And note that we do not have that nasty issue of negative numbers.

An item analysis is not a difficult task to accomplish. If you take just a little bit of time to examine the questions you have included on a test, you will be able to "clean up" questions that need a little work, identify good and bad test items, and build greater confidence in the efficacy of your classroom assessment program.

Generally, look for

- discrimination values above 0.3
- difficulty values between 0.3 and 0.7

Summary

There you have it. The strength of assessment in your classroom will be decided by you. There is nothing secret about it, no supercomputer calculations involved, and nothing that anybody could do better than you. In fact, you are the most appropriate person in the classroom to take care of instruction, assessment (formative and summative), and interpretation of the assessment results. Use a TOS as your blueprint for test design, select the most appropriate method for testing based on the context of your particular classroom, design strong assessment instruments, and put the results to work for you and for your students. In essence, become the *total* educator!

■ FINALLY: ASSESSMENT AND THE HIGH-STAKES ENVIRONMENT

Standardized testing has been a mainstay in education for a very long time. School districts have used annual testing programs to gauge their successes, to evaluate their students, and to monitor their own strengths and weaknesses for decades upon decades. But today's use of testing as a mechanism for generating accountability data has ushered in an era of urgency—some might say anxiety—known as **high-stakes testing**.

Many would cite the No Child Left Behind Act of 2001 as the primary impetus for this situation; on the other hand, Nichols and Berliner (2008) suggest that high-stakes testing "is the engine that drives No Child Left Behind (NCLB) Act" (p. 41). The practice of using standardized testing not only to assess student progress but also to make decisions about the employment of teachers and the administration of schools and districts is one that will likely remain throughout a significant portion of your career. Testing generates numbers, and people tend to put a lot of stock in what numbers might tell them. According to Foote (2007), "The number of students tested annually has skyrocketed as all 50 states have exams in operation, with even more grades—seven in all—required to administer tests" (p. 359). Despite all of this you might keep in mind that the movement toward high-stakes testing is still in its infancy as a measure of educational performance. Supon (2008) suggests that the emerging culture of assessment has changed the role of educators so that while "teachers and principals are responsible to enhance and measure student learning within their classrooms/ schools, they are also responsible to prepare and motivate students for high-stakes testing" (p. 306). And this leads to another issue in contemporary education.

Teaching, but Not to the Test

It would be foolish to expect that a culture could change and not affect the behavior of those within the culture. What we see happening is that as we change from teaching for learning to teaching for the test, the result is a narrowing of the curriculum, lost instructional opportunities, and a loss of teacher autonomy (Campbell, 2002; Vacca & Vacca, 2001). Nichols and Berliner (2008) conclude, "The pressure to score well on a single test is so intense that it leads to nefarious practices (cheating on the test, data manipulation), distorts education (narrowing the curriculum, teaching to the test), and ends up demoralizing our educators" (p. 42). Perhaps of greatest concern considering our focus on the classroom teacher is the unsanctioned though almost implicit suggestion of teaching to the test. There is validity to standardized testing in education, and there is credence to an argument for accountability, but the pressure toward teaching to the test is a blatant example of the test running the curriculum rather than the curriculum determining the test.

Posner (2004) offers the following observation about this perplexing issue:

> Opponents of this so-called high-stakes testing complain that such intense pressure causes teachers to devote virtually all classroom time and resources to preparing students for the standardized test. This phenomenon is called "teaching to the test." Proponents of high-stakes testing respond that that is exactly as it should be. They argue that the tests measure success in teaching the curriculum and so "teaching to the test" is "teaching to the curriculum." And after all, isn't that what we want teachers to do? (p. 749)

As much as we would like to, we cannot resolve this issue in a few pages of this book. However, as the authors of the *Educator's Field Guide*, we would suggest to you that assessment is most effective and most meaningful when it reflects what actually occurred in the classroom rather than what someone thinks should occur. That is to say, take the curriculum requirements that are presented to you and use your own assessment program to see that your students have the opportunity to learn that curriculum. Note that we say "have the opportunity to learn." We do that because in the final analysis it is only the student who can do the learning. There will be nothing you can do as a teacher to force information or understanding into a student. Your task is to provide the opportunities to learn, to monitor their progress with formative assessments, to provide more opportunities based on your formative assessment data, and then to conduct well-constructed summative assessments that offer meaningful documentation of student achievement.

How Classroom Assessment Makes Your Life Easier

All of this discussion of assessment leads to one of the professional facts of a teacher's life—the assigning of grades. When the grades are good, and everyone can smile, this is not a particularly difficult situation. However, for a wide variety of reasons there will be many times when the grades are not so good, and the teacher will agonize over what to do. Despite the fact that this would seem to be a very clear-cut issue, education is nonetheless a human and personal experience. When you consider that grades are not always just a communication between the teacher and the student but also between the teacher and the parent or caregiver, it starts to become obvious that grading can involve more than counting up the correct responses on a test.

An "A" for Effort?

Let's assume for a moment that one of the children attempting to meet an objective comes in for help after school each day for the week prior to the test. Let's also assume that this student stays up late studying and practicing, and you have even heard from the parent that the child is working diligently to succeed. Now the big day comes, and try as that student might, the result is only 67 percent of the questions answered correctly. Would you say the student has failed to meet the standard, or would you boost that score just a bit in view of the extraordinary effort and commitment the student has shown? After all, dedication to a task and working beyond what is asked are both characteristics of a strong work ethic, something that schools try to encourage.

Whether you choose to report the grade as is or instead provide those few extra points, you would not be alone. The debate over awarding points for effort has raged for a long time and likely will continue. It must be admitted that work ethic, character, citizenship, and cooperation are all virtues that schools very definitely attempt to foster in students. Yet it is also true that those same characteristics are not assessed on the yearly achievement tests or on tests such as the SAT or any of the standardized tests that you will take on your way to certification as a professional teacher. The establishment of clear objectives is supposed to clear up this dilemma, but the humanistic side of education is one that cannot be ignored. So what are you to do? Well . . .

Grade Inflation

Grades, like money, are only as valuable as the standards upon which they are based. **Grade inflation** is what happens when the questions that we have been raising remain unanswered. You have probably found already that students from other high schools seem to have received higher or lower grades than your own in the same subjects, yet you find yourself superior (or inferior as the case may be) and wonder how this could happen.

Grade inflation is a function of the humanistic side of education. It would be easy enough to say that a student receives credit for correct answers, and the percentage correct will dictate the grade. But it is also true that education, or learning, occurs in a context. That is, rather than being something that can be separated from all other influences, there are real and extenuating circumstances that affect human performance on any task. The problem is that we have yet to find a way to account for the humanistic side in a fair way. Should the child who overcomes a substantial obstacle (recent illness, the death of a close family member, etc.) be given special consideration when it comes time for grading? Sounds fair for that child, but is it fair for the child who doesn't have to overcome some peculiar obstacle but receives a higher score based purely on performance?

This is a real problem because grades are supposed to be reflective of a standard. You might think of it this way: Would you want to trust your life to a surgeon who made it through medical school with inflated grades? This may sound like a drastic example, but the example has credence when you consider that the precedent for grade inflation would have been established long ago in elementary school when that surgeon was just a child. Also, keep in mind that this problem is national in scope, not confined to just the local or state levels (Wildavsky, 2000). Grades represent the "currency" by which students gauge their own academic achievement and by which the achievement of students is gauged against other students, schools, and even nations.

When assigning grades, you will find it difficult to completely separate the humanistic aspect of this situation from the established objectives. Students will always ask if they can do extra-credit work, if they can have more time, if they can do things over. Yet the classroom teacher needs to be able to balance extenuating circumstances against whether or not a student has actually learned what it is necessary for the student to know. A focus on earning points has shifted the educational emphasis from *learning* to the *completion of requirements.* If all of those requirements add up to learning, so be it. If, however, those requirements add up to little more than completing a variety of activities, then the difficulties of assigning grades can be expected to persist.

As someone just beginning to join the educational profession, you should start thinking about how to combine the humanistic and academic aspects of education in a way that truly reflects the learning that is accomplished in school. We would encourage you to think about what your own approach will be to ensuring that grades you assign will be truly representative of what you intended, expected, *and announced in advance* that your students should be able to do as a result of instruction in your class. By far, our most important recommendation is that you include a robust use of formative assessments in your teaching so that you can identify student strengths and weaknesses and then design appropriate instruction, so that when it becomes time to assign a grade, your students will be ready. Assessment, much more than an instructional afterthought, is an integral component in the development of an educational strategy. However, a teacher's greatest ally when the time for grading arrives is a well-planned and well-executed strategy for high-quality assessment. Indeed, a well-implemented classroom assessment program will make your life much easier when it comes time to make those difficult decisions that teachers face.

Unit IV Appendix

Table IV.1 Blank Table of Specifications

Name of Test						Totals
Totals						

Table IV.2 Table of Specifications for Unit IV Assessment

Assessment Unit Test	Aims/Basic Terms	Making Assessment Part of Instruction	Writing Tests	Analyzing the Results	The High-Stakes Environment	Totals
Knowledge	8	3	4	0	0	15
Comprehension	5	32	0	3	5	45
Application	2	0	16	7	0	25
Synthesis	0	0	15	0	0	15
Totals	15	35	35	10	5	100

Table IV.3 Test Format Matrix and Levels of Thinking From Bloom's Taxonomy

	Knowledge	Comprehension	Application	Analysis	Synthesis	Evaluation
Personal Communication	Good choice for assessing knowledge	Follow-up questions can allow for demonstrating understanding	Can indicate when to apply, but not necessarily a demonstration of the applied skill	Can allow a student to analyze but may call for too much abstraction to be considered at once	Synthesis of new ideas possible, but not of products	Can allow students to make and defend judgments and evaluations
Essay	Requires carefully constructed prompts to assess particular items of knowledge	Can provide student with opportunity to demonstrate understanding	Unless the application is a written skill, not the best choice for this level of thinking	Format allows student to consider information and keep track of thoughts while constructing a response	Synthesis of ideas or story lines possible, but not of products	Can allow students to make and defend judgments and evaluations
Performance	Not well suited to the assessment of knowledge	Not well suited to the assessment of comprehension	Good choice for assessing the application of a skill	Not well suited to the analysis of information	Good choice for assessing the demonstration of a skill or the development of a product	Not well suited to demonstrating evaluation
Selected Response	Can assess a large amount of discrete, specific information	Of limited use in assessing understanding, more so than knowledge	Can assess whether a skill might be appropriate, but not the application of the skill	Of limited value other than to select the results of an analysis from choices	Not well suited to the synthesis of information or products	Of limited value other than to select the results of an evaluation from given choices

Table IV.4 Strengths and Limitations of the Four Test Formats

Format	Strengths	Limitations
Personal Communication	• Can attend to nonverbal responses • Can avoid misunderstanding of question or response • Allows for elaboration • Can take advantage of "teachable moments"	• Time-consuming • Can be difficult to document responses • Requires verbal fluency • Test taker must hold responses in "abstraction" (i.e., cannot see the responses and make changes)
Essay	• Provides opportunity to construct responses that demonstrate understanding and identify relationships • Allows for elaboration • Test taker can see a response and make changes as necessary • Can address several topics at once	• Can be time-consuming to score • If prompts not well constructed, can allow responses that attempt to "surround" an answer • Limits the amount of information that can be addressed during the testing session
Performance	• Not dependent upon verbal ability (unless the skill being assessed involves speaking/singing) • Allows the demonstration of the actual skill or development of an actual product	• Difficult to document demonstration of a skill (with no tangible product) • Can be difficult to score while performance is in progress • Can be time-consuming if many students must perform
Selected Response	• Can address broad range of information • Easily and quickly scored • Multiple formats to meet different needs	• Time-consuming to develop strong questions and viable response options • Impossible to know whether a student has guessed at an answer • Provides students with answers rather than soliciting answers from them

ASSESSMENT

Glossary

Academic self-concept—perceptions students hold of their own academic ability. Students who have become accustomed to succeeding and who feel academically competent are generally successful in a variety of scholastic activities. Those who become accustomed to failure and who feel academically inferior tend to continually fail in scholastic endeavors.

Accountability—the perspective that there are specific things that the schools are supposed to accomplish with children, and that district personnel, school administrators, and teachers are to be held responsible for ensuring that those objectives are met.

Affective perspective—an approach to curriculum that emphasizes not only presenting information to students but also helping them to see the value of that information and to concern themselves with matters more "human" than the mere acquisition of knowledge.

Alternate forms reliability—in regard to test reliability, using two or more versions of a test to be certain that an assessment yields consistent results.

Ancillary personnel—people other than the teacher who need to be "in the loop" with a classroom-management plan. For instance, this can include administrators, other teachers, and parents.

Assessment—whether teacher designed for use in the classroom or those districtwide high-stakes standardized versions, the means by which information is gathered to make a variety of decisions.

At-risk students—those students who, for a variety of reasons, statistically have a high probability for dropping out of school or failing to acquire the competence needed to function in the larger society.

Attention Deficit/Hyperactivity Disorder (AD/HD)—characterization of students who just can't seem to focus on what's going on or, alternatively, who just can't seem to settle down long enough to find out what's going on. For a student to be diagnosed with AD/HD, the symptoms must be manifested before age seven, continue for at least six months, and occur in at least two social settings, such as at school and at home.

Bilingual education—an approach to education for nonspeakers of English in which instruction is provided daily in both English and the student's native tongue.

Blended family—family structure when both partners (whether married or not) bring children to the relationship from prior relationships.

Block scheduling—a scheduling technique to create longer periods of student engagement, such as for project work or science labs. An example of this would be to designate Mondays, Wednesdays, and Thursdays with hour-and-a-half periods while Tuesdays and Fridays would have the regular fifty-minute periods.

Child abuse and neglect—defined as the physical or mental injury, sexual abuse, negligent treatment, or maltreatment of a child under the age of eighteen by a person who is responsible for the child's welfare under circumstances that indicate that the child's health or welfare is harmed or threatened thereby.

Child-centered education—a perspective of curriculum that uses subject matter as the context around which student growth and development will be facilitated. This entails at least two considerations: what subjects will be taught to foster that development, and what we, as a society, want to develop in our children.

Classroom assessment—as opposed to standardized testing, means that a classroom teacher uses to assess progress based on specific classroom experiences/lessons.

Classroom lessons—from the four general formats for arranging educational experiences, brings experiences and knowledge to the students.

Classroom management—refers to those activities in which a teacher engages before, during, and after instruction to allow instruction and learning to take place.

Cognitive perspective—an approach to curriculum that focuses on the acquisition of knowledge. To that end, curriculums are typically divided among several distinct subject-matter areas.

Concept categories—on a Table of Specifications, each column indicates the major concepts, chapters, or topics that are the subject of the assessment.

Consequences—the results that follow from the making of a choice. For *every* choice there is a consequence. In classroom management students are aware of the consequences for their behavior.

Construct validity—in regard to test validity, these are areas that can't be assessed by just asking for knowledge-based responses (e.g., musical ability, creative thinking, intelligence). For these areas, and others like them, an assessment instrument will ask a variety of questions or perhaps require the demonstration of various skills.

Content validity—in regard to test validity, refers to a test of knowledge or comprehension of knowledge.

Convergent questions—questions that typically have one correct answer.

Criterion-referencing—an approach to evaluating assessment data in which the norm group is assessed and the results are compiled. The results (often referred to as the *baseline data*) are examined and the passing grade for future test takers is determined based on the how the norm group performed.

Culture—represents the values, attitudes, and beliefs that influence the behavior and the traditions of a people.

Curriculum—the means and materials with which students will interact for the purpose of achieving identified educational outcomes.

Demographics—socioeconomic characteristics of a group of people (e.g., the students in a teacher's class).

Demonstrating—an active instructional approach to teaching that is strongly teacher oriented. The teacher is the one who touches the materials and manipulates the objects while students observe the demonstration.

Difficulty—with regard to item analysis, this calculation gives an indication as to whether a test item is appropriately challenging.

Direct instruction—from the taxonomy of instructional techniques, the teacher explains or demonstrates a lesson.

Direct reinforcement—in the context of classroom management, this is when one tells an individual or the entire group that a particular behavior was good, or well done, or much appreciated, or impressive.

Directing—an instructional approach that is more student oriented than is **demonstrating**. The teacher may present a new concept, provide examples on the board, direct students to read in the appropriate book, and then have students participate in an activity which clarifies the concept or reinforces understanding.

Discipline—in the context of classroom management refers to actions a teacher will take *after* misbehavior has occurred.

Discovery learning—from the taxonomy of instructional techniques, uses students' personal experiences as the foundation for building concepts.

Discrimination—with regard to item analysis, this calculation is used to determine whether a test item is distinguishing between the higher-scoring students and the lower-scoring students.

Discussion—from the taxonomy of instructional techniques, an exchange of opinions and perspectives between teachers and students or students and peers.

Divergent questions—also called open-ended questions, are used to encourage many answers and generate greater participation of students.

Document camera—a device used in conjunction with a computer to display magazine pages, books, graphics such as charts and maps, and even three-dimensional objects.

Drill and practice—from the taxonomy of instructional techniques, repetition to hone a skill or facilitate memorization of information.

Emotional/behavioral disorders—refers to a condition exhibiting one or more of the following characteristics over a long time and to a marked degree that adversely affects a student's educational performance: (a) an inability to learn that cannot be explained by intellectual, sensory, or other health factors; (b) an inability to build or maintain satisfactory interpersonal relationships with peers and teachers; (c) inappropriate types of behavior or feelings under normal circumstances; (d) a general pervasive mood of unhappiness or depression; (e) a tendency to develop physical symptoms or fears associated with personal or school problems. The term includes schizophrenia.

Essay—from the four general assessment formats, a written exercise that provides the test taker with an opportunity to construct a response that can include great detail and elaboration.

Ethnicity—a sense of common identity based upon common ancestral background, unique physical or cultural characteristics, and the sharing of common values and beliefs.

Evaluation—when *value* is placed on accumulated assessment data.

Explicit curriculum—subjects that will be taught and the identified "mission" of the school.

Extended family—the presence of several generations in the home and can include aunts and uncles or other relatives as well as grandparents.

Extra curriculum—school-sponsored programs that are intended to supplement the explicit curriculum. Participation is voluntary.

Field trips—from the four general formats for arranging educational experiences, taking students to real-world experiences in their natural environment (that is, away from the classroom).

Formative assessments—collecting data to make instructional decisions.

Gender—refers to the social aspect of sexuality, that is, behaviors that are considered masculine or feminine.

Grade inflation—raising grades for nonacademic reasons (e.g., the teacher felt the grades were too low or wanted to reward a student's effort).

Group referencing—comparing a student's score and assigning a grade based on a standard set by a norm group.

Guest speakers—from the four general formats for arranging educational experiences, individuals who can bring expertise, knowledge, and insight representing particular skills, abilities, and responsibilities.

High-stakes testing—with regard to standardized assessments, testing as a mechanism for generating accountability data.

Immersion—with regard to nonspeakers of English, all instruction is in English. The idea is that students need to be immersed in English all day long.

Implicit curriculum—the lessons that arise from the culture of the school and the behaviors expected of the students.

Inclusion—seeks to bring children with special needs into the general education program at every opportunity.

Inclusive learning environments—teachers provide appropriate instruction for *all* students through differentiating instruction in a heterogeneous classroom.

Inquiry—from the taxonomy of instructional techniques, this approach allows students to generate the questions that they will investigate and then answer.

Interactive whiteboard (IWB)—an electronic whiteboard writing surface that can capture writing electronically. The IWB is designed to allow interaction with a computer display.

Internal consistency—refers to matters about the integrity of an assessment instrument (the test) for doing what it is supposed to do.

Item categories—on a Table of Specifications, each row indicates what sort of test items will be included in the assessment instrument.

Item analysis—based on the results of a test, an examination of items on a test to determine whether they were appropriately difficult and discriminating.

Latchkey children—children who come home to empty houses after school because the parents are still at work.

LCD projectors—used with a computer to project an image onto a screen or wall. LCD projectors coupled with computers can access a large amount of text and a great variety of images for instruction.

Learning cycle—an inquiry-oriented lesson plan format based upon a *constructivist* perspective on learning.

Learning disability—as defined by the Individuals with Disabilities Education Act (IDEA), refers to "a disorder in one or more of the basic psychological processes involved in understanding or in using language, either spoken or written, which manifests itself in imperfect ability to listen, think, speak, read, write, spell, or do mathematical calculations" (20 U.S.C., Sec. 1400).

Learning styles—learning modalities such as visual, auditory, tactile/kinesthetic, vocalic, field dependent, field independent, impulsive, and reflective.

Lecture—from the taxonomy of instructional techniques, an approach in which the teacher provides information to students in a one-way verbal presentation.

Lesson plans—conceptualizing how to teach something. There are various formats.

Long-range planning—semester- or yearlong plans for what is to be presented in class. More general than short-range planning (e.g., lesson plans).

Mandated reporters—status of teachers with regard to reporting child abuse/neglect. That is, if required by law to report suspected child abuse to state authorities, teachers are protected by law in so doing.

Mean—from the measures of central tendency, the arithmetic middle of a distribution, also known as the average of the scores. In mathematical shorthand, a score is represented as X and the mean is represented as $\bar{X}$.

Median—from the measures of central tendency, the score that falls in the very middle of the distribution when the scores are arranged in sequence.

Mental modeling—from the taxonomy of instructional techniques, assists students in managing their own learning by modeling a problem-solving technique.

Mission statement—in the context of classroom management, this particular statement is about classroom management, not about instruction, and articulates the person the teacher intends to be, the environment the teacher intends to establish, as the *manager* of behavior in the classroom.

Mode—from the measures of central tendency, the score that occurs most often in a distribution of scores.

Motivation—an intrinsic desire to accomplish some task.

Multimedia presentations—from the four general formats for arranging educational experiences, bring depictions of people and events to the classroom.

Normal curve—also called the *bell curve*, anticipates a particular, symmetrical, distribution of test scores.

Norm group—a group of test takers who were identified as being representative of the population that would be using the test, and whose scores will be used to set the standard for the test.

Nuclear family—consists of one or more parents or guardians or foster parents and may include one or more children.

Null curriculum—topics or perspectives that are specifically excluded from the curriculum.

Objectives—drawn from the broader goals of the unit plan but are more specific and often stated as learning outcomes that are achieved over a defined time period.

Orchestrating—the most student-centered instructional approach. Students are not only actively engaged in the learning; they are also encouraged to assume responsibility for their own learning. In this situation the teacher is not determining the questions and making decisions about seeking answers to the questions.

Overhead projector—will show a series of images (overhead transparencies) in sequence. Not computer dependent.

Percentile—refers to the percentage of scores from a norm group that fall *at or below* the particular score.

Performance assessment—from the four general assessment formats, is used when a product is created or a skill is demonstrated.

Personal communication—from the four general assessment formats, is a circumstance in which a teacher speaks directly with an individual student.

Predictive validity—in regard to test validity, refers to a test designed to predict future academic success.

Problem-solving conference—a one-on-one discussion with a student intended to develop a plan to remediate inappropriate behavior.

Procedures—in the context of classroom management, detail the manner in which particular activities are to be carried out.

Question and answer—from the taxonomy of instructional techniques, requires reflection as information is exchanged in response to a question.

Raw score—an individual's actual result on a test as a function of correct/incorrect answers.

Reliability—refers to whether or not a test gets consistent results.

Role models—individuals (e.g., teachers) who display traits or characteristics that others may choose to emulate.

Routines—in the context of classroom management, are those procedures students use to the point of being accomplished without the teacher's direction.

Rules—represent the code of behavior that a teacher expects the students to follow.

School vandalism—aggressive or destructive acts toward school property.

School violence—aggressive acts against people.

Selected response—from the four general assessment formats, assessments using multiple-choice, true/false, matching, or short-answer items that either provide the test taker with response options or are structured to allow only one correct and appropriate response.

Self-reinforcement—in the context of classroom management, when students follow the rules and accomplish procedures and routines because they find it personally gratifying to do so.

Sex—the biological distinctions of male or female.

Short-range plans—include unit plans and daily planning or lesson plans.

Special needs—represents a category of students with special needs ranging from learning disabled to the gifted and talented.

Split-half reliability—in regard to test reliability, using questions that are parallel in what they assess (e.g., a math test that could have twenty or thirty variations of two-digit by three-digit multiplication problems), scoring the test as two halves, and then comparing the results for each half.

Standardized testing—a system of assessment that is typically administered to a broad population of students. Such assessments can be used with individuals, districtwide, statewide, nationally, or even tests used internationally.

Stanines—uses the normal curve, but divides it into nine equal segments, thus a *sta*ndard *nine*-point *s*cale (stanines).

Strategy—planning some course of action *and* coordinating the implementation of that plan.

Summative assessments—assessments intended specifically for the purpose of assigning a grade.

T score—converts z scores to a 100-point scale thus eliminating negative scores.

Table of Specifications (TOS)—an outline, or blueprint, for designing a test.

Temperament—anger, happiness, sadness, confidence, introvert or extrovert, appreciation of or difficulty with novelty (things being different or changing often), and competitiveness are temperamental trends that you may notice in different students.

Test–retest reliability—in regard to test reliability, administering a test twice, the key element being that *no* instruction (on that particular topic) occurs between the test and the retest, and then comparing the results.

Thematic unit—a unit that integrates, for example, reading, math, and science through the study of a broad area, such as "energy," or "the environment." The rationale for the thematic approach is that it demonstrates the interdisciplinary nature of learning itself.

Tort law—refers to incidents where negligence or breach of contract or trust results in injury to another person or damage to property.

Transitions—time spent bringing one activity to an end and moving efficiently to the next. Transitions may not be instructional periods, but they are very much management zones.

Validity—a matter of whether a test measures what it is supposed to measure.

Vicarious reinforcement—when an individual or perhaps a small group is recognized for an appropriate behavior with the intent that others hear the praise and modify their own behavior to receive some of that same recognition.

z score—translates a raw score into units of standard deviation along a normal curve.

References

Amato, P. (2001). Children of divorce in the 1990s: An update of the Amato and Keith (1991) meta-analysis. *Journal of Family Psychology, 15,* 355–370.

Amato, P., & Keith, B. (1991). Parental divorce and adult well-being: A meta-analysis. *Journal of Marriage and the Family, 53,* 43–58.

American Academy of Pediatrics. (2000). Clinical practice guidelines: Diagnosis and evaluation of the child with attention-deficit/hyperactivity disorder. *Pediatrics, 105* (5), 1158–1170.

American Psychiatric Association. (2000). *Diagnostic and statistical manual of mental disorders* (4th ed., rev.). Washington, DC: Author.

Anderson, L., & Krathwohl, O. (2001). *A taxonomy for learning, teaching, and assessing.* New York: Longman.

Atkins, J., & Karplus, R. (1962, September). Discovery or invention? *Science Teacher, 29*(5), 45–51.

Bandura, A. (1986). *Social foundations of thought and action: A social cognitive theory.* Englewood Cliffs, NJ: Prentice Hall.

Banks, J. (1994). *An introduction to multicultural education.* Boston: Allyn & Bacon.

Banks, J. (1997). *Teaching strategies for ethnic studies* (6th ed.). Boston: Allyn & Bacon.

Barbe, W., & Swassing, R. (1988). *Teaching through modality strengths: Concepts and practices.* Columbus, OH: Zaner-Bloser.

Beller, A., & Chung, S. (1992). Family structure and educational attainment of children: Effects of remarriage. *Journal of Population Economics, 5,* 309–320.

Bentley, M., Ebert, C., & Ebert, E. (2000). *The natural investigator: A constructivist approach to teaching elementary and middle school science.* Belmont, CA: Wadsworth.

Berliner, D. (1985). Effective classroom teaching: A necessary but not sufficient condition for developing exemplary schools. In G. R. Austin & H. Garver (Eds.), *Research on exemplary schools.* Orlando, FL: Academic.

Black, S. (1998, August). Facts of life. *The American School Board Journal, 185*(8), 33–36.

Bloom, B., Englehart, M., Furst, E., Hill, W., & Krathwohl, O. (Eds.). (1956). *Taxonomy of educational objectives: The classification of educational goals. Handbook I: The cognitive domain.* New York: Longman.

Board of Education. (2003, 2010). *Science standards of learning for Virginia public schools.* Richmond: Commonwealth of Virginia. (Original work published 1995)

Borich, G. (1996). *Effective teaching methods* (3rd ed.). Englewood Cliffs, NJ: Merrill.

Borror, D. J., & White, R. E. (1998). *A field guide to insects* (The Peterson Field Guide Series). Boston: Houghton Mifflin.

Brendtro, L., Long, N., & Brown, W. (2000). Searching for strengths. *Reclaiming Children and Youth, 9*(2), 66–69.

Brophy, J. (1983, March). Classroom organization and management. *Elementary School Journal, 83*(4), 265–285.

Bruner, J. (1960). *The process of education.* Cambridge, MA: Harvard University Press.

Burden, P. (2003). *Classroom management: Creating a successful learning community.* Hoboken, NJ: Wiley.

Burns, R. (1984). How time is used in elementary schools: The activity structure of classrooms. In L. W. Anderson (Ed.), *Time and school learning: Theory, research, practice* (pp. 91–127). London: Croom Helm.

Campbell, M. (2002). Constructing powerful voices: Starting points for policy driven literacy assessment reform. *Journal of Reading Education, 27,* 17–23.

Cangelosi, J. S. (2004). *Classroom management strategies: Gaining and maintaining students' cooperation* (5th ed.). Hoboken, NJ: Wiley.

Canter, L., & Canter, M. (1976). *Assertive discipline: A take charge approach for today's educator.* Santa Monica, CA: Canter and Associates.

Carbo, M. (1996, February). Reading styles: High gains for the bottom third. *Educational Leadership, 53*(5), 8–13.

Center for Disease Control and Prevention. (2007, June 6). *Youth risk behaviors surveillance—United States.* Atlanta: Centers for Disease Control and Prevention.

Chaillé, C., & Britain, L. (1991). *The young child as scientist: A constructivist approach to early childhood science education.* New York: HarperCollins.

Chauvin, I. (2006, February). Recognizing child abuse. *Teaching for Excellence, 25*(6), 1–2.

Child Abuse Prevention and Treatment Act, P.L. No. 104-235, 111, 42 U.S.C. 5105g (1996).

Cizek, G. (2002–2003, Winter). When teachers cheat. *Streamlined Seminar, 21,* 1–2.

Coutinho, M., Oswald, D., & Best, A. (2002). The influence of socio demographics and gender on the disproportionate identification of minority students as having learning disabilities. *Remedial and Special Education, 231*(1), 49–60.

Culyer, R. (1987). *Suggestions for improving comprehension: Recommendations based on classroom observations.* Mt. Gilead, NC: Vineyard Press.

Darling-Hammond, L., & Bransford, J. (Eds.) (2005). *Preparing teachers for a changing world: What teachers should learn and be able to do.* San Francisco: Jossey-Bass.

Deshler, D., Ellis, E., & Lenz, B. (1996). *Teaching adolescents with learning disabilities: Strategies and methods.* Denver, CO: Love Publishing.

Druck, K., & Kaplowitz, M. (2005, April). Preventing classroom violence. *New Jersey Education Association Review, 78,* 10–11.

Dunn, R. (1995). *Strategies for educating diverse learners.* Bloomington, IN: Phi Delta Kappa Educational Foundation.

Dunn, R. (2001). Learning style differences of nonconforming middle-school students. *NASSP Bulletin, 85*(626), 68–74.

Dunn, R., Griggs, S., Olson, J., Beasly, M., et al. (1995). A meta-analytic validation of the Dunn and Dunn learning styles model. *Journal of Educational Research, 88*(6), 353–361.

Eisencraft, A. (2003). Expanding the 5E model. *The Science Teacher, 70*(6), 57–59.

Eisner, E. (1994). *The educational imagination: On the design and evaluation of school programs* (3rd ed.). New York: Macmillan.

Eisner, E. (1997). *The enlightened eye: Qualitative inquiry and the enhancement of educational practice.* New York: Merrill.

English, J., & Papalia, A. (1988, January). The responsibility of educators in cases of child abuse and neglect. *Chronicle Guidance,* 88–89.

Evans, G. (2004, February–March). The environment of childhood poverty. *American Psychologist, 59*(2), 77–92.

Evertson, C. M., Emmer, E. T., Clements, B. S., & Worsham, M. E. (2000). *Classroom management for elementary teachers* (5th ed.). Boston: Allyn & Bacon.

Fagan, J. (2001, May). There's no place like school. *Principal, 80*(5), 36–37.

Federal Interagency Forum on Child and Family Statistics. (2008). *America's children in brief: Key national indicators of well-being.* Washington, DC: Author.

Fisher, B. (1992, August–September). Starting the year in a first grade classroom. *Teaching K–8,* 57–58.

Flaxman, S. (2000, August). Opening bell: Get organized for the first day of school with this handy checklist. *Scholastic Instructor,* 20–21.

Foote, M. (2007). Keeping accountability systems accountable. *Phi Delta Kappan, 88*(5), 359–363.

Gambrell, L. (1983). The occurrence of think-time during reading comprehension instruction. *Journal of Educational Research, 77*(2), 77–80.

Gerber, B. L., Cavallo, A. M. L., & Marek, E. A. (2001). Relationship among informal learning environments, teaching procedures, and scientific reasoning abilities. *International Journal of Science Education, 23*, 535–549.

Gilroy, M. (2001, October 23). Bilingual education on the edge. *The Hispanic Outlook on Higher Education, 12*, 37–39.

Glasser, W. (1997, April). A new look at school failure and school success. *Phi Delta Kappan, 78*, 596–602.

Golden, O. (2000, September). The federal response to child abuse and neglect. *American Psychologist, 55*(9), 1050–1053.

Gordon, E., & Gordon, E. (2003). *Literacy in America: Historic journey and contemporary solutions.* Westport, CT: Praeger.

Gronlund, N. E. (1999). *How to write and use instructional objectives* (6th ed.). Bellevue, WA: Merrill Press.

Jackson, N. (1991). Precocious readers of English: Origin, structure, and predictive significance. In A. J. Tannenbaum & P. Klein (Eds.), *To be young and gifted* (pp. 171–203). Norwood, NJ: Ablex.

Jencks, C., & Phillips, M. (1998). *The Black–White test score gap.* Washington, DC: Brookings Institution Press.

Jensen, M., Moore, R., & Hatch, J. (2002). Cooperative learning part II: Cooperative group activities for the first week of class: Setting the tone with group web pages. *American Biology Teacher, 64*(2), 87–91.

Johnson, D. W. & Johnson, R. T. (2009). Energizing learning: The instructional power of conflict. *Educational Researcher, 38*(1), 37–51.

Jones, V., & Jones, L. (2001). *Comprehensive classroom management: Creating communities of support and solving problems* (6th ed.). Boston: Allyn & Bacon.

Jurmaine, R. (1994). *Baby Think It Over®.* (Available from Baby Think It Over®, Inc., 2709 Mondovi Road, Eau Claire, WI 54701).

Kids Count Data Book. (1997). *State profiles of child well-being.* Baltimore, MD: Annie E. Casey Foundation.

Kids Count Data Book. (2008). *State profiles of child well-being.* Baltimore, MD: Annie E. Casey Foundation.

Koblinsky, S., Gordon, A., & Anderson, E. (2000). Changes in the social skills and behavior problems of homeless children during the preschool years. *Early Education & Development, 11*(3), 321–338.

Kohn, A. (2003). Almost there, but not quite. *Educational Leadership, 60*(6), 26–29.

Kominski, R., Jamieson, A., & Martinez, G. (2001, June). At-risk conditions of United States school-age children (Working Paper Series 52). Washington, DC: U.S. Bureau of the Census, Population Division. Retrieved from http://www.census.gov/population/www/documentation/twps0052/twps0052.html

Korenman, S., Kaestner, R., & Joyce, T. (2001). Unintended pregnancy and the consequences of nonmarital childbearing. In L. Wu & B. Wolfe (Eds.), *Out of wedlock: Causes and consequences of nonmarital fertility* (pp. 259–286). New York: Russell Sage Foundation.

Kounin, J. (1970). *Discipline and group management in the classroom.* New York: Holt, Rinehart & Winston.

Lasley, T. J., Matczynski, J. J., & Rowley, J. B. (2002). *Instructional models' strategies for teaching in a diverse society.* Belmont, CA: Wadsworth.

Lewis, S., & Allman, C. (2000). *Seeing eye to eye: An administrator's guide to students with low vision.* New York: American Foundation for the Blind Press.

Long, N., & Morse, W. (1996). *Conflict in the classroom: The education of at-risk and troubled students.* Austin, TX: Pro-Ed.

Mager, R. (1997). *Measuring instructional results.* Atlanta, GA: Center for Effective Performance.

Manning, M. L., & Bucher, K. (2007). *Classroom management: Models, applications, and cases.* Upper Saddle River, NJ: Pearson Education.

Mayer, M., & Leone, P. (2007, September). School violence and disruption revisited: Equity and safety in the school house. *Focus on Exceptional Children, 40*(1), 1–28.

McCubbin, H., Thompson, E., Thompson, A., & Futrell, J. (Eds.) (1999). *The dynamics of resilient families.* Thousand Oaks, CA: Sage.

Mercer, C. D., Jordan, L., Allsop, D. H., & Mercer, A. R. (1996). Learning disabilities definitions and criteria used by state education departments. *Learning Disabilities Quarterly, 19,* 217–231.

Moravcsik, M. J. (1981). Creativity in science education. *Science Education, 65,* 221–227.

National Center for Education Statistics. (2003). *Digest of Education Statistics, 2002.* Washington, DC: U.S. Department of Education.

National Center for Education Statistics. (2008a). *Digest of Education Statistics, 2007.* Washington, DC: U.S. Department of Education.

National Center for Education Statistics. (2008b). *Indicators of school crime and safety: 2007.* Washington, DC: U.S. Department of Education.

Nehring, J. (1992). *The schools we have: The schools we want.* San Francisco: Jossey-Bass.

Nichols, S. L., & Berliner, D. (2008). Why has high-stakes testing so easily slipped into contemporary American life? *Education Digest, 74*(4), 41–47.

Nicholson, S. (1973). The theory of loose parts. *Man/Society/Technology—A Journal of Industrial Arts Education, 32*(4), 172–175.

Novelli, J. (1995, September). Learning centers that work. *Instructor, 105*(2), 82–85.

O'Connor, R. (2008). Teen suicide. *Focus Adolescent Services.* Retrieved January 25, 2009, from http://www.focusas.com/Suicide.html

Oswald, R. F. (2002, May). Resilience within the family networks of lesbians and gay men: Intentionality and redefinition. *Journal of Marriage and Family, 64,* 374–383.

Parkay, F. W., & Stanford, B. H. (2003). *Becoming a teacher.* Boston: Allyn & Bacon.

Payne, R. (1998). *A framework for understanding poverty.* Baytown, TX: RFT Publishing.

Posner, D. (2004). What's wrong with teaching to the test? *Phi Delta Kappan, 85*(10), 749.

Powell, D., Needham, R. A., & Bentley, M. L. (1994, April). *Using big books in science and social studies.* Paper presented at Annual Meeting of the International Reading Association. Toronto, Canada.

Ramsey, J. (1993). Developing conceptual storylines with the learning cycle. *Journal of Elementary Science Education, 5*(2), 1–20.

Riley, J. (1996). *The teaching of reading.* London: Paul Chapman.

Roan, S. (1994, September 28). Square pegs? Being rejected by peers is not only hurtful, it can cause emotional problems and bad behavior. *Los Angeles Times Home Edition,* p. E1.

Rowe, M. B. (1978, March). Give students time to respond. *School Science and Mathematics, 78,* 207–216.

Schroeder, K. (1999, January). Education news in brief. *Education Digest, 44*(5), 73–76.

Shank, M. (2002). Making curriculum sparkle for students with AD/HD. Unpublished manuscript.

Shannon, S., & Milian, M. (2002, Fall). Parents choose dual language programs in Colorado: Survey. *Bilingual Research Journal, 26*(3), 681–696.

Sherman, L. W. (2000). Sociometry in the classroom: How to do it. Retrieved October 4, 2009, from http://www.users.muohio.edu/shermalw/sociometryfiles/socio_are.htmlx

Shuler, D. (1998, Summer). Beginning teachers' classroom management problems and teacher preparation concerns. *Florida Educational Research Council's Research Bulletin, 29*(2), 11–34.

Stiggins, R. (2001). *Student-involved classroom assessment* (3rd ed.). Upper Saddle River, NJ: Prentice Hall.

Substance Abuse and Mental Health Services Administration. (2008, September). *Results from the 2007 national survey on drug use and health: National findings.* Rockville, MD: Office of Applied Studies.

Supon, V. (2008, September). High-stakes testing: Strategies by teachers and principals for student success. *Journal of Instructional Psychology, 35*(3), 306–308.

Tomlinson, C. (2000, August). *Differentiation of instruction in the elementary grades.* EDO-PS 00–7. Washington, DC: Office of Educational Research and Improvement, U.S. Department of Education.

Turnbull, R., & Cilley, M. (1999). *Explanations and implications of the 1997 amendments to IDEA.* Columbus, OH: Merrill.

Turnbull, R., Turnbull, A., Shank, M., & Smith, S. (2004). *Exceptional lives: Special education in today's schools* (4th ed.). Upper Saddle River, NJ: Pearson Education.

U.S. Census Bureau News. (2008, July 28). *Family and Living Arrangements: 2007.* Washington, DC: U.S. Census Bureau.

U.S. Department of Health and Human Services. (2008). *Child maltreatment 2006.* Washington, DC: Author.

Vacca, R., & Vacca, J. (2001). *Content area reading: Literacy and learning across the curriculum* (7th ed.). Boston: Allyn & Bacon.

Vail, K. (2003, December). Grasping what kids need to raise performance. *American School Board Journal, 190,* 46–52.

Vygotsky, L. S. (1978). *Mind in society.* Cambridge, MA: Harvard University Press.

Weber, W. (1990). *Classroom Teaching Skills* (4th ed.). Lexington, MA: Heath.

Weinstein, C., & Weber, W. (2011). Classroom management. In J. Cooper (Ed.), *Classroom teaching skills* (9th ed.) (pp. 215–251). Belmont, CA: Cengage.

Wildavsky, B. (2000, February 7). At least they have high self-esteem. *U.S. News and World Report, 128*(5), 50.

Willert, H., & Lenhardt, A. (2003, Winter). Tackling school violence does take the whole village. *The Educational Forum, 67,* 110–118.

Wong, H., & Wong, R. (1991). *The first days of school: How to be an effective teacher.* Sunnyvale, CA: Harry K. Wong Publications.

Wong, H., & Wong, R. (2009). *The first days of school: How to be an effective teacher* (4th ed.). Sunnyvale, CA: Harry K. Wong Publications.

Yager, R. E., & McCormack, A. J. (1989). *Science Education, 73*(1), 45–58.

Young, J., & Brozo, W. (2001, July–September). Boys will be boys, or will they? Literacy and masculinities. *Reading Research Quarterly, 36,* 316–325.

Index

CORWIN

A SAGE Company

The Corwin logo—a raven striding across an open book—represents the union of courage and learning. Corwin is committed to improving education for all learners by publishing books and other professional development resources for those serving the field of PreK–12 education. By providing practical, hands-on materials, Corwin continues to carry out the promise of its motto: **"Helping Educators Do Their Work Better."**